THE QUEST FOR IDENTITY

AMITAV ACHARYA

INTERNATIONAL RELATIONS OF SOUTHEAST ASIA

OXFORD
UNIVERSITY PRESS

OXFORD
UNIVERSITY PRESS

Oxford University Press is a department of the University of Oxford.
It furthers the University's objective of excellence in research, scholarship,
and education by publishing worldwide in

Oxford New York

Athens Auckland Bangkok Bogotá Buenos Aires Calcutta
Cape Town Chennai Dar es Salaam Delhi Florence Hong Kong Istanbul
Karachi Kuala Lumpur Madrid Melbourne Mexico City Mumbai
Nairobi Paris São Paulo Shanghai Singapore Taipei Tokyo Toronto Warsaw

with associated companies in Berlin Ibadan

Oxford is a registered trade mark of Oxford University Press
in the UK and in certain other countries

Published in Singapore
by Oxford University Press Pte Ltd

© Oxford University Press Pte Ltd 2000

First published 2000

Printed in Singapore

All rights reserved. No part of this publication may be reproduced,
stored in a retrieval system, or transmitted, in any form or by any means,
electronic, mechanical, photocopying, recording or otherwise,
without the prior permission of Oxford University Press Pte Ltd.

This book is sold subject to the condition that it shall not, by way
of trade or otherwise, be lent, re-sold, hired out or otherwise circulated
without the publisher's prior consent in any form of binding or cover
other than that in which it is published and without a similar condition
including this condition being imposed on the subsequent purchaser

ISBN 0 19 588709 3

1 3 5 7 9 10 8 6 4 2

Acknowledgements

The idea of this book was conceived when I organised a panel on "Reconceptualising Southeast Asia", with Ananda Rajah of the National University of Singapore at the Third ASEAN Inter-University Seminar on Social Development in Pekan Baru, Indonesia during 16–19 June 1997. I would like to thank the organisers of the conference as well as the University of Toronto-York University Joint Centre for Asia Pacific Studies for sponsoring me and Tony Reid to participate in the conference.

The project benefited from the generous advice and encouragement of Ananda Rajah and Tony Reid. Valuable research assistance was provided by Shawn Morton, Darshan Vigneswaran, Ken Boutin, Bhubindar Singh, Sinderpal Singh and especially Cheng Pei Fong, at various stages of the research and writing process. The Department of Government, Sydney University; the Institute of Defence and Strategic Studies, Singapore, and the Asia Center at Harvard University, provided pleasant and hospitable settings for the completion of the manuscript at various stages.

Richard Stubbs and Hari Singh read complete drafts of the manuscript. Kwa Chong Guan offered advice on historical issues and helped with the selection of maps. I am deeply indebted to all of them for their valuable comments and criticisms, although none of them bears any responsibility for the contents of the book.

A special note of thanks to the owners of the Budyong Beach Resort, Bantayan Island, Cebu, Philippines, where I spent several memorable weeks around the Christmas of 1997 working on the manuscript. The friendliness and hospitality of the Zaspa family and the people of Bantayan Island will always remain with me.

Asha Kumaran of Oxford University Press, Singapore, provided much encouragement when I first proposed the idea of the book to her in the summer of 1997. Her colleagues, Magdalene Ng and later, Jocelyn Lau efficiently guided the manuscript through the publication process. I am grateful that none lost patience with me even though I missed various deadlines repeatedly.

Preface

This book is a landmark in the process it describes. Southeast Asia's "quest for identity", its imagining of a common destiny, has found a worthy chronicler and analyst in Amitav Acharya.

Two decades ago, it was common for Southeast Asia to be portrayed as essentially a construct of Western academia, its coherence perceptible only from the great distance of a US classroom. The differences between the Islamic, Buddhist, Christian and Confucian traditions of different countries of the region, their very distinct language families, colonial experiences and Cold War alignments, appeared to vitiate any common identity beyond geographic propinquity. But the 1960s and 70s brought to completion the decolonisation of the region, and the 1980s saw the gradual erosion of its Cold War polarisation. As Dr Acharya shows in Chapter 4, Southeast Asian governments were themselves important actors in resolving the Cambodia crisis which was the principal Cold War issue in the region. Once Vietnamese troops were withdrawn from Cambodia in 1989, measures of reconciliation led swiftly to the incorporation of first Vietnam (1995), then Laos, Burma and Cambodia (1997–99) into the Association of Southeast Asian Nations (ASEAN). The governments of Southeast Asia themselves became chief advocates of the idea of a common regional destiny.

Once governments ceased to pull their countries in radically different directions, it became easier to perceive the high colonial era (roughly 1870–1940) as an unusually divided period in a longer term pattern in which interactions within the region were generally more important than those beyond it. *The Quest for Identity* represents a new readiness, particularly novel in the political science literature, to adopt such a long-term perspective as a means to understanding the coherence of the region.

As a specialist in contemporary international relations, Dr Acharya is concerned above all to explain how ASEAN came to represent all ten countries of Southeast Asia. He reviews the history of ASEAN; its strengths and weaknesses; successes and failures. For the first time in this field, he has pursued the origins of Southeast Asian identity and diplomacy into a distant pre-colonial past. He is able thereby to show that contemporary analysts can learn more from Southeast Asia's past than the "procrustean bed" of authoritarian and primordial elements which commentators in the 1950s and 60s identified as in conflict with modern democracy. In contrast to those views, he traces back to pre-colonial roots the pluralism and resistance to central hegemony which characterise ASEAN today.

Historians of early Southeast Asia have epitomised the flexible inter-state and intra-state relations of the region in terms of *mandala*, galaxy, or commercial zones. Clifford Geertz proposed in *Negara* a model for pre-colonial Bali which has been widely used elsewhere to explain how labour could be mobilized on a large scale without the appearance of a strong state. Without endorsing any one model, Dr Acharya reviews this literature effectively to demonstrate that "region-wide patterns of inter-state relations and a degree of interaction and interdependence did exist" in the pre-colonial past.

This is a timely book and an important one. It not only documents the fortunes of ASEAN and the rebirth of a sense of region in Southeast Asia. It also persuasively links past and present to show how a region can be coherent without a dominant power at its core.

Anthony Reid
University of California, Los Angeles

List of Tables

Table 0.1:   Selected Indicators of Southeast Asian States, 1997   xi
Table 1.1:   Selected Pre-Colonial States of Southeast Asia   19
Table 2.1:   Major Armed Communist Movements in Early
             Post-Colonial Era, 1946–76   56
Table 2.2:   Major Armed Separatist Movements in
             Early Post-Colonial Era, 1946–76   56
Table 2.3:   Ethnic Composition of Southeast Asian States, 1976   57
Table 5.1:   Intra-ASEAN Exports as a Percentage of
             Total Value of Exports, 1970–97   149

List of Maps

1.   Map of Southeast Asia   xi
2.   Selected Pre-Colonial States of Southeast Asia   18

List of Acronyms

ADB	Asian Development Bank
AMDA	Anglo-Malaya Defence Agreement
ANS	Armee Nationaliste Sihanoukienne
APEC	Asia-Pacific Economic Cooperation
ASA	Association of Southeast Asia
ASEAN	Association of Southeast Asian Nations
ASEM	Asia-Europe Meeting
ARF	ASEAN Regional Forum
CEPT	Common Effective Preferential Tariff
CGDK	Coalition Government of Democratic Kampuchea
COMECON	Council for Mutual Economic Assistance
CPM	Communist Party of Malaya
DK	Democratic Kampuchea
DRV	Democratic Republic of Vietnam
EAEC	East Asian Economic Caucus
EAEG	East Asian Economic Grouping
EEC	European Economic Community
EC	European Community
EOI	Export-Oriented Industrialisation
ESCAP	Economic and Social Commission on Asia and the Pacific
EU	European Union
FAO	Food and Agriculture Organization
FDI	Foreign Direct Investment
FPDA	Five Power Defence Arrangement
GATT	General Agreement on Tariffs and Trade
ICK	International Conference on Kampuchea
IMF	International Monetary Fund
ISI	Import-Substituting Industrialisation
JIM	Jakarta Informal Meeting
KPNLF	Khmer People's National Liberation Front
MAPHILINDO	Malaysia, Philippines, Indonesia
NATO	North Atlantic Treaty Organization
NICs	Newly Industrialising Countries
OAS	Organization of American States
OAU	Organization of African Unity
SEAC	South East Asia Command (Southeast Asia Command)
SEANWFZ	Southeast Asia Nuclear Weapon-Free Zone
SEATO	Southeast Asia Treaty Organization
SLORC	State Law and Order Restoration Council
TAC	Treaty of Amity and Cooperation
USSR	Union of Soviet Socialist Republics
ZOPFAN	Zone of Peace, Freedom and Neutrality

Contents

Acknowledgements	iii
Preface by Anthony Reid	v
List of Tables	vii
List of Maps	vii
List of Acronyms	viii

INTRODUCTION
Region and Regionalism in the Making of Southeast Asia — 1

Introduction	1
Unity in Diversity	3
Interactions and Identity	9
Structure of the Book	11

CHAPTER 1
Imagining Southeast Asia — 17

Introduction	17
Southeast Asian States and State-System in the Pre-Colonial Era	18
Commerce, Colonialism and the Regional Concept	29
After the War: (Re)Inventing the Region	34
Conclusion	37

CHAPTER 2
Nationalism, Regionalism and the Cold War Order — 43

Introduction	43
The Nationalist Vision of Regionalism	43
Development, Legitimacy and Regional (Dis)order	51
Great Power Rivalry and Regional Autonomy	63
Conclusion	72

CHAPTER 3
The Evolution of Regional Organisation — 78

Introduction	78
ASA and Maphilindo	78
The Establishment of ASEAN: Motivating Factors	83
Dimensions of ASEAN Regionalism	91
Conclusion	98

CHAPTER 4

Southeast Asia Divided: Polarisation and Reconciliation   105

   Introduction   105
   Vietnam and ASEAN   106
   ASEAN and the Cambodia Conflict   111
   Towards Regional Reconciliation   117
   East Asian Regionalisation and Southeast Asian Regionalism   123
   The "ASEAN Way"   127
   Conclusion   129

CHAPTER 5

Managing "One Southeast Asia"   133

   Introduction   133
   Towards "One Southeast Asia"   134
   Southeast Asia and Asia Pacific Security Cooperation   143
   Southeast Asia and Asia Pacific Economic Cooperation   148
   Globalization and the Crisis of Regional Identity   154
   Conclusion   157

CONCLUSION

The Making and Possible Unmaking of Southeast Asia   163

Bibliography   170
Index   185

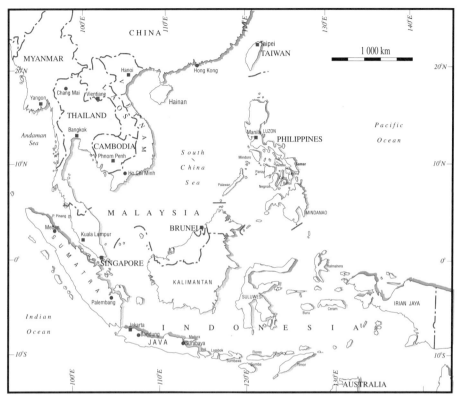

Map 1 Map of Southeast Asia

Table 0.1: Selected Indicators of Southeast Asian States, 1997

Countries	Land Area Sq kms	Population ('000)	GDP billion US$	GDP/Cap US$	Exports million US$	Imports million US$
Brunei	5,765	305	5.3	17,377.0	2,608.9	2,505.2
Cambodia	181,000	10,960	3.1*	297.9*	624	1,114.0
Indonesia	1,919,317	200,000	222.5	1112.5	49,814.7	42,928.5
Laos	236,800	4,800	2.1	437.5	313.1	678.1
Malaysia	329,758	21,170	99.2	4686.1	76,703.0	72,691.2
Myanmar	676,577	45,570	121.0	2,655.0	885.6	1,829.2
Philippines	300,000	71,900	83.8	1165.4	20,543.0	31,885.0
Singapore	648	3,612	94.1	26,041.0	125,006.7	131,326.4
Thailand	514,000	60,000	186.7	3,111.7	55,770.6	72,386.9
Vietnam	330,955	75,350	23.5	311.7	6,800.0	10,200.0

* for 1996

Source: ASEAN Secretariat; *UN Statistical Yearbook for Asia and the Pacific 1998* (Bangkok: UN Economic and Social Commission for Asia and the Pacific, 1998); International Monetary Fund, *Direction of Trade Statistics Yearbook 1998* (Washington, DC: International Monetary Fund 1998).

INTRODUCTION

Region and Regionalism in the Making of Southeast Asia

This book, as the title suggests, explores the issue of "identity" in the international relations of Southeast Asia. The term "identity" is understood here as a "regional identity", and is examined with specific reference to two basic propositions. The first holds that the international relations of Southeast Asia has much to do with conscious attempts by its leaders (with some help from outsider scholars and policy-makers) to "imagine", delineate, and organise its political, economic, social and strategic space. In this sense, the politics among the states of Southeast Asia can be understood as a quest for common identity in the face of the region's immense diversity and myriad countervailing forces, including the ever-present danger of intra-regional conflict and the divisive impact of extra-regional actors and events. The second proposition holds that regional cooperation, in various conceptions and guises, has played a central role in shaping the modern Southeast Asian identity. By seeking to limit external influences and developing a regulatory framework for managing inter-state relations, it has made the crucial difference between the forces of conflict and cooperation that lie at the core of the international relations of Southeast Asia.

By emphasising the idea of "region", this book seeks to overcome what John Legge once described as "the almost universal tendency of historians to focus on the constituent parts of Southeast Asia rather than to develop a perception of the region as a whole as a suitable subject of study."[1] While some historians have now overcome this tendency (notably Anthony Reid in his two-volume *Southeast Asia in the Age of Commerce* and Nicholas Tarling in his *Nations and States in Southeast Asia*)[2], regional perspectives on Southeast Asian politics and international relations remain scarce. Scholarly work on the foreign policies of individual Southeast Asian states, as well as studies of regional security and regional political economy, are often undertaken without regard to the question of what constitutes the region and the issue of regional identity. Through its analysis of the international relations of Southeast Asia, this book seeks to ascertain where there are regional patterns and characteristics which could validate or negate Southeast Asia's claim to be a region.

By emphasising the role of "regionalism", the book highlights one of the defining features of the international relations of Southeast Asia in the post-World War II period. The history of Southeast Asia's international relations is to a great extent a history of attempts to forge regional unity and the success and failure of these attempts. Yet most studies of Southeast Asian regionalism, analysed in subsequent chapters of this book, deal with political, strategic and economic aspects of regional cooperation without attempting to assess their cumulative impact on regional identity. A specific aim of this book is to investigate the impact of regionalism on the idea of regional identity.

The task of analysing Southeast Asia in terms of region and regionalism has assumed a new importance in view of several developments. First, intra-regional linkages within Southeast Asia have been transformed. For the first time in its history, there is a regional organisation that claims to represent the "entire" region of Southeast Asia. The political division of Southeast Asia based on the relative intensity of nationalism and competing ideological orientations of regimes, which characterised intra-regional relations since the end of the Second World War, has come to an end. Notwithstanding differences among Southeast Asian states in terms of their openness to the global economy, their domestic social and political organisation, and their relationship with outside powers, Southeast Asia today arguably displays far more homogeneity and convergence than at any other time in the modern era.

Second, we have seen the emergence of new ways of thinking about regions and regionness. As discussed later in the Introduction, the earlier "scientific" or positivist approaches that "measured" regionness by using concrete empirical indicators, and then by adding in levels of interaction and inter-connectedness, have given way to efforts that view regions primarily as "imagined" constructs. If the nation-state can be an "imagined community", to use Benedict Anderson's classic formulation, why not regions?

Third, there has been a shift from external, imperial and orientalist constructions of Southeast Asia to internal, indigenous and regional constructions. As John Legge points out, much of the pre-war study of Southeast Asia (largely done by outside observers) saw "events [in the region] being shaped by external influences".[3] This is not surprising for a region where outsiders have, since the classical period, played a dominant role in defining its regional space. Indeed, the main references to the area now regarded as Southeast Asia were coined by outsiders, such as the term *Suvarnabbhumi* (covering areas east of the Bay of Bengal) found in Indian Buddhist writings, or the Chinese concept of "Nanyang" (the Southern Ocean), or "Nanhai" (the Southern Sea), an area extending roughly in the west from the port of Foochow to Palembang, and in the east from Taiwan to Borneo's west coast. In the past, Southeast Asian scholars have been justly accused of being "interested ... primarily in external stimuli, to the detriment of the study of indigenous institutions."[4] Today, there is a greater sense that the affairs of Southeast Asia, including its international relations, are to a larger extent being shaped by local actors and processes of interaction. The shift is from a simplistic Cold War geopolitical view of Southeast Asia prevailing in the West to a regionalist conception of Southeast Asia as a region-for-itself, constructed by the collective political imagination of, and political interactions among, its own inhabitants.

Looking at the main forces of continuity and change in Southeast Asia, I have been struck by the way in which debates about "regionness" and regional identity have lurked beneath the surface of major issues in the foreign policy and international relations of Southeast Asian states. This is true of the principal geo-strategic events, such as the end of the Vietnam War, the Vietnamese invasion of Cambodia, or the establishment of the Association of Southeast Asian Nations (ASEAN) which have shaped Southeast Asian history since World War II. It is also true of the way in which economic and political issues, be they economic globalisation, or contemporary debates over human rights and democracy have been perceived and debated within the region. In all these cases, questions about where/who/what is Southeast Asia (where is Southeast Asia?; who is Southeast Asian?; and what is the typical and appropriate Southeast Asian way of doing things?) have been crucial factors influencing both Southeast Asia's intra-regional international relations and its relationship with the outside world. Thus, no serious study of Southeast Asia's international relations can afford to ignore the question of regional identity.

Unity in Diversity

But what makes Southeast Asia a "region"? Any scholar writing a book on Southeast Asia is immediately confronted with this difficult question. Any generalisations about the region run the risk of being branded as over-simplification. A principal reason for this has to be the sheer diversity — geographic, ethnosocial, political etc. — of the region. Clark Neher, a political scientist, argues that the diversity of Southeast Asia is the main reason why there have been so few scholars who have attempted to study the region systematically.[5] But diversity can be a unifying theme as well. One could even argue that it is this very diversity which underlies Southeast Asia's claim to be a distinctive region.

The noted historian of Southeast Asia, Wang Gungwu, raises such a possibility in his preface to a famous volume on Southeast Asian history during the period between the 9th and 14th centuries. During this era, Wang notes, the boundaries of Southeast Asia were not so clearly defined. Moreover, "local peoples during this period showed little consciousness of strong cultural commonalities". As a result, "(t)here was no sense of belonging to a region, and it is probably anachronistic to expect such feelings." But then he wonders, "(w)as that very lack of consciousness of boundaries itself a major common trait that distinguished the region from others?"[6]

From this perspective, one could argue that diversity is what gives Southeast Asia its distinctiveness and makes Southeast Asian studies interesting and worthwhile. Certainly, diversity is not a deterrent to applying the label of "region" to Southeast Asia. Sociologist Hans-Dieter Evers suggests that diversity provides a useful focus for studying the region:

> There is, undoubtedly, some unity ranging from a certain 'South-East Asianism' in culture and social organization to a commonality of political interest expressed in the recent formation of ASEAN. But there is no need ... to deny the obvious diversity in the South-East Asian region. In fact, this diversity should be recognized and analyzed.[7]

While some may dismiss it as a mere "academic" question, the "regionness" of Southeast Asia is a matter of considerable significance for its states and societies. It is a crucial issue for those who want to study the international relations of the region, including, as with this author, those assessing not only the pattern of conflict and cooperation within the region but also the relationship between the region and the outside world.

Regions are contested notions. There is nothing "natural" about regionness. There are any number of ways in which regionness can be explored, identified and established, but no single attempt is likely to prove definitive and universally acceptable.

Most traditional definitions of regions base themselves on relatively fixed attributes, such as proximity, shared cultural characteristics, and a common heritage. Such approaches seek to determine what is common among the peoples and political units that inhabit a given geographic space. Attempts to focus on more dynamic factors are not uncommon but have not yielded any generally acceptable definition. For example, a classic study by Cantori and Speigel on "regional sub-systems" (a code word for regions among international relations scholars of that period) published in 1970 identified geographic proximity, international interaction, common bonds, including ethnic, cultural, social and historical, and a sense of regional identity which may be enhanced by attitude and the role of external actors.[8] Another well-known study by Russett suggested five criteria: social and cultural homogeneity, political attitudes or external behaviour, political institutions, economic interdependence and geographical proximity.[9] A survey of the work of 22 scholars on regions by Thompson found three clusters of necessary and sufficient attributes of "regional sub-systems": general geographic proximity, regularity and intensity of interactions and shared perceptions of the regional sub-system as a distinctive theatre of operations.[10] But none of these studies have proven definitive and laid to rest the debate over the ambiguities surrounding the concept. Nor have they resolved the tension between the geographic and perceptual, fixed and dynamic, rationalistic and discursive, variables that define regionness.

In addressing the question of the regionness of Southeast Asia, scholars writing on the region have usually begun with a "unity in diversity" approach, which relies heavily on a consideration of the geographic and cultural elements that are common to states and societies inhabiting the general area. This approach assumes the existence of a region despite conceding important differences between states and societies that comprise it. Thus, Donald McCloud, one of the pioneers of a regional approach to Southeast Asian affairs, notes: "an understanding of Southeast Asia must begin with the balancing of ... often divergent and overlapping characteristics."[11] In a similar vein, Milton Osborne describes "South-east Asia" as "an immensely varied region marked by some notable unities and containing great diversity."[12]

Foremost among the sources of diversity in Southeast Asia is the division between mainland and maritime/archipelagic segments. This division has been important to studies of the classical inter-state relations of Southeast Asia. Mainland Southeast Asia consists of a series of mountain chains enclosing major depressions — the Mekong Valley, Central Plain of Thailand and the Irrawaddy Basin. Interestingly, each of these depressions has been at the heart of major polities. While the mountains are not high enough (only the Arakan Yoma exceeds 3,000 metres) to have offered a serious barrier to communication, they create a sufficient enclosure to allow for the consolidation of political systems. These core areas fostered imperial states which dominated much of the mainland as well as parts of island Southeast Asia. Indeed, the very first major classical state of Southeast Asia, Funan, provides a good example of this; reaching its height at the end of the fifth century, it extended control over much of the Malay Peninsula.[13]

Island Southeast Asia presents a different (although how different is a matter of debate) and more complex picture. Here the river valleys are not as large, and the alluvial lowland areas (except for eastern Sumatra and Kalimantan) are also relatively small in size. This meant that the agricultural resources available to early states were limited. It also explains why political systems in island Southeast Asia were much more fragmented and volatile than the mainland, and why it is only through the control of sea routes that small states could transform themselves into larger empires. The rise of the port city state of Srivijaya between the seventh and thirteenth centuries attests to this. Command over the sea route between India and China, especially control of the Straits of Malacca, was the basis of its strength and prominence. This example would be followed in later periods by Malacca, Aceh, Penang and Singapore, all port city states.[14]

Other sources of Southeast Asia's diversity are well-known and range from the religious — represented in the presence of Islam, Buddhism, Hinduism, and Confucianism — and the ethnic (mainland Southeast Asia is home to more than 150 distinct ethnic groups; Indonesia alone has some 25 major languages and 250 dialects) to assorted non-ethnic factors such as agricultural practices (upland versus lowland), domicile, belief systems, and communications patterns. On the other hand, diversity in the linguistic field is now thought to have been overstated, as scholars sympathetic to the notion of Southeast Asia as a distinctive region like to point out. This is evident not just from the fact that the Malay/Indonesian language is spoken, with expected variations, in Malaysia, Indonesia, Brunei, southern Philippines and southern coastal regions in Thailand, Cambodia, and Vietnam. Recent research has led to the discovery of a common ancestry among mainland languages as well including modern Vietnamese and Khmer languages.[15] The Vietnamese and the Tai (comprising Thai, Lao, Shan, and others), once thought to belong to the Sino-Tibetan school, are now understood to be closer to the Austro-Asiatic school, which is related to the Mon-Khmer languages of Southeast Asia spoken in Pegu and Cambodia (as well as other parts of mainland Southeast Asia) in older times. Clearly, if a common language was to be the basis of shaping political structures, then the modern "national" boundaries of Southeast Asia would appear to be very artificial indeed.

While language may provide a clear example of the "unity in diversity" approach, other elements are no less important. Anthony Reid, for example, points to water and forest as the "dominant elements" in the physical environment of Southeast Asia. Rice, fish, and betel are quintessentially Southeast Asian, while meat and milk products are not. The human element is important too. Reid writes that while the "bewildering" range of language, culture, and religion in Southeast Asia and its exposure to commerce from outside the region may make it difficult to generalise about the region, there exists a greater similarity and congruence of human characteristics at the level of "popular beliefs and social practices of ordinary Southeast Asians".[16]

It is important to bear in mind that many scholars who have made important contributions to the development of Southeast Asian studies have not found it worthwhile to discover a unity from the apparent diversity of the area. Such scholars have shied away from developing a comparative or regional approach to studying Southeast Asian states and societies. D.G.E. Hall, the author of one of the earliest and most influential books on Southeast Asian history, devoted a mere paragraph to the controversy surrounding the emergence and usage of the term.[17] Characterising the area as a "chaos of races and languages",[18] Hall observed that the term "South-East Asia" only "came into general use during the Second World War to describe the territories of the eastern Asiatic mainland forming the Indo-Chinese peninsula and the immense archipelago which includes Indonesia and the Philippines". Hall did refer to the various usages of the term. This included "South-East Asia "(used by the British Royal Navy); "South East Asia" (used by the Southeast Asia Command most of the time, but not always); and "Southeast Asia" (preferred by many American writers as well as the British scholar, Victor Purcell). But he found "no valid reason" why the latter should be considered better than the others. For him, all these were terms of convenience and like many other large areas, open to objections. But further discussion of these controversies, Hall contended, would be "unnecessary, since our use of the term is dictated solely by convenience".[19] Hall was not alone in choosing to ignore the controversies surrounding the definition of the region. One of the most important post-Second World War collections of essays on the politics of the region, *Government and Politics of Southeast Asia*, published by Cornell University Press in 1964, consisted of country studies and contained no attempt to develop a regional or a comparative (cross-country) perspective involving more than one Southeast Asian state.[20]

A different approach emerged from the works of some pre- and post-Second World War scholars of Southeast Asia. Confronted with the diversity of the region, they responded by formulating new analytic concepts and theories, such as J.S. Furnivall's "plural societies" and J.H. Boeke's "dual organisation". While not necessarily applicable to the whole of Southeast Asia as we understand it today, these concepts nonetheless provided the impetus to view the region systematically as a single framework of analysis. As such, they transcended country-specific perspectives while helping to bring out Southeast Asia's distinctiveness vis-a-vis other regions.[21] Even more directly concerned with Southeast Asia's regional characteristics was Charles A. Fisher, who in his 1964 book, *South-East Asia: A Social, Economic and Political Geography*, found it important to discuss "The Personality of South-east Asia", and to distinguish it from that of neighbouring civilisations. Fisher characterised "South-east Asia" as a "collective name for the series of peninsulas and islands which lie to the east of India and Pakistan and to the south of China". Before the advent of European colonialism, Fisher noted, the region had been overshadowed by the cultural and civilisational influence of India and China, receiving recognition as a distinctive region only after the Second World War.[22] Fisher highlighted the two older terms used for referring to this geographic region, "Further India" and "Far Eastern Tropics", the former connoting "an eastward extension of India", while the latter took the area to be "a tropical appendage of the Far East proper."[23]

8   THE QUEST FOR IDENTITY: INTERNATIONAL RELATIONS OF SOUTHEAST ASIA

Justifying a regional concept, Fisher spoke of a double unity of Southeast Asia. The first, "the inherent geographical unity of South-east Asia", had always been negative in character.[24] He identified three ways in which the area can be differentiated from the rest of Asia. The first is the fact that Southeast Asia straddles the equator and lies wholly within the humid tropics, while only part of the Indian sub-continent is strictly tropical and the whole of the Far East within the temperate zone. A second factor is its remoteness from human settlements in the vast continental interior of Asia and the related fact of its location as a maritime crossroads exposed to repeated sea-borne invasions. The third is the geographic and geological complexity of Southeast Asia when compared to India and China. Southeast Asia is a region "deeply interpenetrated by arms and gulfs of the sea, and further broken up by its intricate and rugged relief."[25]

Apart from the geographical unity of Southeast Asia, Fisher also referred to the "underlying cultural unity" of its lowland peoples, which constitute the majority of the populations of all the states of the region. In his view, the "most important common denominator within the region" was similarities in their "folklore, traditional architectural styles, methods of cultivation, and social and political organization".[26] These were supplemented by the similarity in physical and mental characteristics of the region's population, including the Burmans, Thais, Cambodians, Vietnamese, Malays, most Indonesians, and Filipinos. These peoples were described as being of "the same predominantly Mongoloid cast of countenance, yellow-brown skin colour, and rather short stature, as well as a natural elegance of bearing and an apparently innate cheerfulness and good humour".[27]

Like many Southeast Asianists of the period, Fisher cautioned against over-emphasising the historical influence of India and China in shaping the culture and civilisation of Southeast Asia (this point will be discussed in greater detail in Chapter 1).[28] He concluded that Southeast Asia ought to be regarded as a distinct region within the larger unity of the Monsoon Lands as a whole, and worthy to be ranked as an intelligible field of study on its own account".[29] As he summed up, "tropical and maritime, focal but fragmented, ethnically and culturally diverse, plural alike in economy and society, and demographically a low-pressure area in an otherwise congested continent, South-east Asia clearly possesses a distinctive personality of its own and is more than a mere indeterminate borderland between India and China."[30]

Despite its wide acceptance by scholars, the "unity in diversity" approach is ultimately an inconclusive effort to establish Southeast Asia as a regional unit. Apart from a lingering question whether it overstates the geographic and socio-cultural similarities among its constituent units, this approach only provides a static conception of the region. If regions are defined by a common heritage and a shared history, then one must look not only at the relatively fixed elements constituting that heritage, as the "unity in diversity" approach does, but also the dynamic and interactive factors that create a regional pattern. To address this shortcoming, we need to turn to other, more recent approaches to defining regionness that are relevant to analysing Southeast Asia as a regional concept.

Interactions and Identity

Recent scholarship on Southeast Asia seems to be adopting a wider range of perspectives when considering its claim to be a region than the traditional unity in diversity approach. Some of these reflect developments in the wider social sciences where a variety of new approaches to defining "regionness" has emerged. For example, a recent body of work on regions takes a political economy perspective, attempting to conceptualise them as by-products of the process of globalisation. In this view, regionness is determined by location and specificity within the world economy or transnational production structures.[31] Other scholars have focused on the role of a hegemonic power as the crucial factor in region formation,[32] while yet another approach has defined regionness in terms of patterns of interaction, especially conflict and cooperation.[33] The existence of intense regional conflicts may be as important to establishing a claim to regionness as regional associations and the development of cooperative economic and political approaches. And an increasingly fashionable way of studying regions is to view them as clusters of shared identity, both self-conceived and perceived as such by outsiders. In this sense, regionness depends as much on representation as on "reality". Like nation states, regions are conceptualised as "imagined communities".[34]

To be sure, even the traditional literature on Southeast Asia was not totally incognizant of such understanding. For O.W. Wolters, constructing a regional history of Southeast Asia means investigating "cultural similarities and intra-regional relationships".[35] For Fisher, Southeast Asia's regionness is a matter of geographic location and geostrategic vulnerabilities.[36] Anthony Reid has done more than most scholars to highlight the pattern of pre-colonial commercial linkages in the regional construction of Southeast Asia.[37] More recently, several scholars have turned to identity politics. Thus, Leonard Andaya observes that "region may be defined as an area incorporating ethnonations and nation-states which perceive or 'imagine' common bonds that unite them and distinguish them from others".[38] Applying this definition to Southeast Asia, he concludes that "'Southeast Asia' is no longer simply a term of convenience. Southeast Asians themselves now think regionally."[39]

These various ways of looking at regions are not mutually exclusive. For example, a recent collection of essays on the regional concept of

Southeast Asia combines insights from comparative politics, international relations, history and anthropology, thereby explicitly acknowledging the need for methodological pluralism.[40] Moreover some scholars have tried to trace the evolution of the regional concept by identifying stages in which different factors — domestic politics, academic scholarship, and extra-regional developments — may have been most influential. A good example of this approach comes from Russell Fifield, who identified five steps in the evolution of Southeast Asia as a regional entity, including the creation of the Southeast Asia Command (SEAC); the development of Southeast Asian Studies, especially in the US in the 1940s and 50s; the first and second Indochina wars and the articulation of the "domino theory" by successive US administrations; the decolonization process; and the acceptance and development of the regional concept by the region's governing elites.[41]

For the purpose of this book, one of the main catalysts of the evolution of Southeast Asia as a region can be found in intra-regional perceptions and interactions. The historian O.W. Wolters was among the first to speak of intra-regional relationships in defining the regional concept of Southeast Asia, but as discussed in Chapter 1, he was mainly referring to cultural interactions in pre-colonial times. The approach of this book is more explicitly political, as evident in its emphasis on the role of regionalism.

Regionalism can shape the idea of region in a variety of ways. It may reduce diversity and accentuate homogeneity, especially in the political, economic and social spheres, if not in the geographic and cultural domains. This can be achieved through a diffusion of norms, policies and practices of regional organisations and associations, formal or informal. For example, regional organisations can promote common ideologies and political values, adopt convergent development policies and facilitate their implementation and take steps to reduce inequity among members. This could produce greater homogeneity and commonality that are essential to regional identity.

In addition, regionalism can generate unity through interactions. It can help manage differences and conflicts among states and contribute to greater regional cohesion, an important aspect of regionness. The perception of region can be strengthened through the peaceful management of intra-mural conflicts and disputes over territorial, political and economic issues. Furthermore, regionalism can contribute to the idea of a region by enhancing the commitment on the part of countries of a given geographic area to present a unified front vis-a-vis the outside world. Such a quest for regional autonomy is often revealed through policies of inclusion and exclusion, and by adoption of common policies that secure the interests and identity of the region from larger global forces.

In exploring the regional concept of Southeast Asia, the book argues that regions are socially constructed, rather than geographically or ethno-socially pre-ordained. Southeast Asia's regionness cannot be established by simply looking at its geographic proximity or shared cultural attributes. Regions, like nation-states, are imagined communities. This by itself is no longer a novel argument, although few people have provided a systematic historical study of the construction of Southeast Asia's regional identity. It is attempted here based on the belief that such an approach can be useful in understanding the international relations of Southeast Asia. Southeast Asia's international relations represent a quest for regional identity. Success or failure in developing this identity explains a great deal of the pattern of conflict and cooperation among countries professing to be part of the region.

Structure of the Book

The book is divided into five chapters. The first discusses, in broad historical terms, some of the key features of the pre-colonial pattern of inter-state relations within the area which is roughly considered to be Southeast Asia today. The analysis centres on the insights of a few scholars — none of whom is a political scientist — who have discerned patterns of statehood and interactions within varied historical and geopolitical settings. The key patterns include O.W. Wolters' concept of the *mandala* state, Clifford Geertz's notion of the "theatre state" and Stanley Tambiah's concept of "galactic polity". While selectively time-specific, these "imagined" frameworks do provide an immensely useful base upon which to begin a study of the modern inter-state and international relations of Southeast Asia. Then the chapter looks at the impact of commerce and colonialism on the regional concept of Southeast Asia and the regional pattern of inter-state relations that developed during the classical period. It ends by examining the factors which contributed to a "resurrection" of the Southeast Asia concept and pattern in the aftermath of the Second World War.

Chapter 2 looks critically at the inter-relationship between nationalism, regionalism and the Cold War international order in Southeast Asia and its contribution to the idea of region. The main historical force examined here is nationalism. Regionalism played only a secondary role, although it was clearly an ascending force. Moreover, the concept of region and regionalism which best described the relations among the new nation-states of Southeast Asia was Asia-wide, rather than Southeast Asian. Nonetheless, the convergence and divergence among nationalist movements, the debates about the appropriate form of regional organisation and the impact of Cold War alignments on these concepts were influential in shaping Southeast Asia's claim to be a region.

12 THE QUEST FOR IDENTITY: INTERNATIONAL RELATIONS OF SOUTHEAST ASIA

Chapter 3 deals with an era in which the forces of nationalism outside of Indochina and Burma were yielding slowly to a new regional consciousness born out of common fears of communism and a pragmatic concern with economic development. This was the period of the birth of ASEAN, after earlier experiments in regional unity had faltered. The chapter looks at the circumstances surrounding the emergence of ASEAN, the development of its political, security and economic cooperation geared to management of intra-regional relations as well as the relationship between Southeast Asia and the outside powers.

While the emergence of ASEAN gave a powerful boost to the concept of Southeast Asia, it did not solve the problem of regional unity and integration. The Vietnamese invasion of Cambodia and ASEAN's efforts to resist it and roll it back, the defining events of Southeast Asian international relations through the 1980s, had paradoxical effects on regional identity. While confirming the polarisation of the region into two ideologically competing blocs, it also gave Southeast Asia greater international recognition. By creating a common purpose among the ASEAN regimes, the Cambodia conflict helped to accelerate the process of socialisation and norm-setting in the region. While Vietnam remained isolated and excluded from this process, these norms and the "ASEAN Way" of socialisation would constitute the basis of regional reconciliation during the following decade. Chapter 4, which focuses on the ASEAN-Indochina divide, concludes by discussing the domestic, intra-regional, and international forces which ended polarisation of Southeast Asia.

Chapter 5 examines the international relations of Southeast Asia following the end of the Cold War in general and the Paris Peace Agreement on Cambodia (1991) in particular. The 1990s saw dramatic twists in the fortunes of Southeast Asia. It began on a highly optimistic note: the end of superpower rivalry, the political settlement to the Cambodia conflict, and the surge of global recognition for, and confidence in, ASEAN's ability to manage regional order. The idea of region seemed triumphant. The dream of "One Southeast Asia", comprising the ten states which are officially recognised as Southeast Asian, was reinvented and pursued. But the region also faced new perils threatening to undermine its unity and coherence. Part of these came from inter-state conflicts "swept under the carpet" during the Cold War and now brought to the surface with the lifting of the superpower strategic blanket. But the problems facing the region resulted also from the forces of globalisation which had dominated the economic and political landscape of Southeast Asia. These forces included economic linkages that tied the fate of Southeast Asian economies to those of the wider Asia Pacific, and new regional production structures and multilateral institutions that went beyond the Southeast Asian inter-state system. In building a regional identity, ASEAN had clearly underestimated the burdens imposed by the "One Southeast

Asia" concept. The Asian economic crisis from mid-1997 brought to the fore many of the latent contradictions and tensions in the regional concept of Southeast Asia, and posed a critical test of regionalism in shaping international relations of the region in competition with wider regional and global trends. The future of the idea of Southeast Asia as a region depends very much on how it survives and overcomes these challenges.

Although the chapters follow a rough historical sequence, I have avoided dividing them into distinct periods or phases. Any attempt to so divide Southeast Asian history is bound to be arbitrary. Some of the chapters in the book clearly overlap with one another. For example, Chapter 1 ends with a look at post-war efforts to intellectually reconstruct Southeast Asia as a region while Chapter 2 discusses the more material relationships between nationalism, regionalism and Cold War geopolitics during roughly the same period. Similarly, Chapter 3 begins with a discussion of the emergence of Southeast Asian regional organisation (ASA, Maphilindo) in the early 1960s, although this period is also previewed in Chapter 2 which contains discussions of mostly pan-Asian (as opposed to Southeast Asian) conceptions of regional unity. Because ASA and Maphilindo were direct precursors to ASEAN, it is more useful to discuss them in the chapter that deals primarily with ASEAN's formation and early evolution. On the whole, the chapters are organised on the basis of a thematic, rather than strictly chronological approach. Thus, the main theme of Chapter 1 is the intellectual reconstruction of Southeast Asian state-system and regional identity from a historical perspective, that of Chapter 2 is the impact of nationalism on regionalism, of Chapter 3 is the evolution of Southeast Asian regionalism that of Chapter 4 is the ASEAN-Indochina divide, and that of Chapter 5 is the prospects for regional order in Southeast Asia in the post-Cold War period.

Before we turn to the chapters, it is important to state what this book does not seek to accomplish. It is not a political history of Southeast Asia. Nor does it intend to provide a comprehensive historical narrative on the evolution of regionalism or the various frameworks of regional organisation, although these are important and continuous themes of the book. Rather, what follows is a selective historical analysis of the broad political, economic and strategic forces which have influenced the international relations of Southeast Asia *at the intra-regional level.* Moreover, this book does not purport to describe the place and role of Southeast Asia in the international system. That would require a much more detailed analysis of great power policies and the impact of global events on regional relationships. Instead, this book adopts a bottom-up approach, focusing on the evolution of intra-regional interactions which determine how external actors and events are perceived in the region, and which shape their impact on the region as a whole.

14 THE QUEST FOR IDENTITY: INTERNATIONAL RELATIONS OF SOUTHEAST ASIA

Notes

[1] J.D. Legge (1992) "The Writing of Southeast Asian History", in *The Cambridge History of Southeast Asia vol.1*, Cambridge: Cambridge University Press, pp.4–5.

[2] A. Reid (1988, 1993) *Southeast Asia in the Age of Commerce 1450–1680, Volumes One and Two*, New Haven: Yale University Press; N. Tarling, (1998) *Nations and States in Southeast Asia*, Cambridge: Cambridge University Press. In subsequent years, studies assuming a region of Southeast Asia have appeared. The introduction to a recent collection of essays on the regional concept of Southeast Asia noted a move from an "area studies" approach to what it called a "regional studies" approach to Southeast Asia studies. This was helped by the work of scholars who had looked *reflexively* at a "region" of Southeast Asia. A. Acharya and A. Rajah (1999), "Introduction: Reconceptualising Southeast Asia", Special issue of *Southeast Asian Journal of Social Science*, vol. 27, no.1, p.1.

[3] J.D. Legge (1992) "The Writing of Southeast Asian History", op cit, p.6.

[4] D.J. Steinberg, ed. (1987) *In Search of Southeast Asia*, Honolulu: University of Hawaii Press, p.1.

[5] C.D. Neher (1984) "The Social Sciences" in Ronald A. Morse, ed., *Southeast Asian Studies: Options for the Future*, Lanham: University Press of America, p.130.

[6] G. Wang (1986) "Introduction", in D. Marr and A.C. Milner, eds. (1986) *Southeast Asia in the 9th to 14th Centuries*, Singapore: Institute of Southeast Asian Studies, p.xviii

[7] H. Evers (1980) "The Challenge of Diversity: Basic Concepts and Theories in the Study of South-East Asian Societies", in Evers, ed. (1980) *Sociology of South-East Asia*, Kuala Lumpur: Oxford University Press, p.2.

[8] L.J. Cantori and S.L. Spiegel, ed. (1970) *The International Politics of Regions: A Comparative Approach*, Englewood Cliffs, N.J.: Prentice Hall.

[9] B.M. Russett (1967) *International Regions and the International System: A Study in Political Ecology*, Chicago: Rand McNally; B.M. Russett, (1968) "Delineating International Regions" in J.D. Singer, ed. (1968) *Quantitative International Politics: Insights and Evidence* , New York: Free Press, pp.317–352.

[10] W.R. Thompson (1973) "The Regional Subsystem: A Conceptual Explication and a Propositional Inventory", *International Studies Quarterly*, vol.17, no.1, March 1973, pp.89–117

[11] D.G. McCloud (1986) *System and Process in Southeast Asia: The Evolution of a Region*, Boulder, Co, Westview Press, p.5. This book reappeared in a revised edition in 1995 under the title: *Southeast Asia: Tradition and Modernity in the Contemporary World*.

[12] M. Osborne (1990) *Southeast Asia: An Ilustrated Introductory History*, St. Leonards, NSW: Allen and Unwin, 5th Edition, p.13.

[13] C. Dixon (1991) *South East Asia in the World-Economy: A Regional Geography*, London: Cambridge University Press, p.36.

[14] The only exception to the sea-based political strength can be found in east-central Java, where states could achieve centralisation and authority similar to the mainland states by exploiting highly fertile river basins to produce resources like the mainland states. M.J. Murray (1980) *The Development of Capitalism in Colonial Indochina, 1870–1940*, Los Angeles: University of California Press; J.E. Spencer (1973) *Oriental Asia: Themes Towards a Geography*, Englewood Cliffs, New Jersey: Prentice-Hall ; C.A. Fisher (1964) *South East Asia: A Social, Economic and Political Geography*, London Methuen; B. Harrison (1963) *South East Asia: A Short History*, London: Macmillan; B.W. Andaya and L.Y. Andaya (1982) *A History of Malaysia*, London: Macmillian; J.C. van Leur (1955) *Indonesian Trade and Society*, van Hoeve, The Hague.

[15] The Tai language, with dialectic variations, is spoken in Thailand, southern China, Vietnam, the Shan states of Burma, Laos, Cambodia (western and north-eastern) and to a lesser extent in the northern parts of pennisular Malaysia. M. Osborne (1990) *Southeast Asia: An Ilustrated Introductory History, op.cit.,* pp.7–8.

[16] A. Reid (1988) *Southeast Asia in the Age of Commerce 1450–1680, Volume One: The Lands Below the Winds,* New Haven: Yale University Press, p.3.

[17] D.G.E. Hall (1968) *A History of South East Asia,* London: Macmillan, p.3.

[18] Ibid., p.5.

[19] Ibid., p.3.

[20] G.M. Kahin (1964) *Governments and Politics of Southeast Asia,* Ithaca: Cornell University Press.

[21] Evers points to a number of concepts developed by Southeast Asian Studies scholars which provided the basis not just for the comparative study of Southeast Asian countries, but also came to be used for social research elsewhere and became "standard concepts of textbook social science." H. Evers, "The Challenge of Diversity", op.cit., pp.2–7. These concepts included J.S. Furnivalls' "plural societies", outlined in a work published in 1939, which described a distinct Southeast Asian form of social organisation which had developed in Burma, Malaya, and the Netherlands Indies towards the end of colonial rule. This organisation consisted of three social orders: the natives, the Chinese and the Europeans, "living side by side, but separately and rarely meeting, save in the material and economic sphere". Another concept was J.H. Boeke's "dualistic economies" or "dual orgainisation". Originally published in 1940, it presented a model describing how capitalist economic development under colonial rule, including the influx of mass products from the metropolitan countries, produced an economic duality in which the lower stratum of society sank into greater poverty while the upper stratum became richer, urbanised and Westernised. See: J.S. Furnivall (1956) *Colonial Policy and Practice: A Comparative Study of Burma and Netherlands India.* New York: New York University Press; J.H. Boeke (1953) *Economics and Economic Policy of Dual Societies as Exemplified by Indonesia,* New York, Institute of Pacific Relations. Other concepts identified by Evers include Geertz's "agricultural involution" (comparing Javanese social development with that of Japan and J. Embree's "loosely structured social systems" (contrasting Japanese and Thai rural society).

[22] C.A. Fisher (1964) *South-East Asia: A Social, Economic and Political Geography,* London: Methuen and Co., p.3.

[23] Ibid., p.3.

[24] Ibid.

[25] Ibid.

[26] Ibid., p.5.

[27] Ibid., p.7.

[28] Ibid.

[29] Ibid., p.8.

[30] Ibid., p.9.

[31] See for example, M. Bernard (1996) "Regions in the Global Political Economy: Beyond the Local-Global Divide in the Formation of the Eastern Asian Region", *New Political Economy,* vol.1, no.3 , pp.335–353. See also R. Stubbs and G.R.D. Underhill, eds. (1999) *Political Economy and the Changing Global Order,* 2nd Edition, Toronto: Oxford University Press.

[32] H. Singh (1999) "Hegemonic Construction of Regions: Southeast Asia as a Case Study", in Sarah Owen, ed., *The State and Identity Construction in International Relations*. London: Macmillan.

[33] An influential formulation is Barry Buzan's notion of "regional security complexes". See B. Buzan (1990) *People, States, and Fear: An Agenda for International Security Studies in the Post-Cold War Era*. Boulder: Lynne Rienner. See also, D. Lake and P. Morgan (1997) eds., *Regional Orders: Building Security in a Modern World*. University Park: The Pennsylvania State University Press.

[34] See, A. Dirlik (1992) "The Asia-Pacific Region: Reality and Representation in the Invention of the Regional Structure", *Journal of World History*, vol.3, no.1, 1992; O. Weaver (1993)"Culture and Identity in the Baltic sea Region", in P. Joenniemi, ed. (1993) *Cooperation in the Baltic Sea Region*, London: Taylor and Francis.

[35] O.W. Wolters (1982), *History, Culture and Region in Southeast Asian Perspective*, Singapore: Institute of Southeast Asian Studies. p.x. A revised and expanded edition of this book was published in 1999 by Cornell University Southeast Asia Programme and the Institute of Southeast Asian Studies.

[36] C. A. Fisher (1964) *South-East Asia: A Social, Economic and Political Geography*. London: Methuen and Co.

[37] A. Reid (1988, 1993), *Southeast Asia in the Age of Commerce 1450–1680*, op.cit.

[38] L.Y. Andaya (1996) "Ethnonation, Nation-State and Regionalism in Southeast Asia", in Proceedings of the International Symposium, "Southeast Asia: Global Area Studies for the 21st Century", Organized by Project Team: An Integrated Approach to Global Area Studies" (funded by Monbusho Grant-in-Aid for Scientific Research on Priority Areas), and Center for Southeast Asian Studies, Kyoto University, Kyoto International Community House, October 18–22, 1996, p.131.

[39] Ibid., p.135.

[40] See A. Acharya, and A. Rajah (1999) Introduction: Reconceptualising Southeast Asia, op. cit.

[41] R. Fifield (1984) 'Southeast Asia' and 'ASEAN' as Regional Concepts in Ronald A. Morse, ed., *Southeast Asian Studies: Options for the Future*, op. cit. pp.125–26.

CHAPTER 1

Imagining Southeast Asia

Introduction

For most students of the "international relations" of Southeast Asia, the
starting point of investigation is often the end of the Second World War.
This is also the beginning of the international recognition of Southeast
Asia as a distinctive region. Political scientists examining the international
relations of Southeast Asia have paid little attention to its pre-colonial
inter-state system. The latter has largely been left to historians and to a
lesser extent, anthropologists. And it is the historians who account for
much of the scholarship on the diplomatic interactions and inter-state
relations of the pre-colonial period.

To some extent, this reflects a general bias in the literature of
international relations, much of which sees the roots of the modern
international system to lie in the European political order that emerged
from the Peace of Westphaila in 1648. From this perspective, the modern
state-system in Southeast Asia is but an extension of the Westphalian
model of sovereign, equal and territorial nation-states, scarcely modified
by any indigenous political tradition and institutional framework that
might have existed before the advent of European colonialism. The long
period of European colonial rule not only saw the erosion of traditional
polities, but at the time of their departure, the colonial powers also ensured
that the newly created polities would at least possess the nominal
attributes of "nation-states" that had become the centerpiece of the modern
international order. Since the concept of the nation-state in Southeast Asia
is very much a post Second World War phenomenon, it seems therefore
proper to begin one's understanding of the "international relations" of
the region from the post-1945 period.

But the tendency to ignore the pre-colonial inter-state system of
Southeast Asia has three unfortunate consequences for scholarship on the
region's international relations. The first is to ignore the possibility that
an indigenous and "regional" pattern of inter-state relations did exist in
Southeast Asia before the advent of colonialism. This possibility in itself
is enough to challenge the view that those seeking to study the idea
of Southeast Asia need not look before the Southeast Asia Command
(SEAC) established in 1945. The second is to miss an opportunity to
remedy the essentially Eurocentric and Americanocentric nature of
contemporary international relations theories and concepts. The third
consequence is the unwillingness or inability of most international
relations scholars to use the past to understand the present. As Wolters

tells us, anyone seeking to understand the sources and patterns of conflict and cooperation (the staple of international relations studies) in Southeast Asia, can benefit from insights available from its pre-colonial state-system.[1]

Southeast Asian States and State-System in the Pre-Colonial Era

But is it possible to think in terms of a regional state-system in precolonial Southeast Asia? Lucian Pye, the noted American political scientist, categorically denies such a possibility. In his view, "there was never a Southeast Asian system of inter-state relations" before the colonial period.[2] The idea of a state-system implies a certain degree of similarity among the major political units of a given period as well as a certain level of interaction among them based on mutually recognised patterns of statecraft. But "the story of Southeast Asia before the Europeans arrived", argues Pye, "was one of the rise and fall of kingdoms and dynastic wars of conquest between separate and isolated kingdoms."[3]

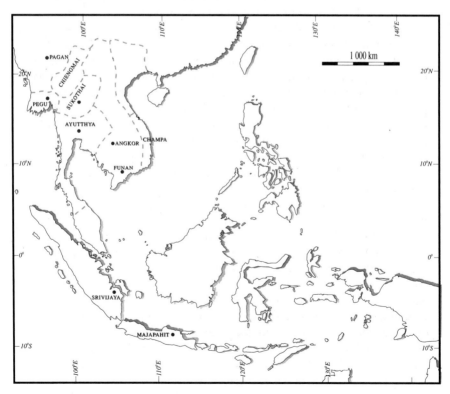

Map 2 Selected Pre-colonial States of Southeast Asia

IMAGING SOUTHEAST ASIA **19**

Table 1.1: Selected Pre-colonial States of Southeast Asia

Empire	Time Period	Geographical Scope
Funan	1–6th Century AD	Ancient Hindu state extending over the Mekong delta, the greater part of modern Cambodia, the lower Menam area and the coastal regions of the Malay peninsula.
Champa	2–17th Century AD	Ancient state in central and southern coastal region of Vietnam.
Pagan	1044–1287 AD	An ancient empire of Myanmar in the Irrawady River region. The Pagan empire extended its influence over a region roughly the size of modern Myanmar.
Srivijaya	7th–13th Century AD	A powerful maritime empire with hegemony over Bangka, Sumatra and the Malay peninsula.
Angkor	9th–15th Century	Ancient Cambodian empire which extended from the tip of the Indochinese peninsula northward to Yunnan and from Vietnam westward to the Bay of Bengal. The Angkor empire was one of the largest, most prosperous and most sophisticated kingdoms in the history of Southeast Asia.
Majapahit	13th–16th Century AD	Major maritime empire covering Bali, Madura, Sumatra and the Malay peninsula, Borneo and the Lesser Sunda Islands, the Celebes and the Moluccas.
Sukhothai	1238–1350 AD	Ancient Thai kingdom in north central Thailand. The Sukhothai kingdom was the first independent Thai state in Thailand's central plain and its hegemony extended north into Laos, west to the Andaman Sea and south to the Malay peninsula.
Ayutthya	1350–1767 AD	Powerful state in continental Southeast Asia. Its influence extended over most of modern Thailand, the Menam basin and a substantial part of the Malay peninsula.

Adding to the difficulty of identifying a pre-colonial state-system in Southeast Asia is the sheer diversity among the classical Southeast Asian polities identified by historians. While external cultural influences, such as "Indianisation" and "Sinicisation" brought about a degree of cultural unity to the area east of India and south of China, they also entrenched

20   THE QUEST FOR IDENTITY: INTERNATIONAL RELATIONS OF SOUTHEAST ASIA

broader cultural-political divisions between the Indianised and Sinicised parts, with the Philippines, relatively untouched by either force, constituting a third distinctive segment.[4] Trade, as the chief medium of the transmission of Indian and Chinese cultural influences, was polarising as well. Among other things, it was responsible for the division of Southeast Asia's political economy into an inland-agrarian "hydraulic" segment (Angkor and the early Mataram), and a riparian or coastal commercial segment (Srivijaya being the most important example).

Yet, other scholars of Southeast Asia disagree with Pye (whose point of reference for comparing precolonial Southeast Asian polities, it may be noted, was the far more developed Chinese state-system and political order) in acknowledging the possibility of a regional framework of interstate relations. In rejecting the popular Western view that the recognition of Southeast Asia as a distinctive region began with the establishment of the Southeast Asia Command during the Second World War, Milton Osborne has argued that as early as in the 1920s and 30s, historians and anthropologists had already begun to take note of similarities among the states and societies of what is now called Southeast Asia. Among these were not only similarities in rituals and family structure, but also evidence of a "regional pattern of international relations within Southeast Asia from its earliest historical periods."[5] This inter-state (I use the term "inter-state" system instead of Osborne's "international relations" to reflect the fact that the latter is a more modern construct that connotes the existence of "nation-states") system of Southeast Asia was loosely defined, and its constituent units and boundaries shifted almost continuously. But it did cover, at various points of the precolonial era, much of what we call Southeast Asia in the postcolonial period.

In looking for the outline, however vague, of a precolonial inter-state system in Southeast Asia, one can turn to the work of some of the most noted Southeast Asianists of our time. Of particular importance here is the contribution of O.W. Wolters, a historian, and Stanley Tambiah, an anthropologist. Wolters's concept of *mandala* (covering both maritime and mainland Southeast Asia),[6] and Tambiah's notion of "galactic polity" (derived mainly from mainland Southeast Asian history) are among the most serious attempts by Southeast Asian specialists to "construct" a regional pattern of statehood and inter-state relations during the pre-colonial period. These constructs not only draw our attention to the shared politico-cultural attributes among the units, but also to the meaningful levels of interaction and interdependence among them. The anthropologist Clifford Geertz's "theatre state" in Bali is another relevant construct, notwithstanding the fact that it describes the politics and inter-state relations of 19th century Bali, compared to the late "classical" era of Southeast Asian history (roughly 4th to 14th century A.D.) featured in the works of Wolters and Tambiah. Indeed, the close affinities between the "theatre state" and the *mandala* has been noted by C. Reynolds who argues that both represent "indigenous, culturally-oriented" models of state which ought to be differentiated from "the Marxian and Weberian notions of the state with fixed boundaries and the rule of law over a given territory."[7]

Common to the three constructs is the idea of loosely organised states existing side-by-side without clearly defined territorial limits. The central political authority exercised by the king generally permitted a considerable amount of autonomy to vassals and lower kings, especially those not in the immediate vicinity of the capital. This is the core of Wolters' formulation of the *mandala* (literally "circle") state. A *mandala* system consists of overlapping "circles of kings" in which the king, "identified with divine and universal authority and defined as the conqueror", could claim personal hegemony over his allies and vassals.[8] The important feature of the system is that the authority of the king over the latter is rarely direct and absolute. Thus, each *mandala* itself is composed of concentric circles, usually three in number, describing centre-periphery relations. The capital and the region of the king's direct control form the centre. This is surrounded by a circle of provinces ruled by princes or governors appointed by the king. These again are surrounded by a third circle comprising tributary polities.[9] Those in the outer circle remain more or less independent kingdoms; while acknowledging the overlordship of the centre, they escape the direct political control of the latter.[10]

Within a *mandala*, statehood was defined not by its "territorial scale", but by sets of "socially definable loyalties that could be mobilsed for common purposes".[11] Wolters provides a number of examples of *mandalas* between the 7th and 14th centuries, the most prominent examples being Srivijaya, Angkor, Ayutthya, and Majapahit. Of these, the *mandala*'s lack of fixed territorial limit is best exmplified by Srivijaya, distinguished by its "notorious uncertainty about its geographical span and political identity".[12] (Indeed, the location of the capital of Srivijaya has not been precisely established to date.) It may be instructive to note that the concept of statehood underlying the *mandala* system was markedly different from the Chinese conception of state featuring fixed boundaries and strict rules of dynastic succession.[13] This, especially the boundary system, was not to be found anywhere in Southeast Asia except Vietnam.

In describing the modern international system, political scientists, especially those identifying with the Realist school, often use the "billiard ball" metaphor. In this imagery, units (states) of similar characteristics relate to one another while maintaining their independent and distinctive existence on the basis of the twin attributes of sovereignty and territoriality. The *mandala*, on the other hand, has been likened to the light of a torch radiating outwards from the centre "gradually fading into the distance and merging imperceptibly with the ascending Power of a neighboring sovereign."[14] For Wolters, the state-system of early Southeast Asian history is akin not to a table full of billiard balls, but to a "patchwork of often overlapping *mandalas*". Because of the vagueness of his territory and the uncertain political loyalties of his vassals, the ruler in the *mandala* system could make no clear distinction between the purpose and conduct of "internal" and "external" relations.[15] The *mandala* thus "represented a particular and often unstable situation in a vaguely definable geographic area without fixed boundaries and where smaller centers tended to look in all directions for security." They would expand and contract in an almost continuous manner as vassals and tributary rulers shifted their loyalties from ruler to ruler when opportunity presented itself.[16]

Weak territoriality and loose central political authority are also key features of Tambiah's construction of "galactic polity". Drawing on examples such as the kingdoms of Pegu, Pagan, Chiangmai, Sukhothai, Ayutthya, Laos, and Cambodia,[17] the concept of "galactic polity" refers to the domain of a universal king (*chakravartin* in Sanskrit) who rules not as an absolute monarch, but rather as a "king of kings". Within his domain are numerous lesser kings who are permitted to remain autonomous after having submitted to the center. Just as a *mandala* consists of concentric circles of authority, the "galactic polity" is "a center-oriented arrangement". The satellite principalities and provinces which exist within this arrangement "reproduced the features of the center on a decreasing scale in a system of graduated autonomies."[18] In describing the inter-state system, Tambiah highlights the "pulsating nature" of galactic polities: "(I)t was part of a large field of coexisting galaxies which mutually inflected one another, and thus expanded or shrank their outer frontiers according to their success in attracting, and then keeping, the outermost satellites within their orbits."[19] As a region of "galactic polities", mainland Southeast Asia consisted of "several core domains and satellite regions that continually changed their affiliation according to the fortunes of war and diplomacy."[20]

Geertz develops a similar conception of inter-state relations in his study of the "theatre state" (*negara*) in Bali. Analysing politics in 19th century Bali and relations among the major states — Den Pasar, Tabanan, Badung, Karengasem, Klungkung — Geertz found that no single state possessed the power to exercise hegemony over the others. Moreover, the major states had to live with "dozens of independent, semi-independent, and quarter-independent rulers" within and beyond their domain.[21] In such a situation, rulers resorted to the use of ceremony and ritual as a tool of power and authority. While Geertz's emphasis on ritual reflects the distinctive situation in Bali and sets his work apart from that of Wolters and Tambiah, in essence it conjures up the same image of states with limited hierarchical organisation, weak internal political and administrative control and blurred and overlapping territorial domains.

In these states, boundaries were not "clearly defined lines but zones of mutual interest". They did not insulate states but served as transition areas "through which 'neighboring' power systems interpenetrated in a dynamic manner". The rulers could not practice "ritualized formal relations across standardized borders".[22] Instead, through exemplary state ritual, they sought to command the loyalty of their subjects and unify their domain even as their state's political and territorial structure remained highly centrifugal. Rulers competed for prestige, rather than property, for people, rather than land.[23] Disagreements and conflicts were seldom over territory, but over "delicate questions of mutual status, of appropriate politesse". Rulers fought over their right to "mobilize particular bodies of men" for state ritual, rather than warfare, although as Geertz notes, the two objectives often converged.[24]

Looking at the *mandala*, the "galactic polity" and the "theatre state", one may get the impression that the early states of Southeast Asia were not in a position to consolidate their domains and expand their political and territorial reach. What then explains the emergence of several powerful states such as Angkor and Ayutthya, which conquered many of their neighbours and controlled vast territories? This has led some scholars to question the historical validity of the *mandala* concept. Kulke argues that while the *mandala* may describe inter-state relations before 1000 AD, the later states of Southeast Asia were more centralised. Based on research into state formation in Java and the modern eastern Indian state of Orissa (which under its ancient name of Kalinga, had extensive maritime links with Southeast Asia and hence might have possessed political systems similar to Southeast Asian kingdoms), Kulke presents an evolutionary model of state formation in Southeast Asia, thereby challenging the essentially static nature of the *mandala*. He traces the evolution of the Southeast Asian state from the "local" to the "regional" and then finally to the "imperial" (or "nuclear areas", "early kingdom", and "imperial kingdom"). It is the second type which most resembles the *mandala* in the sense of being characterised by "a 'multiplicity' of local political centres and shifting loyalties of their leaders, particularly at the periphery of their systems."[25] But beginning with Angkor in the early 9th century, there emerged in Southeast Asia a trend towards a small number of "supra-regional" powers, which was to become a dominant feature of continental Southeast Asia from the 11th century onwards. After the decline of Angkor, the Thai Kingdom of Ayutthya took over the role of imperial kingdom in continental Southeast Asia. The kingdom of Pagan also covered vast areas of western continental Southeast Asia from the middle of the 11th century to the end of 13th century, while Java saw the emergence of a similar entity in the form of Majapahit in the 14th century.

But the existence of certain "imperial" states in Southeast Asia may not constitute a significant exception to the basic features of the inter-state system associated with the *mandala* or the "galactic polity" constructs. Even with their larger territorial domain and greater military strength, the imperial states continued to exhibit considerable centrifugal tendencies and uncertain and overlapping territorial jurisdictions vis-à-vis neighbouring powers, a far cry from the Westphalian principles of sovereignty and territorial integrity.

Assuming that the *mandala*, the "galactic polity" and the "theatre state" constituted accurate, if somewhat crude, representations of state-hood in Southeast Asia before the advent of the nation-state, one could imagine a *regional pattern* of inter-state relations in classical Southeast Asia based on essentially similar political forms. But what about political and cultural interaction and transmission among these units that would have been essential to the creation of a *regional identity*? That this too occurred is a crucial claim of Wolters, who argues that the *mandala* system helped to establish a common pattern of intra-regional authority in a region that was "demographically fragmented", politically "multicentered", and socially "characterised by stubborn small-scale sub-regional identities".[26] For Wolters, the overlapping physical, political and cultural space of the *mandalas* assumes crucial importance:

> Sometimes...a mandala would only comprise a group of states on the island of Java, but a mandala could also be geographically extensive and comprise peoples whose descendants live today in separate nation-states. The Malay rulers of Srivijaya exercised some kind of authority in Sumatra and the Malay Peninsula from the seventh to at least the eleventh century. The Angkoran kings at intervals during the eleventh and twelfth centuries had similar authority in the Chao Phrya basin and the Malay Peninsula and also in parts of what is today southern Vietnam. The mandala of the Thai state of Ayudhya was to some extent, the same mandala of Majapahit in the forteenth century comprising Java, much of Sumatra, and no doubt other Indonesian islands.[27]

Wolters highlights the impact of overlapping *mandalas* in increasing the flow of communications between contiguous areas and reducing the cultural cleavages of the earlier period.

> A glance at some of the famous mandalas which adorn the textbooks of earlier Southeast Asian history shows that each of them increased flow of communications between some of the many centers in different parts of the region. We may too often tend to strike contrasts between these earlier states and the modern states as though great men in the past made exciting impressions in their own day but left nothing behind them of consequence. But there were some enduring consequences which helped to reduce the multicentric character of earlier Southeast Asia.[28]

Elaborating on how the *mandala* system might have contributed to the regional coherence and unity of Southeast Asia, Andaya observes:

Communities large and small retained their independent existence, while acknowledging the superior political and spiritual talents of a wo/man [sic] of prowess. In a mutually beneficial arrangement, the wo/man of prowess offered economic favors, spiritual knowledge and protection to subordinate rulers in return for local products and human resources in times of warfare or crisis. The looseness of the political arrangement was nevertheless reinforced by the general adherence by all to a supralocal religion from India or China in which the *mandala* ruler was equated with the supralocal deity of the new religion. But while individual communities were now becoming incorporated, though loosely, within the larger mandalas, there were no centralized institutions of reinforcement of central values and no fixed boundaries. Common cultural values were forged through interaction within and among the mandalas, thus preparing the way for the growth of nation-states and the concept of a Southeast Asian region.[29]

While the imperial kingdoms differed from the *mandalas* in terms of their size and power, they too contributed to a greater homogeneity within Southeast Asia. The *mandala* system created intra-regional homogeneity by virtue of their being "overlapping circles or spheres of influence". The imperial kingdoms emerged through and fostered "a continuous process of interlocal or interregional integration.[30]

Attempts to develop a regional concept of statehood and inter-state relations by using such categories as the *mandala*, "theatre state", or the "galactic polity" do invite considerable skepticism. One obvious question is whether the *mandala* pattern marked the entirety of what we call Southeast Asia today. Some critics have argued that the *mandala* system was a phenomenon of lowland Southeast Asia, not found in the uplands, such as in large parts of Burma, Laos and northern Thailand.[31] Vietnam and the Philippines raise major problems in using the *mandala* concept as the basis of a regional inter-state system. Vietnam, under Chinese rule for the first thousand years of the first millennium AD, has been described as a centralised bureaucratic state, in contrast to the loosely integrated Indic states of other parts of Southeast Asia. The Chinese-style polity in Vietnam made for a political order that was less volatile and more centralised than what was characteristic of the *mandala* system.[32] (One must, however, bear in mind that parts of the south were physically located within the Angkoran *mandala*,[33] and Vietnamese rulers, despite adopting Chinese-style diplomatic practices, retained an essentially "Southeast Asian" way of relating to people with "tolerance and closeness" that were characteristic of the *mandala* polity.[34] In the case of the Philippines, Wolters identifies Mindoro on the Luzon coast as one of the earliest examples of a Philippine *mandala* which emerged around the second half of the 10th century. After it disappeared, another *mandala* began to take shape on the Luzon coast as an extension of the Islamic *mandala* in Brunei. Thus, half a century before the arrival of the Spanish, the spread of Islam to the southern Philippines areas of Sulu and

Mindanao was beginning to extend the *mandala* pattern in the area.[35] But others challenge this view. In pre-colonial Philippines, political authority rested with too many small chiefs, lacking a central figure of a king around which a *mandala* could be constructed. As a political form, the Philippines *barangay* consisted of villages with a chief whose status and authority was almost entirely locally determined, without linking it to a source from above or from another realm, as with the God-king in the *mandala* system. These were politically autonomous units until they were incorporated into the colonial state apparatus. The *barangay* may be the main reason why the Philippines could not fit into the pre-modern regional concept of Southeast Asia.

Other problems confront the usefulness of the concept of *mandala* as the basis of constructing a regional view of the classical Southeast Asian polity and inter-state system.[36] The *mandalas* were not always culturally or ethnically homogenous. For example, in Sukhothai, the *mandala* comprised Tais almost entirely, but the Pagan *mandala* consisted of Burmans, Shans and Mons.[37] The *mandalas* might have increased the flow of communication within particular subregions and reduced the "multi-centric" character of the region.[38] But this effect was countered by the fact that while the *mandalas* were overlapping in terms of space, they were less so in terms of time. They rose more or less in succession. For example, the Srivijaya *mandala* lasted from the seventh to the eleventh century, while the Angkoran *mandala* extended to Lopburi in Thailand only periodically during the eleventh and twelfth centuries, and the Ayutthya *mandala* (as was the Majapahit) was founded in the mid-fourteenth century. Since the political influence of the *mandalas* did not last for very long, it is not certain that the cultural communalities they generated could be enduring.[39]

Apart from the overlapping *mandalas*, other forces were needed to engender communality and homogeneity in classical Southeast Asia. These include the role of religion. Thus the advent of Buddhism, and the various rulers' zeal in establishing their polities as the leading centres for Buddhist learning in the Thai kingdom of Ayutthya, founded in 1350, brought about a sense of communality in advance of institutional centralisation, which did not occur until the end of the 18th century.[40] Wolters himself points out several other factors at work in homogenising and unifying the region. One crucial factor was the sea, which provided "an obvious geographic framework for discussing possibilities of region-wide historical themes".[41] Maritime commerce helped to increase the material resources and geographic reach of at least some of the *mandala* rulers, thereby enabling them to spread the values and political structures associated with the *mandala* system. Another factor is Indian literature, which according to Wolters, engendered a certain "catholicity of outlook" in Southeast Asia. Indian literary models, such as *Arthasastra* which was used in Java by King Erlangga in the 11th century, brought Southeast Asia "closer to an intra-regional communality of outlook" among the rulers.[42]

An important factor in deciding whether a given area constitutes a region or not must be one's ability to identify structures or practices within the area that are markedly different from other parts of the world. In making generalisations about the classical states of Southeast Asia, scholars have also sought to draw distinctions between the precolonial state-system in Southeast Asia and that in Europe. Tambiah has argued that his idea of "galactic polity" which connotes "an exemplary center pulling together and holding in balance the surrounding polity", is "a far cry from a bureaucratic hierarchy in the Weberian sense."[43] This in itself is true, but it must be borne in mind that the two are not comparable. The "galactic polity" (which is similar to the *mandala*), resembles the European state of the pre-Westphalian period, while the Weberian state is a post-Westphalian construct. But a more controversial claim about the "distinctiveness" of the precolonial Southeast Asian state-system concerns the place of warfare. The work of Wolters and Geertz play down the role warfare and violence in the exercise of political authority and the management of inter-state relations.[44] Moreover, they also suggest that while the classical state-system of Southeast Asia was not entirely free from war, there was less coercion of the vanquished. Thus, Wolters argues that "victories rarely, if ever, led to the permanent obliteration of local centres either by colonization or through the influence of centralized institutions of government."[45] The reason why the *mandala* system, with few exceptions, did not expand into large imperial states through conquest may be that the system of *mandala* rule was relaxed, not coercive. As Wolters put it, the "*mandala* rulers coerced as well as wooed."[46] Citing the case of Majapahit, Wolters points out that its vassals offered tribute and sought investiture. If they ignored the ruler, punishment was mild as long as they all acknowledged the overlordship of Majapahit. Wolters suggests that this loose relationship between lord and vassal was a prime example of an inter-state system and intra-regional relations in earlier Southeast Asia based on a minimum use of force.

The value placed upon consensus in Southeast Asia's precolonial inter-state system contrasts with the emphasis in European inter-state relations on use of force. To be sure, the *mandala* system of overlapping sovereignty, patrimonial authority, and vaguely definable and continuously shifting territorial boundaries was not unlike the European state-system before Westphalia. But the possibility of conflict resolution represented a key difference between the two. Wolters notes that "confrontations between the *mandalas* are unlikely to have brought persisting prejudices in their wake comparable with those associated with the history of European nationalisms."[47] Southeast Asia, in this view, was not prone to the internecine warfare that characterised the European continent both before and after Westphalia. Moreover, there is an implication in Wolter's earlier work that inheriting a pacific tradition might have been a big help in Southeast Asia's quest for regional unity in the postcolonial period. In Southeast Asia's case, "(n)othing prefigures a European-style contrast between a past that bristled with "national" rivalries and a present that is groping towards regional consensus."[48] Thanks at least in part to the *mandala* system, differences among Southeast Asian cultures in the past were not significant enough to preclude the development in modern times of a regional consciousness and regional cooperation.

Geertz's generalisations about the "theatre state" in 19th century Bali provides a somewhat more ambiguous basis for considering a pacific tradition in Southeast Asia. In the "theatre state", what mattered in the hierarchical organisation of the state system was not relative preponderance of material power, military or economic, but relative claims of ritualistic and symbolic authority, and "the scale on which those pronouncements [about divine representation] could be mounted". The struggle for power was but a "competitive display" of ritual and symbol, not accumulation of instruments of warfare.[49] When the ruler faced centrifugal tendencies, he resorted to ritual and symbol to hold the state together, instead of by carrying out a military expedition. He also reduced the need for use of force to maintain unity through highly decentralised local administrative structures. "What was high centralization representationally was enormous dispersion institutionally, so that an intensely competitive politics, rising from the specificities of landscape, custom, and local history, took place in an idiom of static order emerging from the universalizing symbology of myth, rite and political dream."[50]

The use of ritual and symbol, rather than force and coercion, may be seen as representing a fundamentally different view of the state and the inter-state system than found in Western political tradition.[51] However this claim about the precolonial Southeast Asian inter-state system can be over-stated. The Angkoran kings, such as Jayavarman II and Suryavarman II were able to wage massive warfare. This belies the impression that they shunned force because their executive power in a day-to-day government was limited to being an umpire, securing material resources for themselves and their religious establishment. The role of force within the *mandala* system could also be deceptive. Here, the ruler was not just an umpire who communicated with divinity and ruled by example and ritual through possession of divine knowledge and representation of god. He was also able to mobilise massive resources from a network of loyalties. This could be used to prepare for wars.[52]

The above observations lead to serious questions about the role of Western academic scholarship in restoring Southeast Asia's regional past. Concepts such as the *mandala* and the "theatre state", could be criticised for being simplistic and Orientalist. As Reynolds puts it, the picture of the *mandala* as a non-coercive cultural form of authority perpetuates "an exotic, idealist, Orientalist construction of the Southeast Asian past."[53]

Critics have attacked the tendency to claim a Southeast Asian past free from conflict or warfare. To quote Reynolds again, "the historian's desire to return to a past untrammelled by European intervention may have resulted in an overly benign view of early Southeast Asia, a time in which the region is not seen as conflictual, as warlike, nor as ridden by social, economic, and environmental problems as in more modern periods."[54] Tambiah contrasts the idyllic picture of Geertz's *negara* with the "perennial warfare, interregional conflicts, and litigious treaties"[55] among the Balinese states which itself emerges from other parts of Geertz's account.[56] Yet, claims about the "pacific" nature of statecraft in Southeast Asia are by no means unique to the *mandala* and the "theatre state" constructs in their own respective timeframes. In some respects, they are a forerunner to attempts in more recent times by Southeast Asian leaders to speak of an "ASEAN Way" of international conduct, which emphasises consensus-building and conflict-avoidance. And just as the *mandala*, the galactic polity and the theatre state could be the basis of an imagined Southeast Asian community during the classical period, the "ASEAN Way" has been at the core of efforts to build a Southeast Asian regional identity in the modern era. Moreover, constructs such as the *mandala* do serve a useful purpose for scholars of Southeast Asia, including political scientists searching for ways to study and compare the politics and international relations of the region. They provide a benchmark for assessing similarities and differences between the pre-modern states and societies of Southeast Asia, which individual country studies could not do.

Commerce, Colonialism and the Regional Concept

The pattern of intra-regional relations which was characteristic of the *mandala* system was transformed by two factors. The first of these was commerce, which had a mixed impact in so far as Southeast Asia's regionness was concerned. The second force, with a more destructive implication for the region, was colonialism.

The importance of trade in the making of Southeast Asia has not always received scholarly attention. Attempts to examine Southeast Asia's political economy, including the once influential "Asiatic Mode of Production" (AMP) school, did not view trade as an important aspect of the domestic economy in classical states. The latter were seen as autarchic, without any significant marketing system. They either produced their needs locally or procured them through fixed reciprocal exchange rates and redistributive relationships, despite the existence of the "bazaar" states of the archipelago.

Yet, there is now substantial evidence to suggest that trade played a major role in creating the state in Southeast Asia. The earliest Southeast Asian states were established along trade routes between India and

China.[57] This included states in the third century in the lower Mekong area and on the isthmus of the Thai-Malay peninsula. In the 6th century, other states emerged in Sumatra and west Java on the maritime route between India and China. In his study of trade relationships from the early Christian era to the beginning of 15th century, K.R. Hall found substantial linkages between maritime trade and early state formation. Control over sources of export products was generally a key feature of coastal states except south-central Java and the ability to benefit from maritime trade was critical to the fortunes of even the so-called "agrarian" kingdoms such as Pagan, Champa, Ayutthya, Sukhothai, Majapahit, and Vietnam.[58]

In Southeast Asia, trade created states in many ways. It provided new resources, such as luxury goods for redistribution, and arms and weapons. Just as importantly, it gave rulers new ideas of political organisation and legitimacy, which they used to expand their authority and control. Control over trade routes was a crucial basis of political organisation. On the Malay peninsula, states came to be organised on the basin of a large river or groups of rivers, with their capital strategically located at the point where the river met the sea. Positioned in such a manner, the ruler could control the movement of persons and goods, defend from external attack, and levy taxes on imports and exports.

Trade helped to transform Southeast Asia by producing unprecedented commercial prosperity, cultural cosmopolitanism, and trends towards centralised polities. Southeast Asian traders (especially Malays) were major players in this. Unlike the later period of rapid urbanisation and economic transformation, a significant proportion of the rural population became dependent on international trade. This process was accompanied by religious revolution, with the expansion of Islam and Christianity creating "more precise religious boundaries, a portable, universally-applicable textual authority, and a predictable moral universe".[59] The political impact of commerce was equally far-reaching, and included a shift in the political centre of gravity from interior to coastal areas in Cambodia, Java, Thailand and Burma. State revenues became the preoccupation of states, with the emergence of trade monopolies and more effective local administrative structures.

According to Anthony Reid, trade created not only states, but also the region. Developing the notion of "the age of commerce" between the 15th to 17th centuries, Reid suggests a high degree of commercial intercourse connecting the great maritime cities of Southeast Asia, such as Malacca, Pasai, Johor, Patani, Aceh, and Brunei. The consequences of increased intra-regional trade included, among other things, reduction of cultural barriers and the spread of the Malay language as the language of commerce. Reid also makes the more far-reaching claim that until the advent of the Dutch East India Company in the 17th century, the "trading links within the region continued to be more influential than those beyond it."[60]:

> [M]aritime intercourse continued to link the peoples of Southeast Asia more tightly to one another than to outside influences down to the seventeenth century. The fact that Chinese and Indian influences came to most of the region by maritime trade, not by conquest or colonization, appeared to ensure that Southeast Asia retained its distinctiveness even while borrowing numerous elements from those larger centers. What did not happen (with the partial exception of Vietnam) was that any part of the region established closer relations with China and India than with its neighbours in Southeast Asia.[61]

Reid's historical research, by creating a picture of how intra-regional trade links contributed to cultural and other linkages in precolonial Southeast Asia, helps us understand the extent to which colonialism disrupted Southeast Asia's evolution as a region. It did so by making various parts of the region individually more interdependent with (or dependent upon) the outside, Western world (especially the colonial masters) at the expense of mutual dependence within the region itself. But trade was a double-edged sword so far as the creation of a regional concept of Southeast Asia is concerned. The trade networks cited by Reid were pan-Asian rather than intra-Southeast Asian, with India and China serving as important nodal points. Moreover, the impact of trade conforms to what Wolters has described as the uniting as well as dividing role of the sea in Southeast Asian history. On the one hand, the "single ocean" concept, involving trading connections linking opposite ends of maritime Asia, created "a fundamental unity of communications".[62] It also created the basis of an intraregional cultural framework based on Indian textual models, thereby supplying "an enduring shape to 'Southeast Asian history'".[63] But trade did not necessarily create a commercial class in Southeast Asia with region-wide economic interests.[64] Instead, accessibility to the sea might more likely have served as a source of localisation as it allowed the emergence of a multitude of landfalls able to thrive independently of each other by taking advantage of both local and foreign trade.[65] Within such a milieu, "each locality saw itself as belonging to a microcosm of the world," rather than as part of a broader regional system.[66]

Here, it may be useful to contrast the perspectives of Wolters and Reid on the evolution of Southeast Asia as a region. Unlike Reid, Wolters views maritime linkages as less significant in moulding Southeast Asia into a regional unit, focusing instead on the importance of the cultural and political space created by the *mandala* system. But it is evident that the two are dealing with rather different stages of Southeast Asian history; Wolters primarily, but not exclusively, with the classical period; Reid

32 THE QUEST FOR IDENTITY: INTERNATIONAL RELATIONS OF SOUTHEAST ASIA

primarily with the post-*mandala*, immediate precolonial period. In this sense, their perspectives may actually be complimentary. The "age of commerce" took up and furthered where the *mandala* system had left the region, until colonialism undermined the homogenising influence of both.

Nonetheless, while acknowledging their critical importance as analytical frameworks for studying Southeast Asia's past, it is hard to escape the conclusion that neither the *mandala* management of political and territorial space nor the "age of commerce" produces an authentic and enduring basis for a regional notion of Southeast Asia. Moreover, with the advent of European colonialism, much of the commonality and shared consciousness created during these periods was disrupted and, in some cases, severely eroded.

Colonialism dealt the decisive blow to the classical inter-state system of Southeast Asia. Among its chief effects was the severe disruption and eventual disintegration of the Asian trade network. This proved to be one of the most significant effects of the Portugese conquest of Malacca.[67] The growth of European influence after 1825 directly inhibited contacts between Southeast Asian societies and polities as each colony became progressively more linked to the metropolitan area. Moreover, the response of Southeast Asia to the colonial expansion was marked by so much diversity that there could be little scope for a sense of common destiny or a community of experience to serve as the basis of regional identity and cooperation.[68] European writings and intellectual thought also overshadowed Southeast Asian cultural and political traditions.[69] A further blow to Southeast Asia's historical intra-regional ties was the colonial authorities' lack of interest in a developing a regional diplomatic framework. For example, there are no recorded meetings between the American governor general of the Philippines and his British, French or Dutch counterparts.[70]

Adding to these forces of fragmentation was the long-range communication system driven by colonial imperatives. One of the clearest examples of this was the Spanish occupation of the Philippines during the period between the 1660s and mid-19th century. As Spain strove to defend its possession against Dutch, Portuguese, and Muslims, it relied heavily on the trans-Pacific link to Mexico as a kind of lifeline. This broke the traditional maritime routes binding Southeast Asia together and linking it commonly to the outside world. The Spanish rule also introduced a new and important religious division into classical Southeast Asia, already fragmented by the advent of Islam.

Another disintegrative impact of colonialism on the regional inter-state system was the drawing of artificial boundaries. This was done on the basis of the geographical location of a particular people, rather than their ethnic spread or loyalties. Since there were few clearly defined geographical boundaries already existing, they had to be drawn arbitrarily, without regard to the network of overlapping hierarchies and personal allegiances existing in Southeast Asia. The colonial powers imposed frontiers on a landscape where the concept of territoriality had not been well established. Thus, the idea of a "national" frontier in Southeast Asia was applied despite the lack of the essential attributes of nationhood.[71] They bore little resemblance to the national frontiers in Europe which had been drawn over a long period of time, through centuries of warfare, conquest, and centralisation of loyalty to the state. The Europeanisation of the international relations of Southeast Asia by drawing boundaries was primarily intended to prevent disputes among the colonial powers. It helped to settle their disputes in Europe, as much as to facilitate governance within a particular geographical area. The territorial limits did not match ethnic, social, political, or economic realities. Boundaries often reflected the accidental nature of colonial takeovers. However, many were consciously designed for the sake of administrative and economic efficiency, or to satisfy the strategic interests of the colonial powers in Europe. The result of the drawing of boundaries was the creation of what J.S. Furnival would call "plural societies", i.e., a single state containing a multitude of racial and ethnic groups, or a single ethnic group divided across many states.[72]

The impact of colonialism in the destruction of Southeast Asia's regional character was to become part of the nationalist thinking in Southeast Asia. Indeed, in the aftermath of colonialism, some Southeast Asian elites would see the task of post-colonial region-building as a matter of restoring the pre-colonial integrity of the region. "The isolation of centuries had to be breached; lost ties had to be restored."[73] But European colonialism did have significant homogenising influences as well. While responses of the various colonial units to Westernisation differed, the clash between Western political, cultural, and economic pressures and indigenous traditions also produced similar changes[74] and led to an increased degree of commonality in social and political structures throughout colonial Southeast Asia. While the delineation and protection of national frontiers was detrimental to regional identity, the influence of Westernization helped to blur the historical differences between the Indianized, Sinicized, and Philippine segments of Southeast Asia.[75] Moreover, colonial heritage and post-colonial developments formed a key part of the basis for thinking about Southeast Asia in regional terms. While the shared experience of colonial rule (with the exception of Thailand) had been offset by differences among colonial regimes and the divergent patterns of retreat of colonial powers, the diversity was moderated by a common sense of nationalism, a common task of nation-building, and efforts towards modernisation. These, as Neher argues, would provide "a general framework for studying Southeast Asia as an entity."[76]

After the War: (Re)inventing the Region

If most international relations scholars tend to view the concept of Southeast Asia as a post-Second World War construct, the origins of this construct must be traced to two defining features of the war itself. The first was the relatively brief era of Japanese colonialism. This period in Southeast Asian history must be regarded as being qualitatively different from that of European domination in terms of its implications for regional identity. The impact of the Japanese victory in encouraging Southeast Asian nationalists has been widely noted. But this was not its only unintended political effect. It also stoked a regional consciousness in several ways. This was the first time that "the region had ever known one common ruler."[77] Japanese rule destroyed the "colonial partition" of Southeast Asia among the various Western powers. It also introduced various Southeast Asian nationalist leaders to one another. For example, President Jose P. Laurel of the Philippines, Prime Minister Ba Maw of Burma, and Prince Wan Waithayakon of Thailand, representing Premier Phibum, attended the Assembly of Greater East Asiatic Nations held in Tokyo in November 1943, the first meeting of three such prominent Southeast Asian political leaders.[78]

To some extent, Japanese policy accorded a greater recognition to the distinctiveness of Southeast Asia. Southeast Asia enjoyed a greater prominence in Japan's concept of a Greater East Asian Co-prosperity Sphere than in Japan's earlier framework of Pan-Asianism. The latter, as Tarling points out, was inspired by a desire to prevent outside powers from exercising domination over East Asia and had focused on China. Its aim was to bring China under Japanese hegemony since, in Japan's view, an independent China, even with Japanese assistance, lacked the strength to stand up to the Western powers. The idea of the Greater East Asia Co-prosperity Sphere, on the other hand, placed more emphasis on Southeast Asia, not just because of Japan's concerns about access to resources, but also because of Japan's frustrations in dealing with China.[79]

While Japanese occupation might have created an incipient basis of a Southeast Asian regional order, it was the powers challenging Japanese hegemony which gave Southeast Asia its name. Of particular emphasis here is the impact of the Second World War and the Southeast Asia Command (SEAC), which in Fifield's view helped to make Southeast Asia a "fixed and practical term even in the United States" during the Second World War.[80] The Southeast Asia Command was created in 1945 embracing Burma, Malaya and Singapore, with its headquarters in Kandy, Ceylon. Its frontiers were extended to Thailand, southern Indochina and much of Indonesia after the Japanese surrender and its headquarters moved to Singapore. Whilst SEAC was intended to serve as a means of accepting the Japanese surrender, repatriating Japanese personnel and restoring order in the formerly occupied areas (including restoration of colonial rule until the determination of their final status), it was forced in this process to become involved in regional politics. Since, with the exception of Britain, the former colonial powers were utterly dependent upon the United States in Southeast Asia, SEAC soon came to represent the total Allied response to regional security and politics.[81]

While SEAC put Southeast Asia in the international spotlight, what contributed to a "rediscovery" of Southeast Asia's regional coherence was the role of academic scholarship inspired by both the Second World War as well as the advent of the Cold War immediately thereafter. To be sure, as Fifield argues, a regional concept of Southeast Asia might have emerged, albeit at a slower pace, had there been no Southeast Asia Command. The concept of Southeast Asia was slowly emerging in academic and policy discourses before the advent of SEAC or even before the outbreak of the Second World War. [82] But there is little doubt that the outbreak of the Cold War gave a major impetus to academic interest on Southeast Asia. Southeast Asia — with the proliferation of communist insurgencies throughout the region — became a focal point of the new global geopolitics. As Western policy-makers concerned with the threat of communist expansionism began to look at the Southeast Asian situation with greater concern, this itself became a major factor behind the increased academic interest in the region.

The outcome was a virtual reinvention of the Southeast Asian concept by imagining it to be a "culturally independent region".[83] Post-war scholarship on Southeast Asia marked the onset of an intellectual endeavour (which continues today) which challenged the historical links between Southeast Asia and the "great" Asian civilisations. Dominated by Sinologists and Indologists or "Sanskritists", Southeast Asian studies had seen the region as a "lesser version" of China and India, and as a receptacle for cultural ideas from the two.[84] The new scholarship focused on exposing the over-emphasis on Indian and Chinese influences and dismissing the notion of this region as a mere cultural hybrid. This in itself might have looked ironic, since, as noted earlier, some works which had portrayed the region as a "weaker and inferior"[85] extension of the great civilisations of India and China, also had a major influence in creating a regional understanding of Southeast Asia. The Indianised and Sinicised ideas did provide a generalised framework to link the diverse cultures of Southeast Asia, and had enabled scholars to "assert the unity of the region" by drawing attention to the "shared ideas of statecraft, architecture and religion through their common link to India and China".[86] Yet, a great deal of the post-war scholarship (while still being undertaken by Westerners) was concerned with identifying and articulating the differences between Southeast Asian societies vis-à-vis the two neighbouring civilisations and establishing what was regarded as distinctive Southeast Asian cultural traits.[87] The emphasis was less on how Southeast Asia adopted Indic or Sinic art, religion, political concepts and practices, and more on how they "adapted these foreign ideas to suit their own needs and values".[88] The new scholarship was devoted to ensuring that Southeast Asians "were not regarded as recipients (or victims) of history, but as makers of it."[89]

It will not be too much of an exaggeration to say the new understanding of Southeast Asia also supported the quest for an "indigenous" framework of regional international politics. It coincided with a redrawing of the boundaries of the region itself. No longer were India and China included in the region; no longer was Southeast Asia considered part of South Asia or East Asia.[90] Moreover, the immediate post-war period saw what Reid has called the "turning away" tendency in states existing in the closest proximity to larger powers, i.e. Burma and Vietnam (as well as the Philippines in relation to the US). Thus, for the elite in Burma and Vietnam, knowing themselves to be part of an ancient Southeast Asian cultural matrix was an immensely useful way of claiming a distinctive national identity vis-à-vis the feared Indian and Chinese neighbour. For the Philippines, imagining a pre-Hispanic past with pan-Malay linkages helped to overcome the sense of being an American appendage. Thus, academic claims about a Southeast Asian cultural identity distinct from that of India or China supported a quest for regional order focusing on a common Southeast Asian political identity.

But whatever positive feelings about the prospects for regional order that the discovery of Southeast Asia's cultural unity might have generated, were offset by the emergence of "nation-states" in the political landscape of Southeast Asia. Expectations of conflict and disorder in this nation-state system exceeded those of peace and harmony. Apart from the conflicts associated with the decolonisation process itself, including anti-colonial wars in Burma, Indonesia and Vietnam, the pessimism about Southeast Asia's future stemmed from the very artificial nature of colonially-imposed boundaries. Nothing illustrated this pessimism more starkly than the designation of Southeast Asia as "the Balkans of the Orient" which came to feature in a great deal of Western thinking about the region in the early post-Second World War period. The scholar who contributed most to this analogy, C.A. Fisher (who had argued for considering Southeast Asia as a coherent region, as discussed in the Introduction), suggested that Southeast Asia, like the Balkans, was located in a "cultural and political fault zone". Both formed a border region between two greater civilisations. Moreover, both regions were characterised by "geographical fragmentation, an area broken up into peninsulas and islands, a characteristically mountainous region, where lowlands are the exception rather than the rule."[91] This, like in the Balkans, would make it difficult to maintain internal stability and invite frequent foreign invasions and attempts by foreign powers to control the sea lanes and straits. Regional disorder would be compounded by the pervasiveness of minority strife, caused by attempts by weaker ethnic groups to seek refuge in the mountains to protect themselves from attack by stronger plains-people. Finally, Fisher predicted, in both regions local memories about past conflicts, abundant in folklore, would render the prospects for cooperation among its countries remote.[92]

Conclusion

This chapter has sketched an outline of an inter-state system in Southeast Asia before the advent of the nation-state. This outline relies heavily on attempts to "imagine" Southeast Asia's pre-colonial past featuring regional patterns of statehood and inter-state relations. It also provides an examination of the historical forces that made and unmade the region, including the seemingly contradictory effects of pre-colonial commerce and colonial rule on the regional system. The major themes of the chapter, including the nature of the state-system associated with the *mandala* and similar constructs, the impact of colonialism in disrupting Southeast Asia's traditional political, cultural and commerical linkages, the emergence of a geopolitical notion of Southeast Asia during and in the immediate aftermath of the Second World War, and the early post-war attempts by regional specialists to "imagine" and delineate a region of Southeast Asia, would have an important bearing on the international relations of the region in subsequent periods. They provide the necessary backdrop to considering the relationship between nationalism and regionalism, the impact of the Cold War international order on intra-regional relations, and the evolution of regional organisation geared to the management of regional conflict.

At the beginning of the post-Second World War period, while efforts to restore Southeast Asia's cultural unity and regional coherence had begun, its political future as a region appeared highly uncertain. The Japanese conquest of Southeast Asia and entities such as SEAC attracted international attention to the region and laid the basis of a regional geopolitical framework that had never existed during the colonial period. The advent of the Cold War furthered the development of this framework. But such sources of a regional international order in Southeast Asia were largely inspired by external events and forces. There was little in the form of an *internal making* of Southeast Asia. To make matters worse, initial efforts to create a Southeast Asian regional identity through cooperation were minimal and unsuccessful.

38 THE QUEST FOR IDENTITY: INTERNATIONAL RELATIONS OF SOUTHEAST ASIA

Notes

[1] See O.W. Wolters (1999) *History, Culture and Region in Southeast Asian Perspectives*, Revised Edition, Cornell University Southeast Asia Program, Postscript p.vi.

[2] L.W. Pye (1998) *International Relations in Asia: Culture, Nation and State*, Sigur Center Asia Papers, no.1, Washington, D.C.: The Sigur Center for Asian Studies, The George Washington University, p.6.

[3] Ibid.

[4] J. Benda (1969) "The Structure of Southeast Asian History: Some Preliminary Observations", in Robert O. Tilman, ed., *Man, State, and Society in Contemporary Southeast Asia*, London: Pall Mall Press, pp.23–24.

[5] M. Osborne (1990) *Southeast Asia: An Illustrated Introductory History*, 5th Edition, St.Leonards, NSW: Allen and Unwin, p.5.

[6] O.W. Wolters (1999) *History, Culture and Region*, op.cit., pp.27–40.

[7] C. Reynolds (1995) A New Look at Old Southeast Asia, *Journal of Asian Studies*, vol.54, no.2, p.426.

[8] O.W. Wolters (1982) *History, Culture and Region*, op.cit., p.27.

[9] I have relied on S.J. Tambiah in describing these features of O.W. Wolters' notion of *mandala*. See, S.J. Tambiah, (1985) *Culture, Thought, and Social Action: An Anthropological Perspective*, Cambridge: Harvard University Press, p.260.

[10] Ibid., p.261.

[11] O.W. Wolters (1999) *History, Culture and Region*, op.cit., p.25.

[12] Ibid., p.32.

[13] Ibid., p.24.

[14] B. Anderson (1972) "The Idea of Power in Javanese Culture", in C. Holt, ed. (1972) *Culture and Politics in Indonesia*, Ithaca: Cornell University Press, p.28.

[15] O.W. Wolters (1999) *History, Culture and Region*, op.cit., p.29.

[16] Ibid., pp.27–28.

[17] S. J. Tambiah (1985) *Culture, Thought, and Social Action: An Anthropological Perspective*, op.cit., p.324.

[18] Ibid., p.323.

[19] Ibid., p.324.

[20] Ibid., p.324.

[21] C. Geertz (1980) *Negara: The Theatre State in Nineteenth-Century Bali*, Princeton, N.J.: Princeton University Press, pp.18–19.

[22] Ibid., p.24.

[23] Ibid., p.24.

[24] Ibid., p.24.

[25] H. Kulke (1986) "The Early and Imperial Kingdoms in Southeast Asian History", in D.G. Marr and A.C. Milner, *Southeast Asia in the 9th and 14th Centuries*, Singapore: Institute of Southeast Asian Studies and Canberra: Australian National University, Research School of Pacific Studies, p.7.

[26] O.W. Wolters "Culture, History and Region in Southeast Asian Perspectives", in R.P. Anand and P.V. Quisumbing, eds (1981) *ASEAN: Identity, Development and Culture*. Quezon City: University of the Philippines Law Center and Honolulu: East-West Center, Culture Learning Institute, p.3.

[27] Ibid., p.9.

IMAGINING SOUTHEAST ASIA **39**

[28] Ibid., p.12. But Wolters took a more cautious view of the homogenising effects of *mandalas* in his revised monograph. See Wolters (1999) *History, Culture and Region*, op.cit., p.31.

[29] L.Y. Andaya (1996) "Ethnonation, Nation-State and Regionalism in Southeast Asia", in Proceedings of the International Symposium, "Southeast Asia: Global Area Studies for the 21st Century", Organized by Project Team: An Integrated Approach to Global Area Studies" (funded by Monbusho Grant-in-Aid for Scientific Research on Priority Areas), and Center for Southeast Asian Studies, Kyoto University, Kyoto International Community House, October 18–22, 1996, p.137.

[30] H. Kulke, "The Early and Imperial Kingdoms in Southeast Asian History", op.cit., p.17.

[31] O.W. Wolters (1999) *History, Culture and Region*, op.cit., p.39.

[32] C. Higham (1989) *The Archeology of Mainland Southeast Asia from 10,000 B.C. to the Fall of Angkor*, Cambridge: Cambridge University Press, chap. 5–6.

[33] Ibid., p.111.

[34] Vietnam scholars warn against analysing the precolonial Vietnamese state entirely in terms of Chinese principles. As Keith Taylor contends in his study of the Ly Dynasty in the 11th century Vietnam, while the state adopted the Chinese model of centralisation and emulated Chinese diplomatic practices, questions of authority and legitimacy were decided on the basis of "patterns of thought shared with other Southeast Asian peoples". K. Taylor (1986) "Authority and Legitimacy in 11th Century Vietnam", in D.G. Marr and A.C. Milner (1986) *Southeast Asia in the 9th and 14th Centuries*, op.cit., p.141. Wolters contends that the similarities between Vietnam and the rest of Southeast Asia, despite the latter's Sinic polity, are striking, and confirm the relative uniqueness of Southeast Asian polity. While Vietnam's polity was based on the Chinese model of a powerful and permanent centre within a fixed territorial space, the Vietnamese rulers were also very unSinic and more Southeast Asian in their high degree of tolerance and closeness to the people, and the simple and informal court customs. O.W. Wolters (1999) *History, Culture, and Region*, op.cit., p.37.

[35] Ibid., pp.33–34.

[36] While the concept of *mandala* may be one of the most far-reaching attempts to think of Southeast Asia in terms of an "indigenous" regional system, it is ironically, also Indic in origin, and hence, is of limited utility as a tool of differentiating Southeast Asia from other societies.

[37] L.Y. Andaya, "Ethnonation, Nation-State and Regionalism in Southeast Asia", op.cit., p.136.

[38] O.W. Wolters (1999) *History, Culture, and Region*, op.cit., p.31.

[39] Ibid., pp.31–32.

[40] Ibid., p.31.

[41] Ibid., p.42.

[42] Ibid., p.47.

[43] S.J. Tambiah, *Culture, Thought and Social Action*, op.cit., p.266.

[44] C. Reynolds, "A New Look at Old Southeast Asia", op.cit., p.427.

[45] O.W. Wolters (1999) *History, Culture and Region*, op.cit., p.28.

[46] Ibid., p.34.

[47] Ibid., p.36.

40 THE QUEST FOR IDENTITY: INTERNATIONAL RELATIONS OF SOUTHEAST ASIA

[48] O.W. Wolters (1981) " Culture, History and Region", op.cit., p.36.

[49] C. Geertz, *Negara: The Theatre State in Nineteenth-Century Bali*, op.cit., p.125.

[50] Ibid., p.132.

[51] O.W. Wolters (1981) " Culture History, and Region," op.cit., p.97.

[52] O.W. Wolters (1999) *History, Culture and Region*, op.cit., p.34.

[53] C. Reynolds, "A New Look at Old Southeast Asia", op.cit., p.427.

[54] Ibid., p.422.

[55] S.J. Tambiah, *Culture, Thought and Social Action*, op.cit., p.324.

[56] C. Geertz, *Negara: The Theatre State in Nineteenth-Century Bali*, op.cit., p.43.

[57] J.W. Christie, "Negara, Mandala, and Despotic State: Images of Early Java", in D.G. Marr and A.C. Milner, *Southeast Asia in the 9th to 14th Centuries*, op.cit., p.69

[58] K.R. Hall (1985) *Maritime Trade and State Development in Early Southeast Asia*, Honolulu: University of Hawaii Press.

[59] V. Lieberman (1995) "An Age of Commerce in Southeast Asia? Problems of Regional Coherence", *The Journal of Asian Studies*, vol. 54, no.3, August 1995, p.797.

[60] A. Reid (1988) *Southeast Asia in the Age of Commerce 1450–1680, Volume One: The Lands Below the Winds*, New Haven: Yale University Press, p.7.

[61] Ibid., p.6.

[62] O.W. Wolters (1999) *History, Culture, and Region*, op.cit., p.p.44–45.

[63] O.W. Wolters (1981) "Culture History, and Region", op.cit., p.27.

[64] Ibid., p.21

[65] Ibid.

[66] Ibid., p.33.

[67] M.C. Ricklefs (1993) *A History of Modern Indonesia Since c.1300*, 2nd edition, Stanford: Stanford University Press, p.26.

[68] D.J. Steinberg, ed. (1987) *In Search of Southeast Asia*, Honolulu: University of Hawaii Press, p.100. While colonialism created greater diversity within Southeast Asia, the colonial period constituted a small part of Southeast Asian history. This raises questions as to whether one should pay too much attention to its impact in moving the countries of Southeast Asia in different political and administrative directions. M. Osborne, (1990) *Southeast Asia: An Illustrated Introductory History*, op.cit., p.12.

[69] D.G. McCloud (1995) *System and Process in Southeast Asia: The Evolution of a Region*, Boulder, CO: Westnew Press, p.5.

[70] R. Fifield (1984) "'Southeast Asia' and 'ASEAN' as Regional Concepts", in R.A. Morse, ed. (1984) *Southeast Asian Studies: Options for the Future*, Lanham: University Press of America, p.126.

[71] Nicholas Tarling describes the differences between the drawing of frontiers in Europe and in Southeast Asia in the following terms:

> In the drawing of the frontiers there was something of a paradox, In Europe the concept dealt with subjects and citizens in terms of their geographical locality rather than their personal allegiance; and the state laid claim to their taxes and imposed their obligations on an impersonal basis. That contrasted with much of the previous Southeast Asian practice, especially in the archipelago where, insofar as geographical frontiers existed, they might be only vaguely defined. Often more important within states, even within some of the larger ones, were personal allegiances, client-patron relations, different

connections between court and core, court and periphery; often more important states were overlapping hierarchies, dual loyalties. Such structures better reflected the conditions of the Southeast Asian past, But the concept that the Europeans sought to apply in Southeast Asia also contrasted with the European present. In Europe frontiers had been created over a long period of time, often as a result of a struggle, and within them new loyalties had been built up. Increasing loyalty was to the state itself, as representing the nation in whose name it had been accepted, its government ruled. No such ideology could apply to the colonial territories; nor was there a clear substitute for it. The colonial powers were utilizing a concept not only drawn from a system of international relations that differed but from one which they themselves were not in fact applying. N. Tarling, ed. (1992) *The Cambridge History of Southeast Asia*,Volume 2, "The Nineteenth and Twentieth Centuries", Cambridge: Cambridge University Press, pp.6–8.

[72] C.A. Trocki, "Political Structures in the Nineteenth and Early Twentieth Centuries", in ibid., p.85.

[73] A. Melchor, Jr. (1975) "Security Issues in Southeast Asia", in *Regionalism in Southeast Asia*, Jakarta: Centre for Strategic and International Studies, pp.46–47.

[74] H. J. Benda, "The Structure of Southeast Asian History", op.cit., p.35.

[75] Ibid., p.35.

[76] C.D. Neher (1984) "The Social Sciences" in R.A. Morse, ed. (1984), *Southeast Asian Studies: Options for the Future*, op.cit., p.129.

[77] A. Vanderbosch and R. Butwell (1966) *The Changing Face of Southeast Asia*, Lexington: University of Kentucky Press, p.340.

[78] Ibid.

[79] N. Tarling (1998) *Nations and States in Southeast Asia*, Cambridge: Cambridge University Press, pp.82–83.

[80] R. Fifield (1992) "The Southeast Asia Command," in K.S. Sandhu et al. *The ASEAN Reader*, Singapore: Institute of Southeast Asian Studies, p.21.

[81] Ibid., pp.20–23.

[82] Ibid., p.23.

[83] M. Osborne (1990) *Southeast Asia: An Illustrated Introductory History*, op.cit., p.5.

[84] L. Andaya, "Ethnonation, Nation-State and Regionalism in Southeast Asia", op.cit., p.133. This old approach was exemplified in Coedes' classic study. See: G. Coedes (1968) *The Indianized States of Southeast Asia*, Kuala Lumpur: University of Malaya Press, 1968 (edited by W.F. Vella, translated by S.B. Cowing).

[85] L. Andaya, "Ethnonation, Nation-state and Regionalism in Southeast Asia," op.cit, p.134.

[86] Ibid., p.134.

[87] Some scholars have cited the absence of the Hindu caste system in Southeast Asia as an example of how the region differed from India. Among the distinctive "Southeast Asian" cultural traits that Southeast Asianists have used to differentiate it from China and India are "the concept of spirit or 'soul stuff' animating living things, prominence of women in descent, ritual matters, marketing and agriculture, and the importance of debt as a determinant of social obligations". A. Reid, *Southeast Asia in the Age of Commerce 1450–1680*, op.cit., p.6. Osborne highlights the contrast between the Indian emphasis on extended family and the Southeast Asian concept of the nuclear or individual family, and the differences between Thai and Indian

Buddha images. In Vietnam, he argues, the impact of Chinese political and cultural traditions was more salient at the level of the court than at societal levels, attesting to the strength of indigenous Vietnamese traditions, which were more Southeast Asian, rather than Sinic in nature. M. Osborne (1990) *Southeast Asia: An Illustrated Introductory History*, op.cit., pp.5-6.

[88] Ibid., p.5. One prominent example of how Southeast Asians adapted, rather than adopted, foreign cultures concerns Islam, an interesting example since it is not associated with either Indic or Sinic civilisations. Islam came to Southeast Asia as an alien culture, but from 16th century onwards, it had become a mass culture, expressing itself in Malay and taking on a "self-conscious" Southeast Asian character. The Islamic people of Southeast Asia, including the Acehnese, Javanese, Makassarese, Filipinos, southern Tais and Chams, distinguished themselves from the rest of the Islamic world. They were recognised at the religious centres of Islam as a distinctive group (as seen from the fact that they were put in the same hostels when they went on pilgrimage). A. Reid (1999) "A Saucer Model of Southeast Asian Identity." Special issue of *Southeast Asian Journal of Social Science*, vol.27, no.1, pp12–13.

[89] G.C. Bentley (1985) Indigenous States of Southeast Asia, *Annual Review of Anthropology 76*, op.cit., p.299.

[90] D.K. Emmerson (1984) Southeast Asia: What's in a Name?, *Journal of Southeast Asian Studies*, vol. XV, No.1, March 1984, p.8.

[91] C.A. Fisher (1962) Southeast Asia: The Balkans of the Orient? A Study in Continuity and Change, *Geography 47*, p.347.

[92] Ibid., p.9.

CHAPTER 2

Nationalism, Regionalism and the Cold War Order

Introduction

The aftermath of the Second World War was a period of profound change in Southeast Asia. The main historical forces shaping Southeast Asia's destiny were nationalism and decolonisation, and the struggle of the newly-independent states to create stable political systems and viable national economies. In the international arena, Southeast Asia became progressively drawn into the Cold War between the US and the Soviet Union. A key feature of this period was the close nexus between domestic politics (including nationalism, national integration, and democracy), prospects for regionalism and international relations. The Cold War helped to polarise the region, and influenced the domestic politics of Southeast Asian states. It contributed to the rise of authoritarianism in the non-communist states of Southeast Asia. At the same time, domestic problems, including weak national integration and regime survival concerns, had major consequences for the foreign policy orientation of the non-communist Southeast Asian states, especially their attitude towards regionalism. The early post-war period saw the first articulation of ideas about regional unity by Southeast Asia's nationalist leaders. Yet, most of these were not concerned with a Southeast Asian identity, but instead focused on larger pan-Asian or Afro-Asian unity. And a range of domestic and international factors ensured the non-fulfillment of these aspirations.

The Nationalist Vision of Regionalism

In her post-war diplomatic history of Southeast Asia, C.M. Turnbull points out that "the two important factors affecting regionalism and international relations in the immediate post-war years were the de-colonisation process itself, and the problems of creating national identity within the (often artificial) former colonial boundaries."[1] Nationalism was the major political force in Southeast Asia during the first two decades of the post-war era. But it had a mixed impact on regionalism. On the one hand, Southeast Asian nationalists recognised regionalism as an inevitable trend; something which was "bound to come" as a way of undoing the artificial divisions and separations among Southeast Asian peoples and territories brought about by colonial rule. Nationalist leaders such as Aung San of Burma and Elpidio Quirino of the Philippines were among the first people to lament that Southeast Asian countries maintained much closer economic, cultural and political links with their metropolitan powers than with each other. Even in the Philippines, despite its relative geographic isolation and different colonial heritage, the discourse of nationalism was not devoid of a regional context. While there was little connection between nationalist movements in the Philippines and in other Southeast Asian countries, references by the Filipino nationalist Jose Rizal to the Filipinos as "Malays" did invoke a regional identity.[2] But it was soon evident that shared nationalism was not an adequate basis for reinventing a notion of Southeast Asia. Regionalism was constrained by differing circumstances of decolonisation, the greater appeal of pan-Asianism and Afro-Asianism as regionalist frameworks, and the tendency among Southeast Asian leaders to use regionalism as a tool of partisan ideology, rather than collective identity.

The decolonisation process in Southeast Asia was unexpectedly sudden and marked by wide variations. Thailand, the only state not to experience colonial rule, used the post-war American ascendancy to break free from the Anglo-French hold, especially as a way of escaping possible retribution from the latter for its war-time collaboration with Japan. Elsewhere in the region, the colonial powers took different approaches to their Southeast Asian possessions. The US fulfilled its pledge to give independence to the Philippines while maintaining close economic and military links with it. France and the Netherlands sought to give their colonies equal status in a French or Dutch union. But these did not match the aspirations of the Vietnamese and Indonesian nationalists, who took up armed struggle as the means of national liberation. The British were in a different position, much stronger in their colonies than the French or the Dutch. Britain came back to its colonies pledging self-government for them. Churchill, like the French and the Dutch, wanted a reimposition of colonial rule, but Britain had allowed independence movements to appear and grow legitimately and pursue a more peaceful constitutional path to independence. The British Commonwealth concept, already tested in the case of the old dominions, helped to persuade the nationalists to seek independence while retaining links with Britain. It also made it easier for Britain to transfer power to the newly independent states. British economic links and defence responsibilities continued to play an important role in the affairs of the new states.

In general, Britain found it easier to carry out an orderly and more "voluntary" transfer of power than the Dutch and the French. In Burma, the British War Cabinet had promised the colony independence with full Commonwealth membership as soon as it was ready. The popularity of Aung San's Anti-Fascist People's Freedom League forced Britain to quicken the process of independence even in the absence of safeguards for Burma's minorities. Notwithstanding the assassination of Aung San in April 1947, Britain granted Burma independence in January 1948, although this "premature" move plunged Burma into a civil war situation. The decolonisation process in the Malayan peninsula evolved relatively smoothly. In 1946, Singapore was separated as a Crown Colony. The Malayan peninsula was organised into a Malayan Union. In 1948, this became the Federation of Malaya. Later, Sarawak and North Borneo were placed under direct colonial rule, while Brunei remained as a protectorate. In contrast, the Dutch attempts to incorporate its colonies into a Netherlands Union and undermine the Republic of Indonesia formed by the Indonesian nationalists failed. In Indochina, the French did not recognise the independent regimes created by Japan and re-established control in Cambodia and Laos in 1946. But its attempt to do so in Vietnam soon led to war.

The contrasting circumstances under which decolonisation proceeded contributed to the differing attitudes of Southeast Asian countries towards regionalism. The initial appeal of regionalism was as an instrument of national liberation. Certainly Ho Chi Minh was keen to use regional cooperation to further the cause of Vietnamese independence.[3] In September 1945, he mentioned to an American official his interest in the creation of a "pan-Asiatic community" comprising Vietnam, Cambodia, Laos, Thailand, Malaya, Greater Burma, India, Indonesia and the Philippines. (China, Japan, and Korea were not included in Ho's vision of an Asiatic community). His ostensible goal at this stage was to foster political and economic cooperation among these countries while maintaining good relations with the US, France and Britain. This was a time when Ho still hoped that the colonial powers, exhausted by war, would voluntarily speed up the process of decolonisation. But when this proved to be a false hope, Ho and other Southeast Asian nationalist leaders began considering the use of regional cooperation to oppose the return of European colonialism. This was clearly evident in Ho's letter to Indonesian Prime Minister, Sutan Sjahrir, in November 1946 urging cooperation between the two countries to advance their common struggle for freedom. In this letter, Ho asked Indonesia to join him in getting India, Burma and Malay to develop initiatives towards a "Federation of Free Peoples of Southern Asia". But Indonesian leaders responded coolly to this idea, apparently worried that cooperating with the Vietnamese communists would give the Dutch an opportunity to use the fear of communism to delay Indonesia's own independence. This incident showed how differences among nationalist strategies in Southeast Asia served as an impediment to regional cooperation.

But the Vietnamese communists would continue to see regionalism as a means to advancing their goal of national liberation. While direct cooperation with their Vietnamese counterparts was troublesome to Indonesian nationalists, cooperation within a larger Pan-Asian framework could be politically more useful. It was in this context that Southeast Asian nationalists saw efforts by India under Nehru to develop a Pan-Asian framework to foster decolonisation and regional cooperation as a welcome opportunity. Apart from the Democratic Republic of Vietnam under Ho and the Indonesian nationalists, support for the idea of using regionalism to advance the cause of national liberation came from the Philippines, where Carlos P. Romulo, then the Philippines delegate to the UN, endorsed the forthcoming Asian Relations Conference in New Delhi as a way of giving encouragement to anti-colonial struggles in Asia.

The unofficial Asian Relations Conference held in New Delhi in 1947 saw all the Southeast Asian states represented amongst the 31 delegations. The tone of the conference was anti-European, pro-liberation and pro-neutrality. The meeting provided a platform for subsequent action by the regionalists in protesting against the second Dutch police action against Indonesia in 1948. But it did not lead to the establishment of regional machinery and organisation. A more explicit call for a regional organisation was made by the Indian Prime Minister Nehru at another conference of Asian countries in January 1949. Nehru urged the participants to emulate emerging trends towards regionalism in Europe and the Americas: it would be "natural that the free countries of Asia should begin to think of a more permanent arrangement than this conference for effective mutual consultation and concerted effort in the pursuit of common aims".[4] But prospects for a Pan-Asian grouping were plagued by differences amongst the pro-communist, pro-Western and neutral-minded delegations. They had little to agree upon apart from the end to direct colonial rule. Moreover, some Southeast Asian leaders viewed the prospects for a pan-Asian community with some unease, fearing its domination by China or India. As one Burmese put it, "It was terrible to be ruled by a Western power, but it was even more so to be ruled by an Asian power".[5]

Southeast Asian nationalists were disappointed at Nehru's mild approach to the colonial powers and India's refusal to provide more than "moral" support to the anti-colonial struggles in the region. This also convinced them of the need for an entirely Southeast Asian subgrouping. Abu Hanifa, one of the Indonesian representatives to the New Delhi conference, wrote later that the idea of a wholly Southeast Asian grouping was conceived at the conference in response to the belief among the Southeast Asian delegates that the lager states, India and China, could not be expected to support their nationalist cause. At the meeting, delegates from Indonesia, Burma, Thailand, Vietnam, the Philippines and Malaya:

> debated, talked, [and] planned a Southeast Asian Association closely co-operating first in cultural and economic matters. Later, there could be perhaps be a more closely knit political cooperation. Some of us even dreamt of a Greater Southeast Asia, a federation.[6]

The idea of a Southeast Asian grouping also received support from nationalist leaders in Burma and Vietnam. It was part of the pan-Asian thinking of Aung San of Burma. Less than a year before his assassination, Aung San explained that "(w)hile India should be one entity and China another, Southeast Asia as a whole should form an entity — then, finally, we should come together in a bigger union with the participation of other parts of Asia as well."[7] When his dream of securing immediate freedom from British rule as a reward for cooperating with the British against the Japanese seemed to be faltering, Aung San called for an Asian Potsdam Conference to "plan a united campaign to achieve freedom within the shortest possible time." He followed this up with a call in January 1947 for the creation of an "Asian Commonwealth", with the objective once again being liberation from colonial rule. But at a more sub-regional level, Aung San also proposed the idea of a Southeast Asian economic union comprising Burma, Indonesia, Thailand, Malaya, and Indochina. Following the New Delhi Conference, he expressed support for a Southeast Asian union consisting of Burma, Indonesia, Thailand, Indochina, and Malaya. But his assassination in July 1947 ended Burma's quest for regional cooperation.[8] After unsuccessfully seeking a Pan-Asian platform, the Vietnamese communists also began thinking in terms of a Southeast Asian grouping. They were urging Thailand, because of its independent status and its geographical location, to take the lead in organising such a group, to be modelled after the principles of the UN charter, to resist the reimposition of European rule.

Discussions about the usefulness of regionalism at this time high-lighted the smallness of Southeast Asian countries and their inability to achieve self-reliance without collective efforts. Vietnamese commentators, juxtaposing a "united and free" posture on the part of Southeast Asian states as a counter to the colonial powers' "divide and rule", also stressed that without regional unity, Southeast Asia would become nothing more than "slaves" of colonial powers producing raw materials for them and buying their expensive manufacturing products.[9] The ethnic and social-cultural similarities and ties among Southeast Asian countries were stressed. Their location between China and India and the existence of common interests in addressing domestic problems, and mutual support in anti-colonial struggles were cited as the rationale for regional unity. A regional grouping, according to *Bangkok Post* newspaper, need not be a "tightly cohesive federation" but a forum for the exchange of policies on agriculture, communications and trade. The *Malayan Tribune* saw regionalism among Southeast Asian countries, including Burma, Thailnd, Indochina, Malaya and Indonesia as a way of safeguarding the "tremendous potential and great riches" of Southeast Asia which might otherwise "tempt the powerful."[10]

Thailand, which had been seen as a leader of a Southeast Asian grouping, found a reason to get involved when it failed to win back disputed territories in French-ruled Laos and Cambodia. An offshoot of this was the Thai support (including such leaders as Pridi Banomyong and Thamrong Nawasawat) in sponsoring the Southeast Asian League on 8 September 1947, with representatives from Vietnam, Laos, Cambodia, Indonesia, Thailand and Malaya (there were no Burmese and Filipino delegates). This was intended to be an "unofficial" and provisional organisation which could later develop into an official body once it secured recognition from the national governments of the region. But the group failed to take off. Delegates from Indonesia, Malaya and Burma were worried that their participation would jeopardise their own negotiations with the Dutch and the British concerning transition to independence, especially given the radical undertone of the grouping and the involvement of the DRV government. This in itself illustrates how differing nationalisms and pathways to independence might have undermined the prospects for regionalism in Southeast Asia. Although it had attracted support from upper-echelon Thais,[11] the Southeast Asia League came to be seen as primarily a support mechanism for communist movements, since one of its activities was gun-running for the Vietminh. Among its active members was Prince Souphanouvong, who became a leader of the Laotian communists under the Pathet Lao.

For many Southeast Asian nationalists, enthusiasm for regional organisation depended on the extent to which it could be seen to support the nationalist cause. Thus, after their initial efforts to use regionalism to advance the national liberation cause proved abortive, Vietnamese nationalists not only lost interest in a Southeast Asian grouping, but also harshly criticised efforts by moderate nations such as Malaya, Thailand, the Philippines, and Indonesia under Suharto, to build a Southeast Asian regional organisation. Hanoi then pursued unity among the Indochinese states, based largely on strategic and ideological considerations. The interest of the nationalist leaders in Indonesia and Malaya in a Southeast Asian grouping that included the DRV was countered by the fear that it could delay their own struggle for independence. This divergence planted the seeds of the future ideological and political polarisation of Southeast Asia.

In this context, Vietnam's vision of Indochina as "one strategic unit", outlined by General Giap in Febraury 1950, merits attention. In a speech before the sixth All-Country Military Meeting in February 1950, Giap stated:

> The war of liberation of the three peoples of Vietnam-Laos-Cambodia cannot be separated; that is: Indochina is one strategic unit, it is one battlefield. That is also why in military terms, the Indochinese battlefield constitutes one block in the enemy's aggressive and defensive projects. For these reasons, and above all for geo-strategic ones, we cannot consider Vietnam to be entirely independent as long as Cambodia and Laos are still ruled by imperialism.[12]

These fateful words would acquire a singular notoriety in the capitals of the non-communist Southeast Asian states as the justification of Vietnamese expansionism and hegemonism. This was especially so in the aftermath of the Vietnamese invasion of Cambodia in 1979, after Hanoi had criticised ASEAN as a tool of Western imperialism. But to consider Giap's notion as an alternative regional or sub-regional framework under Vietnamese hegemony would be a mistake. His concept of Indochina as one strategic unit was context-dependent (Vietnam's struggle against the French) and time-bound ("as long as Cambodia and Laos are still ruled by imperialism"). But the concept did move from being the basis of Vietnam's anti-colonial struggle to being the organisational framework of its revolutionary regional politics. And while not amounting to an alternative regional framework, it remained a powerful barrier to the development of a single regional identity of Southeast Asia. It was not until the 1990s (through the Vietnamese withdrawal from Cambodia in 1989, the Paris Peace Agreement of 1991, and the Vietnamese membership in ASEAN in 1995) that Vietnam came to re-embrace the regional concept of Southeast Asia.

In commenting on the relationship between nationalism and regionalism, Wang Gungwu has argued that "the main obstacle in the way of Southeast Asian regionalism is not so much nationalism itself as the two different types of postwar nationalism."[13] Wang sees the roots of intra-regional discord in Southeast Asia in terms of radically different conceptions of Southeast Asia as a region held by the moderate and the revolutionary nationalists. The revolutionaries rejected the idea of a region dominated by Western powers, while the moderates had more to fear from a region dominated by China. While the revolutionaries hoped for a confederated region, the moderates would only accept regional cooperation based on the principles of equality and sovereignty. The moderates desired a region freely and multilaterally linked to the outside world, while the revolutionaries would accept this only if the communist powers were integral to this external linkage.[14] It is important to note that the framework of regionalism that proved viable in Southeast Asia in the end was the one promoted by the moderate camp led by Thailand, Malaysia, and Suharto's Indonesia, the latter being a significantly more "moderate nationalist" regime than its predecessor.

When nationalist leaders in Southeast Asia expressed interest in regional unity, they also acknowledged that their ties to former colonial powers were often much stronger than those to their own neighbours. Nationalists such as Aung San of Burma and Elpidio Quirino of the Philippines recognised the existence of strong pre-colonial ties,[15] but when they called for regional cooperation, they were not calling for a recreation of pre-colonial geographic and political entities, but for the realisation of a Pan-Asian consciousness.[16] While Aung San's regionalist ideas went beyond Southeast Asia, and the Vietnamese view of regionalism was somewhat tactical, geared to securing regional support for communist-dominated national liberation, Indonesia under Sukarno's stewardship had little interest in the idea of Southeast Asia as a region. While earlier Indonesian nationalists had been reluctant to embrace a Southeast Asian regional organisation out of fear that it would undermine their negotiations with the Dutch, even after achieving independence, Indonesia made little effort to bring together Southeast Asian countries under one grouping. Independent Indonesia saw itself as a leader of the region (thereby supplanting Thailand, which had earlier been seen as a regional leader, and Burma which after Aung San's assassination was too preoccupied with its domestic troubles). But Sukarno's foreign-policy beliefs were too grandiose to fit into a Southeast Asian framework. His vision was for a grouping of the "new emerging forces" to oppose the "old established forces" — a global rather than a regional movement. Moreover, among those who Sukarno considered to be "old established forces" and therefore a target of Indonesia's dislike and opposition's was a fellow Southeast Asian country with which it had substantial ethnic ties, Malaysia. If Sukarno was interested in any regional cooperation, it was well beyond Southeast Asian in scope. Indonesia had derived considerable support for its independence struggle from anti-colonial sentiments in Asia and Africa (especially from India under Nehru's leadership), and naturally saw regionalism covering the newly-independent countries in Asia and Africa as a more important instrument of nationalism than what the idea of Southeast Asia could offer.

Sukarno's approach became evident when he got involved in a grouping known as the Colombo Powers (not to be confused with the Commonwealth-inspired Colombo Plan) that met in Ceylon in 1954 to commit itself to opposing the polarisation of the world into competing blocs. The grouping itself achieved little but put forward a proposal for an Afro-Asian Conference in Bandung the following year. Like at the Asian Relations Conference, Southeast Asian participation at Bandung was quite extensive with only Malaya and British Borneo absent (present were delegates from Burma, Thailand, Cambodia, Laos, The State of Vietnam, The Democratic Republic of Vietnam (DRV), and the Philippines). Yet, no single "Southeast Asian view" could be detected at Bandung. Instead, one of the most pronounced splits at Bandung involved Southeast Asians—the Philippines and Thailand on the one hand and Indonesia and, to a lesser extent, Burma on the other. The former believed that their independence and security were threatened by the communist menace and entering into military pacts with the US was essential to protect their national interests. Indonesia, on the other hand, believed that an "independent foreign policy", which meant not entering into rigid military alliances with any of the two superpowers, was the only way for the newly independent states to safeguard their sovereignty. Given its status as the largest country in Southeast Asia in terms of size and population, even mere indifference on the part of Jakarta was a major obstacle to the prospects for regionalism in Southeast Asia. Sukarno pursued a foreign policy which was nationalist in motivation and internationalist in scope, missing the regional level where cooperation and unity-building were seen to be unimportant (to the internationalist agenda) at best and detrimental (to the nationalist cause) at worst.

As could be seen from the foregoing discussion, many of the ideas concerning regionalism during this period were made in the context of decolonisation and political and ideological considerations linked to the Cold War. The Pan-Asian and Afro-Asian frameworks, despite being largely still-born, did make a contribution to Southeast Asian regionalism. They introduced the concept of regional cooperation and created opportunities for the region's leaders to meet one another. These would prove important steps towards Southeast Asian regionalism in subsequent periods. For the time being, however, a Southeast Asian community remained a distant concept. There were a number of obstacles to the development of such a regionalist framework, even among the moderate nationalist countries which were more inclined to accept identity-based (such as Aung San of Burma), as opposed to ideology-based (as was the case with Vietnam on the one hand and Thailand and the Philippines on the other), Southeast Asian regionalism. Two sets of obstacles are especially noteworthy. The first had to do with the domestic conditions of the Southeast Asian states, where the main problems were those of communist insurgency and ethnic separatism, problems which the governments of the day sought to address through a differing mix of economic development and political control. The second set of obstacles stemmed from the international security environment, where Cold War geopolitics constrained the willingness and ability of Southeast Asian governments to undertake effective regional cooperation.

Development, Legitimacy and Regional (Dis)order

With the departure of the colonial powers from the region, the new governments of Southeast Asia faced a serious challenge in ensuring domestic stability and regime legitimacy. To cope with the challenge, nationalist elites throughout the region emphasised growth and development, and all favoured rapid industrialisation. For them, primary production and import of manufactured goods were associated with colonialism, while industrialisation was seen as the symbol of, and passport to, economic independence. Economic nationalism contributed to efforts to boost national self-sufficiency and reduce foreign influence.

But the focus on domestic economic development left little scope for attention to regional economic cooperation. During the colonial era, the economies of Southeast Asian countries were heavily dependent on tropical products. In 1950, manufacturing accounted for 12% of the Philippines GDP, and 5–10% or less elsewhere in the region.[17] As a result, these economies were competitive, not complementary, a factor inhibiting the motive for regional cooperation.

Moreover, significant differences marked the development policies of Southeast Asian states in the post-colonial era. One area of divergence was openness to the global economy. Singapore was the most open and was the first to develop export-oriented industrialisation (EOI). This reflected Singapore's unique circumstances: a small population, no natural resources and no hope for economic self-sufficiency. The island also sought to capitalise on its strategic location, its bureaucratic efficiency, absence of corruption, and well-disciplined labour force. Singapore also served as a financial centre and took advantage of its modern banking and stock market, helped by overseas Chinese financial networks, whilst also looking to serve international markets. None of the other Southeast Asian countries adopted Singapore's approach. Malaysia, for example, focused on primary production, with its dependence on rubber and tin, the two major exports, continuing for two decades after the Second World War. The oil and timber of Sabah and Sarawak also benefited growth.

Malaysia (in the 1950s), Thailand and the Philippines were among the regional economies to try import-substituting industrialisation (ISI). The Philippines was the first country in Southeast Asia to try ISI. For the first decade and a half after World War Two, the Philippines posted the best economic growth in Southeast Asia, helped by a combination of US aid, a well-educated population and relatively good institutional infra-structure. However, despite the clear problems of over-protection, slowing demand, falling commodity prices and high population growth rates, domestic vested interests in ISI prevented a switch to EOI. The contrasting policies and experiences of Singapore and the Philippines are striking, although both were founding members of ASEAN and thus subscribed to ASEAN's common "free market" orientation.

In addition, Southeast Asian governments adopted different attitudes toward property rights. Here, a threefold classification has been proposed by Norman Owen.[18] The governments of the Philippines, Singapore, Malaysia and Thailand preferred economic systems based on respect for private property throughout the post-war period. South Vietnam (1954–75), the Khmer Republic under Lon Nol (1970–75) and Indonesia under Suharto also fell into this category. On the opposite end were the governments of Democratic Kampuchea (1975–78), North Vietnam after 1954, Burma after 1962, South Vietnam after 1975 and Laos after 1975. A somewhat middle course was taken by Burma under U Nu (1948–62),

Indonesia under Sukarno (particularly the Guided Democracy period of 1957–65), and Cambodia under Norodom Sihanouk (1953–70). Thailand under Nai Pridi Phanomyong (1945-47) and Laos in the 1950s and 60s may also be included in this category which had a socialist orientation, although it did little to actually redistribute wealth.

The differing economic philosophies of the Southeast Asian countries were reflected in their stand on foreign companies. Vietnam, Laos and Kampuchea expropriated all foreign firms, while under Guided Democracy, Indonesia nationalised all Dutch holdings and threatened to do so with respect to other foreign holdings, a policy not reversed until 1965. In the 1960s and 70s, Malaysia and the Philippines adopted laws to develop a higher indigenous stake in the corporate sector, which resulted in foreign firms selling out to locals or the government. Singapore, Thailand and Brunei were the only states not to have tried systematically to curb or diminish foreign investment.

The problems of considering Southeast Asia as a coherent economic region in the immediate aftermath of decolonisation were perhaps best captured by an important study by Burmese economist Hla Myint. The book, entitled *Southeast Asia's Economy in the 1970s*, was the product of an early attempt to develop a regional or sub-regional perspective on Southeast Asia's economic development. In April 1969, the Fourth Ministerial Conference for the Economic Development of Southeast Asia held in Bangkok requested the Asian Development Bank (ADB) to carry out a study of Southeast Asia's economy in the 1970s. (The report was first published by ADB in 1971 and published as a book by Praeger in 1972.) While pointing to differences, the book also laid the basis for a regional perspective on development.[19]

The aim of the study was "to analyse the nature of the major problems which confront the nations in the region in the seventies and explore the possibilities of individual and cooperative action by governments to effect their solution."[20] It sought to provide a "general background of the economic development of the region", highlighting what it called the "colonial pattern of economic development that prevailed before World War II, based on expansion of primary exports and import of cheap consumer goods."[21] Generalising about the region during the post-war period before the 1970s, it identified two key variables: "the importance of exports in the economic development of Southeast Asia, and the importance of appropriate domestic economic policies and improvements in internal organization in enabling these countries to take better advantage of their external economic opportunities."[22]

The study pointed to the diversity of Southeast Asia's economic development patterns, conditioned by historical circumstances as well as political and psychological attitudes of the ruling elite. Historical circumstances played a big part in the Indochinese countries, Vietnam,

Cambodia and Laos, where war and instability impeded economic recovery. But even in the rest of the region, economic performance varied due to differing degrees of economic nationalism. The "moderately minded" countries such as the Philippines, Thailand, and Malaya enjoyed speedy post-war economic recovery, rapid export expansion and high growth rates, while in Indonesia and Burma, which pursued stronger nationalist policies, recovery was slow and growth modest. Thus, the level of aggregate real income in 1960 as a percentage of the pre-war level for the Philippines, Thailand and Malaya was 201%, 191% and 164% respectively, while for both Indonesia and Burma, it was a lowly 111%.[24] The result was "the division of Southeast Asia into two groups of countries", one comprising the Indochinese countries as well as Indonesia and Burma, and the other consisting of the "moderately minded" nations of Malaya, the Philippines and Thailand, all of which achieved growth rates of 5–7% in contrast to the essentially stagnant economies of the former.[25]

The study was not only one of the first attempts in presenting a regional analysis of development patterns and policies, it was also among the first to seriously advocate regional economic cooperation in order to overcome the smallness of domestic markets. The manufacturing sectors in various Southeast Asian countries, noted the report, were producing a similar range of products and were offering similar tariffs and tax concessions to foreign multinationals. Against this backdrop, "there would seem to be a considerable scope for increasing the efficiency of the manufacturing industries if the Southeast Asian countries can be persuaded to open their markets to the manufactured exports of each other."[26] Pointing to the "considerable scope for mutual gain if the Southeast Asian countries can moderate their 'economic nationalism' against each other", the study argued:

> The gains from such regional cooperation arise from two sources. Firstly, even among the Southeast Asian countries, local conditions vary considerably and there is scope for intra-regional division of labour in manufacturing. Secondly, the access to the wider markets will enable these more efficient industries to attain their full economies of scale."[27]

The study drew a close linkage between regional idenity and regionalism: "A friend of Southeast Asia cannot but hope that her distinctive ways of life and culture which already create a sense of unity in the countries of the region may be preserved and strengthened by a movement towards closer regional economic cooperation."[28]

Despite the urging of economic regionalism, the economic divide in post-colonial Southeast Asia meant little prospect for regional governments to develop the necessary political will for mutual economic cooperation. The only possibility for such cooperation would be on a sub-regional basis, such as among the more "moderately minded" governments, but this had to await the stabilization of domestic changes in Indonesia.

While nationalism delivered Southeast Asia from the colonial yoke, it did not remove the problems of national integration or regime legitimacy. Southeast Asian states were typical "weak states" suffering from the problems of ethnic divisions and separatism and challenges to regime survival, which could not be managed through Western-style democratic frameworks. These factors tended to inhibit regionalism by forcing governments to be inward-looking in their political and security outlook, and in the case of Burma, even isolationist. Differing national responses to domestic challenges and inter-state tensions caused by transborder movements of communist and separatist insurgents also undermined the basis of regional unity. Yet, over the long term, these very domestic weaknesses would produce a convergence of political, economic and security predicaments among a group of Southeast Asian states, who would view regional cooperation as a necessary means of coping with internal as well as external vulnerabilities. As in the economic arena, the domestic political and security challenges facing Southeast Asian states would facilitate cooperation only on a sub-regional basis.

Among the most serious domestic challenges facing Southeast Asian states were the twin threats of communist insurgency and ethnic separatism. Communist movements which proliferated throughout Southeast Asia even before the French defeat in Indochina (which led to the establishment of the first communist regime in Southeast Asia, North Vietnam) derived support from China and Russia. But they also depended on cross-border sanctuaries in neighbouring states. For example, the survivors of the Communist party of Malaya (CPM) retreated into Thai territory. The Vietcong's ability to survive depended critically on sanctuaries in Cambodia. North Vietnam's support of the Pathet Lao and the Khmer Rouge in Cambodia was a major source of interstate tensions in Indochina before the communist victories in all three states in 1975. Separatist movements lacked significant extra-regional backing, but derived some support from neighbouring Southeast Asian countries. Examples include the support for Muslim separatists in southern Thailand from elements in Malaysia, similar Malaysian support for Islamic groups in Mindanao and Thai sanctuaries for ethnic rebels in Burma. The impact of these in creating serious friction was evident in Malaysia-Thailand and Burma-Thailand relations.

Moreover, insurgency undermined regionalism by creating a continued pattern of dependency on the part of Southeast Asian states on external military aid. This dependence lessened their interest in regional co-operation as a means of addressing domestic challenges. While the US intervention in South Vietnam and the British role in the Malayan insurgency were examples of direct external intervention, other regimes, in Thailand and the Philippines, also relied on external security support. It was not until the US failure in Vietnam caused governments to realise that seeking foreign support against domestic opponents could prove

56 THE QUEST FOR IDENTITY: INTERNATIONAL RELATIONS OF SOUTHEAST ASIA

Table 2.1: Major Armed Communist Movements in Early Post-Colonial Era, 1946–76

Country	Movement
Burma	1. Burma Communist Party (1948–)
Cambodia	1. Khmer Rouge (1970–75)
Indonesia	1. Madiun Communist Rebellion 2. Partai Kommunist Indonesia
Laos	1. Pathet Lao (1951–75)
Malaysia	1. Communist Party of Malaya (1948–) 2. North Kalimantan Communist Party (1950s–)
Philippines	1. New People's Army (1969–) 2. Huk Rebellion (1946–54)
Singapore	none (The Communist Party of Malaya operated in Singapore before its separation from Malaysia in 1965)
Thailand	1. Communist Party of Thailand (1965)*
Vietnam	1. National Liberation Front (1958–75)

* Approximate year of origin.

Adapted from S. Paribatra and Chai-Anan Samudavanija, "Internal Dimensions of Regional Security in Southeast Asia" in M. Ayoob (1986) *Regional Security in the Third World*, London: Croom Helm Ltd.

Table 2.2: Major Armed Separatist Movements in Early Post-Colonial Era, 1946–76

State	Armed Rebellion
Burma	1. Ethnically-related armed rebellions (1948–)
Indonesia	1. Darul Islam (1948–62) 2. PRRI Permesta (1958–61) 3. Organisasi Papua Merdeka (1963–) 6. Aceh Merdeka (1976–) 7. Fretilin (1976–)
Laos	1. Le Liquede Resistance Meo (1946–75)
Malaysia	none
Philippines	1. Moro National Liberation Front (1972)* 2. Moro Islamic Liberation Front (1984)*
Singapore	none
Thailand	1. Pattani United Liberation Organisation (1967–) 2. Barisan Nasional Pembebasan Pattani (1971–)

* Approximate year of origin.

Adapted from S. Paribatra and Chai-Anan Samudavanija, "Internal Dimensions of Regional Security in Southeast Asia" in M. Ayoob (1986) *Regional Security in the Third World*, London: Croom Helm Ltd.

Table 2.3: Ethnic Composition of Southeast Asian States, 1976

State	Ethnolinguistic Groups	Percentage of Population (%)
Burma	Burman	75
	Karen	10
	Shan	6
	Indian-Pakistani	3
	Chinese	1
	Kachin	1
	Chin	1
Cambodia	Khmer	90
	Chinese	6
	Cham	1
	Mon-Khmer tribes	1
Indonesia	Javanese	45
	Sundanese	14
	Madurese	8
	Chinese	2
Laos	Lao	67
	Mon-Khmer tribes	19
	Tai (other than Lao)	5
	Meo	4
	Chinese	3
North Vietnam*	Vietnamese	85
	Tho	3
	Muong	2
	Tai	2
	Nung	2
	Chinese	1
	Meo	1
	Yao	1
South Vietnam	Vietnamese	87
	Chinese	5
	Khmer	3
	Mountain chain tribes	3
	Mon-Khmer tribes	1
Malaysia	Malay	44
	Chinese	35
	Indian	11

58 THE QUEST FOR IDENTITY: INTERNATIONAL RELATIONS OF SOUTHEAST ASIA

Table 2.3 (continued)

State	Ethnolinguistic Groups	Percentage of Population (%)
Philippines	Cebuano	24
	Tagalog	21
	Ilocano	12
	Hiligaynon	10
	Bicol	8
	Sumar-Leyte	6
	Pampangan	3
	Pagasinan	3
Singapore	Chinese	77
	Malay	14
	Indians	7
	Others	2

* Vietnam unified in 1975 as a result of the communist takeover of the South.

Adapted from S. Paribatra and Chai-Anan Samudavanija, "Internal Dimensions of Regional Security in Southeast Asia" in M. Ayoob (1986) *Regional Security in the Third World*, London: Croom Helm Ltd.

counterproductive, that they turned to regional cooperation, including a common respect for the doctrine of non-interference as a more effective strategy for dealing with domestic insurgencies.

Throughout Southeast Asia in the 1950s and 60s, preoccupation with domestic problems diminished foreign policy capacity, including capacity for regional cooperation ventures and institutions. It also led to a tendency to create foreign diversions to shift attention from domestic problems, as the case of Sukarno's *Konfrontasi* showed.

The ways and approaches employed by Southeast Asian states to deal with their domestic problems and the outcome of these efforts also affected regionalism. The communist victory in North Vietnam ended any possibility of its participation in a regional forum involving the non-communist Southeast Asian states. In Burma, a campaign against insurgency and separatism undermined democracy and led to the advent of a military regime under General Ne Win in 1962, which professed no interest in regionalism and pursued an isolationist policy. In Malaysia, Thailand, the Philippines and Indonesia after Sukarno, on the other hand, domestic problems created a shared predicament. All these states had pursued free-market policies and relied on rapid economic growth to combat communism. They perceived a common internal threat and saw regional cooperation as an important way to combat it.

In this respect, it should be recognised that the pro-Western regimes facing the threat of communist insurgency shared a common perception about its sources. They saw it as essentially domestic. Even as these insurgencies derived support from China and Russia, international support was not their root cause. Communist insurgencies in Southeast Asia established themselves internally by exploiting the nationalist campaign against colonial and external powers, as in the case of Indonesia and Malaysia.[29] In terms of their origins and appeal, the insurgencies corresponded to what Michael Leifer identifies as being the common feature of such insurrections in post-colonial societies: "organized armed opposi-tion to successor elites to colonialism by alternative elites who offer a radically different vision of modernity and social order", and whose "appeal is cast doctrinally in terms of the values of distributive justice and are designed to attract groups alienated by poverty, by gross disparities of private wealth and by intolerance of a dominant culture".[30] To the extent that the socioeconomic patterns in all Southeast Asian countries in the post-colonial period were marked by these features, communist insurgencies in the region were a product, first and foremost, of internal contradictions. It was this realisation which was to prove crucial to the emergence of ASEAN and its inward-looking focus as a group of like-minded regimes. This was further evident when these governments collaborated against the threat of insurgency. In fact, one of the main catalysts of political cooperation among the non-communist Southeast Asian countries leading to the formation of ASEAN was the development of joint counter-insurgency measures along their common borders.

Another important development affecting political cooperation in Southeast Asia was the decline of democratic experiments and the rise of authoritarianism in the pro-Western states of Southeast Asia. Indeed, the linkage between authoritarianism and regionalism has been one of the neglected aspects of study of Southeast Asia's international relations. The decline of constitutional government and the growing authoritarian turn of governments in the region initially dampened prospects for regionalism, but over the longer term, it created the political basis for a common subregional political and ideological framework.

As Chan Heng Chee observes, many Southeast Asian countries "emerged from the colonial era experimenting with Western liberal democracy, but each abandoned the original model for variations of authoritarian forms which accommodate degrees of democracy".[31] A common thread running through the shift toward authoritarianism was its justification by the ruling regimes in terms of communist threat, ethnic unrest, and a belief that economic development required a certain amount of authoritarian control. And it is this thread that provided an important basis for regional cooperation in the 1960s and 70s, especially through the ASEAN framework.

Burma provides the clearest case where the retreat of democracy dampened the prospects for regional cooperation in Southeast Asia. Burma had been swept into independence by revolutionary nationalism. Its nationalist leadership under Aung San was an early advocate of regionalism, although, as noted earlier, this was not necessarily Southeast Asian in scope. But whatever interest Burma had in regionalism ended with the collapse of its democratic experiment in March 1962. The Ne Win regime suspended the constitution, suppressed the opposition and set up a Revolutionary Council which assumed sweeping legislative, executive, and judicial powers under his leadership. The junta set up its own political party called the Burma Socialist Programme Party, and made itself the only legal political party in 1964. The Revolutionary Council announced a programme called "The Burmese Way to Socialism" in April 1962 which aimed at achieving economic self-sufficiency by combining Theraveda Buddhism with Marxism-Leninism. It adopted non-alignment as its foreign policy posture and maintained good relations with both India and China at a time when they were at war, but gradually reduced its contacts with the outside world. This posture of isolationism was Ne Win's way of insulating Burma from external intervention in whatever form. Although it remained a member of the UN, World Bank, International Monetary Fund (IMF) and Asian Development Bank (ADB), Burma scaled down its involvement in these organisations, refused to send students abroad and discouraged tourism. Moreover, it no longer professed an interest in regional cooperation and effectively excluded itself from proposals to form a regional organisation in Southeast Asia.

While in Burma domestic troubles led to foreign policy isolationism, in the case of Indonesia, domestic strife led to expansionism and inter-state tensions. Sukarno's flirtation with democracy weakened after the first national elections held in 1955. Thereafter, Javanese attempts to centralise the country sparked serious separatist campaigns, leading to the setting up of independent governments by local army commanders in Sumatra and Sulawesi in late 1956. Sukarno also had to deal with the communist movement at home. The Indonesian Communist Party (PKI) was rebuilding its strength after the disastrous 1948 revolt, drawing support from China and Russia. The combination of ethnic separatism and communist insurgency led Sukarno to impose martial law in March 1957, followed by the abolition of the parliamentary constitution in 1959 and the declaration of what he called a "Guided Democracy" which placed considerable power in his own hands. These domestic troubles contributed to Sukarno's tendency to divert attention from domestic problems through regional adventures which threatened the security of neighbours.[32] These included his policy of *Konfrontasi*. Sukarno regarded the Malaysian Federation created in 1963 with the merger of Malaya, North Borneo (Sabah), Sarawak and Singapore as an artificial creature of colonialism. The British had seen the federation as the best way to ensure the viability of the small and vulnerable states. But Sukarno took an ideological stand against the Malaysian Federation, arguing that because of its continuing defence and economic links with Britain, including the Anglo-Malaysian Defence Agreement of 1957 which in 1963 was extended to the whole of Malaysia covering Malaya, Sarawak, North Borneo, and Singapore, Malaysia was not genuinely independent. He contrasted Indonesia's armed struggle with Malaysia's constitutional path. Soon after the formation of the Malaysian Federation, Sukarno launched a "Crush Malaysia" campaign, which continued for three years. Indonesia's campaign combined raids on the Sarawak-Kalimantan border with incursions into the Malay peninsula and Singapore. He even took Indonesia out of the UN in 1965 to protest the admission of Malaysia into the UN.

Suharto's "New Order" regime initially promised to be less authoritarian than Sukarno's "Guided Democracy", but hopes for this soon faded. Explaining its actions in terms of the need for national "resilience", manifested through internal stability and economic development, the regime imposed authoritarian rule and put down hopes for the more participatory political climate raised by the 1965 coup. But while Sukarno's foreign policy directly undermined regionalism, the New Order saw regionalism as an important tool for its domestic goals.

A similar turn to authoritarianism in Malaysia and the Philippines, while not crucial to the initial development of regionalist concepts among the pro-Western regimes in Southeast Asia, did help to sustain it later. In Malaysia, the democratic experiment also ran into problems as a result of domestic troubles including communist insurgency and ethnic unrest. Communal riots following the May 1969 elections were blamed on economic injustice and the failure of free market economics to reduce racial inequalities. The government of Tunku Abdul Rahman responded with the suspension of parliament (restored in September 1970), but sought to enlarge and strengthen the corporatist form of governance by creating an even bigger alliance among political groups under the National Front. It also created a national ideology, called *Rukunegara* and banned public debate on sensitive issues such as race relations and the status of the Malay monarchies. While ethnic unrest led to the decline of the Malaysian democratic experiment, communist insurgency masking regime survival concerns contributed to the retreat of democracy in the Philippines. In September 1972, Ferdinand Marcos, approaching the end of his second and last term in office, suspended the constitution and declared martial law citing communist insurgency as the reason. Marcos' "New Society" programme emphasied the need for stability, promised land reform and economic justice, but extracted the price of "constitutional authoritarianism" as the necessary political framework. The army was strengthened and given a place in mainstream Filipino politics for the first time, and political dissidence was suppressed.

Thus, the governments of Malaysia, Singapore, the Philippines and Indonesia came to focus on political stability and continuity of leadership while downgrading the Western model of participatory liberal democracy.

The case of Thailand was not substantially different. Thailand had experienced alternations between democratic experiments and military rule. Democracy seemed to have prevailed in 1946 when Seni Promoj, who became Prime Minister after the defeat of the Japanese, lost the 1946 general elections. But the ensuing government of Pridi Phanomyong was overthrown in 1947 by Fleid Marshall Phibun Songkram. Democracy returned briefly in 1957 when political parties were legalised and general elections were held as a result of domestic and Western pressure. But General Sarit Thanarat, who had been forced out of power as a result of the election, returned the country to military rule in October 1958. The government suppressed the left-wing opposition and promoted economic development, education and social reform to dispel the underlying sources of social discontent. In the late 1960s the military government of Thanom Kittikachorn and Prapat Charusathien faced a serious escalation of the insurgency led by the Communist Party of Thailand, both in the northern and southern parts of the country. The government responded with harsh measures. Although this would lead to massive protests and brief restoration of civilian rule between 1973 and 1976—under Seni Promoj and then his brother Kukrit—an authoritarian and bureaucratic polity continued to shape Thai regional foreign policy for much of the 1950s and 60s.

Facing similar predicaments of communist insurgency, ethnic separatism and challenges to regime survival, the governments of Malaysia, Singapore, Thailand, the Philippines, and Indonesia, responded with a common turn to authoritarianism, emphasising domestic stability and economic development. This became a source of solidarity among these regimes. As Jorgensen-Dahl pointed out:

> the various countries [in ASEAN] ... have the same internal enemy ... the common internal enemy is seen to feed and depend for its success on a cluster of social conditions that are essentially the same in the various countries. From this point of view regional cooperation and organisation is seen as an instrument which will allow the countries involved to more effectively strike at the roots of these conditions, and therefore at the very base of the most crucial support of their common internal enemy".[33]

Among these governments regionalism was seen as a more effective way of dealing with internal threats than external support. In some cases, the turn to regionalism spurred by domestic changes was quite dramatic. In the Philippines, after imposing martial law, Marcos moved to make his country more independent of the US, stressing regionalism in the foreign policy framework. Domestic politics also began to facilitate a shift in Thailand away from the US and toward regionalism. During the fight against the communists in the late 1960s, the fear of a US withdrawal and doubts about its credibility, as well as security concerns raised by the escalation of the Vietnam War caused Thailand to rethink its stance. Indonesia's foreign policy shift was the most dramatic and most influential. Sukarno's anti-colonialism was replaced by Suharto's anti-communism. The Suharto regime shifted its foreign policy not only by cutting off diplomatic ties with Beijing and Moscow (placing the blame for the attempted 1965 coup on Beijing's support for the Indonesian communists), but more importantly by becoming an active promoter of regionalism leading to the formation of ASEAN.

Great Power Rivalry and Regional Autonomy

At the onset of the post-colonial era, the attitude of the great powers and the Cold War geopolitics served to undermine the prospects for Southeast Asian regionalism. The availability of external (Western) security guarantees against both domestic and external threats rendered the need of some Southeast Asian states for regional cooperation less urgent in dealing with security challenges. Thailand and the Philippines, while ostensibly interested in regional defence cooperation, could actually be relaxed about it since their security needs were met, at least partially, by the United States-Philippines mutual defense treaty of 1951 and the beginning of the US military assistance to Thailand in 1950. Moreover there was little agreement among the Western powers on the need for regional security cooperation in Southeast Asia. The French and the British had hoped for some form of collaboration, especially in defence, against popular insurgencies in Malaya and Vietnam backed by China. However, the US was not prepared to support any such proposals, having been stretched by the Korean War. This was to change in the 1950s, but the US would face considerable obstacles to developing a regional defence system in Southeast Asia.

At the end of the Second World War, neither the US nor the Soviet Union considered Southeast Asia to be an area of major strategic significance. Their involvement in the region was minimal. Stalin considered Southeast Asia to be peripheral to his interest in the spread of communism; the Soviet Union had not envisaged the possibility for major geopolitical or ideological gain either in Indonesia or in Indochina. This lack of interest was further confirmed by its failure to support the Indonesian Communist Party's Madiun revolt in 1948.

During the immediate post-war period, the US and Britain had a key influence over the framework of regional associations in Southeast Asia. At the Potsdam Conference of July 1945, the victorious Allied Powers decided to divide the responsibility for administering Japan's colonial possessions in Southeast Asia between the Americans, Chinese, and British. Accordingly, the US would be responsible for the Philippines, the Chinese would have responsibility for North Vietnam, and the Southeast

64 THE QUEST FOR IDENTITY: INTERNATIONAL RELATIONS OF SOUTHEAST ASIA

Asia Command (SEAC), led by Britain, would have responsibility for the remainder of colonial Southeast Asia. This made Britain the only external power to have the opportunity to develop a semi-regional approach to Southeast Asia. By 1948, Britain had become convinced that Southeast Asia would become a major arena of US-Soviet rivalry. The British also came up with one of the first formulations of the "domino theory". The British Commissioner-General in Southeast Asia predicted in 1949 that the fall of China would precipitate communist takeovers in Indochina, followed by Siam (Thailand), Burma and Malaya. Although President Eisenhower expressed belief in the domino theory in April 1954, the US rejected a British proposal to create some sort of Marshall Plan for Southeast Asia. To a certain extent, Britain's interest in developing the Colombo Plan[31] within the framework of the Commonwealth was partly an effort to compensate for its inability to influence the Americans in this regard. The Plan was created at a meeting of the Commonwealth Foreign Ministers in Colombo in January 1950. It was meant to be a framework for the provision of economic and technical aid. Britain had hoped that the scope of the plan be extended to cover security issues, although this failed to materialise.

The US policy towards Southeast Asia in the immediate aftermath of the war was more hesitant about the necessity for a regional organisation. In general, Southeast Asia was not a priority area in American global strategic policy, thanks to the continued streak of hemispheric isolationism and the burdens imposed by the need to police other theatres of the Cold War. US policy did recognise an opportunity for American business to invest in the Southeast Asian colonies created by post-war rehabilitation. There was support for this from the colonial powers; this in turn served to moderate the American interest in seeing a hasty end to the age of empire in Southeast Asia. Thus, while as a champion of national liberation, President Roosevelt proposed in 1942–43 an international trusteeship system for the former Southeast Asian colonies which would prepare them for independence, the stability afforded by the restoration of colonial rule was seen by the US as a more useful tool against communist advance than the instability associated with weak nation-states. Thus, the real US interest in thinking about Southeast Asia as a regional unit and its interest in regional cooperation had less to do with anti-colonialism than anti-communism. Even then, Washington was cautious about being too closely involved in a regional organisation. As a Policy Planning Staff Paper on US policy towards Southeast Asia in March 1949 noted:

> We should avoid at the outset urging an area organization, our effort should initially be directed toward collaboration on joint or parallel action and then, only as a pragmatic and desirable basis for intimate association appears, should we encourage the areas to move step by step toward formal organi-

zation. If Asian leaders prematurely precipitate an area organization, we should not give the impression of attempting to thwart such a move but should go along with them while exerting a cautiously moderating influence ... In order to minimize suggestions of American imperialist intervention, we should encourage the Indians, Filipinos and other Asian states to take the public lead in political matters. Our role should be the offering of discreet support and guidance..."[35]

The US reluctance to support the establishment of an anti-communist security alliance in the Pacific was reflected in its response to one such proposal, made by President Elpidio Quirino of the Philippines and calling for a Pacific equivalent of the North Atlantic Treaty Organization (NATO). This proposal drew support from President Syngman Rhee of South Korea and General Chiang Kai-Shek of nationalist China. A meeting between Chiang and Quirino in Baguio in July 1949 led them to call for a anti-communist front with the involvement of South Korea, India, Australia, New Zealand, Thailand and Indonesia. While Australia, New Zealand and Thailand were willing to consider this idea, the Truman administration was not interested.

But the US attitude shifted in the early 1950s in response to the communist challenge. As the survival of non-communist regimes, whether vestiges of old colonial rule or newly-installed nationalist regimes, was recognised as a major American interest in Southeast Asia, the US began assisting the French against the Vietminh as well as supporting the nationalist regimes which showed a determination to challenge communists, a policy which explained American support for Indonesian independence which became stronger following Sukarno's stand against the Indonesian communists in Madiun. The "loss" of China further strengthened the US decision to extend its containment policy to Southeast Asia. On 18 July 1949, the US Secretary of State, Dean Acheson, expressed American interest in preventing "further communist domination on the continent of Asia or in South-East Asia".[36] This development came in the midst of major developments in the Cold War in Europe, including the formation of the North Atlantic Treaty Organization (NATO) in 1949 and signs of intensified armed struggle by communist movements in Burma, Indonesia, Malaya, the Philippines and Vietnam. Regional alliance-building became an important part of the US containment strategy to prevent the emergence of pro-Soviet regimes in Asia, an objective rendered more urgent by the outbreak of the Korean War and the Vietminh offensive against French forces in September 1950. These developments gave rise to Washington's own "domino theory" which assumed that communist victory in any single country would have a contagion effect leading to communist victories in the rest of the countries of the region. Other strategic interests and objectives also contributed to the US interest in regional security co-operation. These included ensuring access to

66 THE QUEST FOR IDENTITY: INTERNATIONAL RELATIONS OF SOUTHEAST ASIA

strategically located overseas bases and a desire to counter pan-Asian movements, such as the Asian Relations Conference of 1947, the New Delhi Conference of 1949 and the Bandung Conference of 1955, which were seen as being unfriendly and anti-Western.

Washington's attitude towards Asian, including Southeast Asian, regional cooperation in the immediate post-war period was thus marked by contradictory impulses. Having been aware of the growing Asian nationalism, US planners and policy-makers had refrained from taking any initiative in the formation of regional associations in Asia. Any such US initiative, it was thought, might give rise to suspicion of "imperialist intervention". On the other hand, the United States was eager to provide assistance to a regional association born out of Asian initiative that would be pro-West in orientation and anti-communist by nature. In the absence of a desirable Asian initiative and with the growing influence of communist forces in Indochina, Washington took the initiative and was instrumental in the establishment of the Southeast Asia Treaty Organization (SEATO).

While the US began looking for a regional security structure to contain communism, the Eisenhower administration emphasised the development of bilateral alliances with the Philippines and Thailand. But the defeat of the French at the hands of Vietminh forces led by General Vo Nguyen Giap in 1954 at Dien Bien Phu led to an American effort to internationalise the war, and spurred new interest in a regional defence alliance. American support for the French in Indochina had been increased due to China's entry into the Korean War in November 1950 and its backing of the Vietminh. While the Geneva Accords on Indochina in 1954 produced a ceasefire agreement between the French and North Vietnamese governments[37], it did not assuage US concerns over communist expansion. In fact, the Geneva accords sowed the seeds of the ideological and strategic polarisation of Southeast Asia which was to affect the prospects for regional cooperation. As A.J. Stockwell writes:

> In international relations it presented the pursuit of war by other means. Predicated upon a Manichean division of the world into two hostile blocs, it reinforced belief in the existence of Western and communist monoliths. Instead of providing for the agreement of the Great Powers, it set the scene for another phase in their future confrontation. None of the participants (including the co-chairmen, Britain and the USSR) had either the will or the means to stand firm on the implementation of the Geneva settlement and to convert the ceasefire into a political agreement. The United States came to hate everything Geneva stood for; China soon claimed it had been duped as regards the position of Cambodia and Laos; and the opposing Vietnamese felt betrayed by their respective sponsors. Some weeks later the creation of the Southeast Asia Treaty Organization (SEATO) at the Manila Conference (September 1954) introduced a new phase in the conduct of containment in the region by replacing the outworn structures of French colonialism and

military imperialism with a system of collective security. Geneva may have prevented the internationalization of the Vietnam War in the summer of 1954, but it provided for the formal entanglement of Indochina in the international relations of Cold War.[38]

The legal framework for SEATO, the Southeast Asia Collective Defence Treaty (or the Manila Pact) was signed on 8 September 1954 at a meeting in Manila, attended by Britain, the US, France, Australia, New Zealand, Pakistan, Thailand, and the Philippines. The meeting also adopted a Pacific Charter which, among other things, endorsed SEATO's role in deterring threats to the security and stability of the members from aggression and subversion. The establishment of SEATO did contribute to a greater awareness of Southeast Asia as a region in the international arena. However, the concept of "region" embodied by SEATO was loose and flexible. According to Article VIII of the Manila Pact:

> As used in this Treaty, the "Treaty Area" is the general area of South-East Asia, including also the entire territories of the Asian Parties, and the general area of the South-West Pacific not including the Pacific area north of 21 degrees 30 minutes north latitude. The Parties may, by unanimous agreement, amend this Article to include within the Treaty Area the territory of any State acceding to this Treaty in accordance with Article VII or otherwise to change the Treaty Area.[39]

As a regional security framework, SEATO was plagued by several problems. Key differences emerged between its two leading players, the US and Britain. Britian had wanted to delay the consideration of a pact until the Geneva conference was over, hoping that it would produce a settlement and bring about lasting peace. John Foster Dulles, the US Secretary of State who masterminded US Cold War alliances, saw it differently. He did not believe the conference would succeed (this proved to be a self-fulfilling prophecy). Even before the start of the conference, in March 1954, Dulles called for a collective defence treaty against communist aggression. Britain argued that such a treaty would jeopardise the conference's prospects and instead suggested a non-aggression pact which would include India and other Asian countries. In the end the organisation only came about through a compromise, whereby Britain gave up its demand for a non-aggression pact while the US gave up the idea of a unified field command. These undermined SEATO at birth.

The establishment of SEATO was greeted with considerable antagonism by China and Vietnam. Beijing accused the US of destroying the Geneva agreement, despite US-British claims that SEATO was meant to reinforce the Geneva principles. But SEATO's main problem had to do with the gap in expectations between the Asian members on the one hand, and the Western sponsors, especially the US, on the other. The credibility of the alliance suffered as the Asian parties to SEATO were disappointed by the lower level of assurances and security guarantees offered by the US. Adding to this were the divergent security objectives of the Western powers and the Asian parties. For the latter, internal challenges to regime survival were the main threat to security, rather than overt communist aggression or subversion that had been advanced by the US as the major rationale for creating a regional security structure. Moreover, SEATO, like other Cold War alliances, failed to provide any mechanism for conflict-resolution within the region. Given that intra-regional conflicts constituted a serious challenge to the security of Southeast Asia, a regional security system that did not contain a mechanism to deal with such conflicts was questionable in terms of relevance and utility.

For the region's officially non-aligned countries, especially Indonesia and Malaysia, SEATO represented a flawed approach to regional security. For them, while military pacts might be useful against a threat of outright aggression, an unlikely scenario as far as many non-communist Southeast Asian states were concerned, they could not address revolutionary social challenges. Indonesia's Foreign Minister, Adam Malik, drew attention to this danger when he warned that "[m]ilitary alliances or foreign military presence does not enhance a nation's capacity to cope with the problem of insurgency. The price for such commitments is too high, whereas the negative ramifications for the nation are too great."[40] Mohammed Ghazali bin Shafie, a former Malaysian Foreign Minister, later wrote, "External support for internal insurgencies or for governments combating insurgencies, have the effect of raising the level of violence and complicating both conflict management and the peaceful resolution of conflicts through political means. Internal stability cannot after all be imposed from the outside".[41] Seeking the help of external powers in situations of domestic instability could undermine the legitimacy of the threatened regime; after all the most important and painful lesson of the Vietnam War was that relying on external backing in domestic upheavals could "easily serve to insulate it [the threatened regime] from political and economic realities and render it insensitive to the social forces with which in the long run it must come to terms if it is to survive on its own".[42]

A major development affecting SEATO's fortunes was the superpower détente of the early 1970s, which severely undermined the credibility of the American commitment to anti-Soviet regional coalitions in the Third World. Détente also raised the unsavoury prospect of a superpower condominium that might compromise or ignore the security interests of the Third World states in general. Faced with these prospects, some members of Cold War alliances chose to change track and distance themselves from the superpower sphere of influence, thereby rendering them rapidly obsolete. The failure of such alliances in turn led to renewed interest in regional organisations that promised "regional solutions to regional problems".

In Southeast Asia, the US came to acknowledge the limitation of SEATO. President Nixon wrote in October 1967 that "SEATO was useful and appropriate to its time, but it was Western in origin".[43] This suggests that even the US had become convinced that regional cooperation in Southeast Asia could not thrive without an indigenous basis. The decision to dissolve SEATO by mid-1977 was announced in September 1975. By this time ASEAN had come into a life of its own. Some attempt was made by SEATO's protagonists to see ASEAN as a more civilian successor to SEATO. In May 1977, the then Secretary General of SEATO, Sunthorn Hungladarom, said, "I don't think it is possible to revive SEATO. We have to let some organization like ASEAN assume some of SEATO's functions."[44] But ASEAN would be very sensitive to any such comparison. The US did turn its attention to supporting ASEAN. This was consistent with the Johnson administration's 1965 policy declaring its intention to support regional cooperation in Southeast Asia. But the US backing of ASEAN would be mainly indirect, and ASEAN would be very careful about not being seen as a tool of US policy.

In the late 1960s a major shift in the international environment affected the international relations of Southeast Asia. The chief trend was the easing of Cold War tensions and a shift from the rigid bipolarity of the early Cold War period towards a more fluid situation, resulting from the Sino-Soviet rift and the rise of the European Community. US-Soviet relations had steadily evolved towards greater understanding from the Cuban missile crisis in 1962, when the danger of nuclear war was brought home to their leaders.

In Southeast Asia, these developments helped to increase the appeal of regionalism among the pro-Western regimes. They lessened the credibility and usefulness of relying on Western security guarantees, even for the Philippines and Thailand, who had developed close defence links with the US. The Philippines' dependence on the US had increased significantly as a result of US help in suppressing the Huk insurgency which was at its height in the 1950s. The Philippines then became a major link in the US containment strategy, providing troops to fight in the Korean War from August 1950. In August 1951, the US and the Philippines signed a Mutual Defence Treaty. Thailand too had become a close US ally, signing military, economic and technical cooperation and assistance agreements in 1950. Like the Philippines, the Thai government under Phibun sent troops to Korea. Facing a communist insurgency dominated by an ethnic Chinese element, Thailand had adopted some anti-Chinese measures.

Against this backdrop, two developments had a major impact on the attitudes of the pro-Western regimes of Southeast Asia, especially Thailand, the Philippines, Malaysia and Singapore, towards Western security guarantees. The first was the announcement by the Harold Wilson government in 1966 of Britain's "east of Suez" policy, which in effect meant the withdrawal of British military forces "east of Suez" (initially by the mid-1970s, but this was brought forward to 1971). The other development was the Nixon administration's new "doctrine" on regional security, called the "Nixon Doctrine" which ruled out US involvement in a future land war in Southeast Asia, and called upon America's Asian allies to assume a greater burden of their own defence. Despite the different historical roles played by the British and the Americans in Southeast Asia's international relations, both developments had the same effect; they signaled to the pro-Western countries of the region the need for greater self-reliance, through both national effort and regional cooperation.

The British withdrawal was particularly significant for Singapore and Malaysia. Long reliant on Britain and other Commonwealth partners (Australia and New Zealand) for protection against both internal as well as external threats, they received the announcement at a time when the development of their indigenous defence capabilities was still at a rudimentary stage. The British decision to withdraw prompted the replacement of the Anglo-Malaysian Defence Agreement (AMDA) with a regional security system called Five Power Defence Arrangements (FPDA) involving Britain, Australia, New Zealand, Singapore and Malaysia. Mindful of their financial limitations and political constraints, the British produced a greatly watered-down commitment: a consultative arrangement backed by a small air defence (centred on Australian combat aircraft) and ground force component (contributed by New Zealand).[45] Against this backdrop, for both Singapore and Kuala Lumpur, regional cooperation aimed at minimising the potential for intra-regional conflict seemed to be a natural course to follow, complementing the rapid build-up of their military forces in order to achieve greater self-reliance dictated by the weakening Western strategic umbrella.[46]

The British withdrawal contributed to the urgency of regional co-operation on the part of Singapore which saw it as an essential means through which local countries could address the non-military, especially political and economic, requirements of security. The Foreign Minister of Singapore, S. Rajaratnam, observed:

> The British decision to withdraw from the region in the seventies brings...to an end nearly two centuries of dominant European influence in the region. The seventies will also see the withdrawal of direct American influence in Southeast Asian affairs. For the first time in centuries, Southeast Asia will be on its own. It must fill what some people call the power vacuum itself or resign itself to the dismal prospect of the vacuum being filled from the outside. ... we can and should fill it ourselves, not necessarily militarily, but by strengthening our social, economic and political foundations through cooperation and collective effort.[47]

The Nixon Doctrine was a by-product of the Nixon administration's efforts to simultaneously reduce tensions with the Soviet Union while seeking a new opening to China. This meant an easing of the side-effects of the US-Soviet and Sino-US geopolitical rivalry on Southeast Asia. While this contributed to a more relaxed atmosphere in Southeast Asia, the US policy also had the effect of magnifying the evolving Sino-Soviet conflict, especially with the use of the "China card" in the Nixon-Kissinger geopolitical framework. This meant that insofar as Southeast Asia was concerned, Sino-Soviet rivalry would remain an important aspect of the region's international relations. Thus, the pro-Western regimes of Southeast Asia could no longer count on their external security guarantees, while not being totally free from the influence of great power rivalry. It is in response to both these situations that the pro-Western governments in Southeast Asia looked to regional solidarity.

The US failure in Indochina had become apparent by the late 1960s, and the Nixon Doctrine by calling on America's regional allies to assume greater responsibilities for their own security, was a warning signal of the eventual US disengagement from mainland Southeast Asia. One major impact of the shifting US posture was to further stimulate Thailand's efforts to steer a more independent course in foreign policy, a move also in keeping with Bangkok's traditional policy of avoiding "too much dependence on any single power or patron".[48] The impact on the Philippines was similar, spurring Manila's desire to shed its image as a strategic client of the US and assert its "Asian" identity.[49] For these two states, the geopolitical reverses suffered by the US due to its engagement in Vietnam, and the Nixon Doctrine made a drive towards self-reliance in the framework of greater regional cooperation imperative. For Singapore and Malaysia, the US withdrawal was a further blow to the credibility of the Western security guarantees that had already been severely undermined by the announcement of British withdrawal from the region.

These developments in great power relations interacted with developments at the regional level. Here, contrasting trends emerged in Indochina on the one hand, and the rest of Southeast Asia (excluding Burma) on the other. As Indochina's international relations were shaped by war and revolution and continuing great power intervention, the non-communist Southeast Asian countries, alarmed by the developments in Indochina and exposed to the common danger of insurgency and interventionism, closed ranks and launched an experiment in regionalism with a view to reduce great power influence and ensure their political survival.

While the Cold War aggravated a great deal of intra-regional conflict in Southeast Asia, it also helped to bring the region to international limelight. Prior to the advent of the Cold War in Southeast Asia the region had consisted of separate countries that had been linked far more closely to their colonial masters than they were to each other. By identifying the region as a 'trouble-spot', and asserting region-wide solutions to their problems there, the superpowers changed all that. The Cold War also provided a strong impetus for regionalism by creating a common fear of superpower rivalry among the countries of the region.

For much of this early Cold War period, Southeast Asia presented the image of a highly unstable segment of the international system, an image captured by Milton Osborne's famous phrase "region of revolt".[50] The region's proneness to strife became a distinctive feature, prompting comments by Bernard Gordon that one of the factors "which makes Southeast Asia a 'region' is the widespread incidence of conflict, along with some attempts at cooperation", and that "instability is the one feature of Southeast Asia that gives the region much of its contemporary importance."[51] The Cold War geopolitical view of Southeast Asia prevalent in the West, particularly in the US, was that it was a region of likely dominos.

Conclusion

The international relations of Southeast Asia in the 1950s and 60s were deeply influenced by a complex interaction between three fundamental forces: nationalism, the nature of the decolonisation process, and the advent of the Cold War. The main outcome of this was the achievement of only limited national and regional autonomy by the Southeast Asian states. Nationalism had spurred a search for self-reliance and autonomy. However, in reality, the weakness of the nation-state and intra-regional divisions caused by both the pressures of the Cold War and contending nationalisms, served to create a regional pattern of international relations in Southeast Asia which was largely dominated by outside powers and influences. Superpower rivalry gradually replaced colonialism as the chief determinant of international affairs in the region. The newly independent states of Southeast Asia were too weak and disorganised to override these external constraints and resist great power intervention. Attempts to develop "regional solutions to regional problems" faltered due to existing suspicions and rivalries among the Southeast Asian states, as well as their continued dependence on external security guarantees.

The fact that the political, economic and strategic conditions in Southeast Asia remained substantially unfavourable to regional cooperation during the first two decades of the post-war period was confirmed by an important study of regional economic interdependence in Southeast Asia. Although the study was concerned mainly with economic linkages, it helped to identify the obstacles to prospects for regionalism in general. These included:

a. the tendency among Southeast Asian leaders to advance proposals for regional cooperation for domestic and foreign political effect (examples include Sukarno's "Newly Emerging Forces" idea);

NATIONALISM, REGIONALISM AND THE COLD WAR ORDER 73

b. the persistence of intra-regional antagonisms such as *Konfrontasi*,
    the Vietnam-Thailand, Cambodia-Vietnam, and Malaysia-Thailand
    rivalries, which created great sensitivity towards the development
    of political and military institutions of regional cooperation;
c. the impact of the Cold War in polarising national foreign policy
    postures, with countries such as India (which was still being
    regarded as a likely member of a Southeast Asian regional coopera-
    tion framework), Laos, Cambodia and Burma choosing a non-aligned
    posture between East and West, and Malaysia, Singapore, Thailand,
    and the Philippines adopting a pro-Western posture (Indonesia,
    according to this study, was shifting from a neutral to a pro-Western
    stance); and
d. differences in basic economic policy among regional countries, with
    Burma, Indonesia, and India adopting an "inward-looking" trade
    and investment policy while Malaysia, Thailand and the Philippines
    relied on a relatively "outward-looking" approach through private
    enterprise and free trade.[52]

Another pessimistic assessment of the regional situation was provided
by Kenneth T. Young, a former US ambassador to Thailand. Published in
1965, it argued:

> It is doubtful that political regionalism or area-wide defense will emerge
> to play a part in encouraging regional equiibrium or regional institutions
> for political collaboration or collective defense. Centrifugal and divisive
> tendencies are too strong. Leaders will be more interested in relations with
> outside countries than among themselves, and more inclinded to participate
> in Pan-Asian or international conferences and organizations than in
> exclusively Southeast Asian formations. They know that real power and
> resources, which the Southeast Asian countries do not possess, will continue
> to come from outside the region. Even the common fear of Communist China
> and the threat of Chinese minorities will not develop any sense of solidarity
> or serve to coordinate the divergent policies of neutrality and alignment.
> One political dilemma in Southeast Asia is that these new governments are
> trying desperately to become viable nation-states in an area where the
> individual state may, despite internal nationalism and good leadership, be
> turning obsolescent for security and development of the area, and where at
> the same time a sense of regional community and purpose is lacking to
> complement and reinforce the nation-state.[53]

Young was correct in identifying the lack of resources and the divisive
tendencies in Southeast Asia and the negative impact of nationalism on
regionalism. But with the benefit of hindsight, it is clear that he did not
forsee the motivation for cooperation among a sub-regional group of like-
minded regimes fearful of Chinese-backed communist expansion. By the
mid-1960s, there were already indications of a shift in domestic and

74   THE QUEST FOR IDENTITY: INTERNATIONAL RELATIONS OF SOUTHEAST ASIA

external conditions which would culminate in the development of regionalist concepts among the non-communist states of Southeast Asia. Some of these changes were linked to great power policies. The declining willingness and ability of the Western powers, Britain and the US, to maintain their security umbrella in the region, further encouraged the quest for regional cooperation and identity. The non-communist states of Southeast Asia had now to look to themselves for developing a collective political resistance to communism. Thus Singapore's Foreign Minister, S. Rajaratnam, would explain the emergence of ASEAN as a "response on the part of non-communist Southeast Asia to the western abandonment of its role as a shield against communism."[54]

These external developments interacted with the domestic situation in pro-Western Southeast Asian states which was marked by a number of similarities. These included the commonly-faced threat of communist insurgency and ethnic separatism. These challenges also produced a common shift towards authoritarianism, as well as an emphasis on regime legitimisation via rapid economic growth through market capitalism, thereby creating a commonality of predicament and policy outlook among these states. Ultimately, this proved to be the key driving factor behind the formation of ASEAN in 1967.

The first two decades of the post-Second World War period saw a major shift in approaches to regional order in Southeast Asia. The 1950s were marked by a direct or indirect push by the Western powers to involve their Southeast Asian allies in developing regional alliances that could act as bulwarks against communism. In these years, then, Southeast Asian efforts in developing regional groupings were minimal and largely rhetorical. But from the late 1950s, there emerged the first serious initiatives from among Southeast Asian leaders to develop regional associations with an essentially Southeast Asian scope and character. The 1960s saw a growing recognition among the Southeast Asian elite of the dangers and futility of being involved in the kind of regionalism advocated by the West, and their consequent desire to develop a more "self-reliant" form of regionalism geared to managing intra-regional security relationships and shielding the region from the harmful effects of great power rivalry. While the initial efforts in this regard were short-lived, they had an important cumulative effect, moving the countries of the region towards a more viable form of regionalism in 1967.

Notes

[1]   C.M. Turnbull (1992), "Regionalism and Nationalism", in N. Tarling, ed. (1992) *The Cambridge History of Southeast Asia*, Volume 2, "The Nineteenth and Twentieth Centuries", Cambridge: Cambridge University Press, p.589.

[2]   See: A. Reid (1997) "A Saucer Model of Southeast Asian Identity," *Southeast Asian Journal of Social Science*, vol.27, no.1, pp.7–23.

[3] C.E. Goscha (1999) *Thailand and the Southeast Asian Networks of the Vietnamese Revolution, 1885–1954*, Surrey: Curzon Press, p.244.

[4] Cited in C. Mahapatra (1990) *American Role in the Origin and Growth of ASEAN*, New Delhi: ABC Publishing House, p.15.

[5] W. Henderson (1955) "The Development of Regionalism in Southeast Asia", *International Organization* vol.9. no.4, pp.462–476.

[6] Cited in C.E. Goscha (1999) *Thailand and the Southeast Asian Networks of the Vietnamese Revolution, 1885–1954*, op cit., p.255.

[7] A. Vanderbosch and R. Butwell (1966) *The Changing Face of Southeast Asia*, Lexington: University of Kentucky Press, pp.339–340, p.341.

[8] Ibid., p.341.

[9] C.E. Goscha (1999) *Thailand and the Southeast Asian Networks of the Vietnamese Revolution, 1885–1954*, op.cit., p.257.

[10] Ibid, pp.258–59.

[11] Ibid., p.341.

[12] Cited in C.E. Goscha (1999) *Thailand and the Southeast Asian Networks of the Vietnamese Revolution, 1885–1954*, op.cit., p.348.

[13] G. Wang (1964) "Nation Formation and Regionalism in Southeast Asia", in M. Grant, ed., *South Asia Pacific Crisis: National Development and World Community*, New York: Dodd, Mead and Company, p.134.

[14] Ibid., pp.125–135.

[15] B.K. Gordon, (1966) *The Dimensions of Conflict in Southeast Asia*, New Jersey: Prentice Hall, p.145.

[16] Ibid., p.164.

[17] N. Owen (1992) "Economic and Social Change" in N. Tarling, ed., *The Cambridge History of Southeast Asia*, Volume 2, "The Nineteenth and Twentieth Centuries", Cambridge: Cambridge University Press, pp.467–527, p.493.

[18] Ibid., pp.473–74.

[19] H. Myint, (1972) *Southeast Asia's Economy: Development Policies in the 1970's*, New York: Praeger Publishers, 1972. This was of course not the first book on the subject. Books written by Western scholars with a Southeast Asian focus included: F.H. Golay, R. Anspach, M.R. Pfanner, and B.A. Eliezer (1969) *Underdevelopment and Economic Nationalism in Southeast Asia*, Ithaca: Cornell University Press; T. Morgan and N. Spoelstra (1969) *Economic Interdependence in Southeast Asia*, Madison: University of Wisconsin Press.

[20] Cited in H. Myint, (1972) *Southeast Asia's Economy: Development Policies in the 1970's*, op.cit., p.13.

[21] Ibid., p.25.

[22] Ibid., p.23.

[23] Ibid., p.13.

[24] Ibid, p.27.

[25] Ibid., pp.26–27.

[26] Ibid., p.71.

[27] Ibid., pp.71-72.

[28] Ibid., p.159.

[29] J. Lim and S. Vani, (1984) "Introduction," in J. Lim and S. Vani, eds., *Armed Communist Movements in Southeast Asia*, Aldershot: Gower, p.xiii.

[30] M. Leifer, (1980) *Conflict and Regional Order in Southeast Asia*, Adelphi Paper No.162 London: International Institute for Strategic Studies, p.4.

[31] H.C. Chan (1982) "Political Stability in Southeast Asia" paper presented to the Seminar on "Trends and Perspectives in ASEAN", Singapore, Institute of Southeast Asian Studies, 1–3 February 1982, p.11.

[32] C.M.Turnbull (1992) "Regionalism and Nationalism", op.cit., p.610.

[33] A. Jorgensen –Dahl (1982), *Regional Organization and Order in Southeast Asia*, London: Macmillan, p.102

[34] The Colombo Plan which began to function from 1 July 1951 was not strictly a regional organization. Under this plan, seventeen Asian countries were to receive technical assistance and capital aid from the US, Britain, Canada, Australia, Japan and New Zealand. The assistance arrangements were based on bilateral understandings between aid givers and recipients. The US considered expanding the Colombo Plan into a multilateral grouping and sounded out a proposal to this effect privately to some members at the Ministerial Conference of the Colombo Plan in Ottawa. Although the Colombo Plan was useful in facilitating American cooperation with Asian countries without inviting the usual criticism of imperialist intervention, the plan to strengthen the Plan failed to materialise due to the reluctance of the US to agree to the creation of a permanent secretariat.

[35] C. Mahapatra (1990) *American Role in the Origin and Growth of ASEAN*, op.cit., p.21.

[36] Cited in A.J. Stockwell, Southeast Asia in War and Peace: The End of European Colonial Empires, in N. Tarling, ed. (1992) *The Cambridge History of Southeast Asia*, Volume 2, op.cit., p.361.

[37] The Geneva settlement established an International Supervisory Commission to oversee the end of hostilities, divided the country at the seventeenth parallel, ensured French withdrawal and recognised the independence, security and integrity of Laos and Cambodia. The eventual reunification of Vietnam was envisaged pending a political settlement and the holding of elections, to be held in July 1956.

[38] A.J. Stockwell, "Southeast Asia in War and Peace: The End of European Colonial Empires", op.cit., p.373.

[39] *History of SEATO* (Bangkok: Public Information Office, SEATO Headquarters, no date), pp.42–43.

[40] A. Malik (1970) "Djakarta's Conference and Asia's Political Future", *Pacific Community*, Vol 2, no. 1 (October), p.74.

[41] M. Ghazalie bin Shafie (1975) "ASEAN's Response to Security Issues in Southeast Asia", in *Regionalism in Southeast Asia*, Jakarta: Centre for Strategic and International Studies, p.23.

[42] G. McT. Kahin "The Role of the United States in Southeast Asia" in T.S. Lau, ed. (1973) *New Directions in the International Relations of Southeast Asia*, Singapore: Singapore University Press, p.77.

[43] Cited in E. Young (1981) *Development Cooperation in ASEAN: Balancing Free Trade and Regional Planning*, Ph.D. Dissertation, The University of Michigan, Ann Arbor, 1981, p.89.

[44] Ibid., p.89.

[45] K.W. Chin (1974) *The Five Power Defence Arrangement and AMDA: Some Observations on the Nature of an Evolving Partnership*, Occasional Paper No. 23, Singapore: Institute of Southeast Asian Studies, 1974.

[46] K.K. Nair (1975) "Defence and Security in Southeast Asia: The Urgency of Self-Reliance", *Asian Defence Journal*, No.1 (1975), pp. 9–17.

[47] Statement at the Second ASEAN Ministerial Meeting, Jakarta, 6 August 1968, cited in T. Phanit (1980) *Regional Integration Attempts in Southeast Asia: Problems and Progress*, Ph.D Dissertation, Pennsylvania State University, pp.32–33.

[48] B. Pace, et al. (1970) *Regional Cooperation in Southeast Asia: The First Two Years of ASEAN — 1967–1969*, McLean, Va.: Research Analysis Corporation, p.18.

[49] T. Phanit, *Regional Integration Attempts in Southeast Asia*, op.cit., pp.35–36.

[50] M. Osborne (1970) *Region of Revolt: Focus on Southeast Asia*, New South Wales: Pergamon Australia.

[51] B.K. Gordon (1966) *The Dimensions of Conflict in Southeast Asia*, op.cit., pp.1 and 3.

[52] "Introduction", in T. Morgan and N. Spoelstra, eds. (1969) *Economic Interependence in Southeast Asia*, Madison: University of Wisconsin Press, pp.10–11.

[53] K.T. Young, (1965) *The Southeast Asian Crisis*, New York: The Association of the Bar of the City of New York, p.64.

[54] Cited in E. Young (1981) *Development Cooperation in ASEAN: Balancing Free Trade and Regional Planning*, op.cit., p.87.

CHAPTER 3

The Evolution of Regional Organisation

Introduction

In Southeast Asia's international relations, the first two decades after the Second World War were characterised and shaped by nationalism, decolonisation, great power intervention and failed attempts at regional (mainly pan-Asian) cooperation. It is fair to say that attempts at regional cooperation played a marginal role in shaping international order and were overwhelmed by domestic politics on the one hand and externally determined Cold War geopolitics on the other. But the situation during the next two decades would be different. While the domestic strife characteristic of post-colonial states persisted and great power rivalry continued to plague the region, Southeast Asia's international relations during the 1970s and 80s would be marked chiefly by a dynamic involving the competing forces of regional conflict and cooperation. An important factor shaping this dynamic was the establishment of the Association of Southeast Asian Nations in 1967.

During this period, regionalism would have a paradoxical effect on Southeast Asia's unity and identity. On the one hand, it brought together the non-communist Southeast Asian states under a political and security framework to an unprecedented degree. This subregional framework was spurred by a collective quest for security and development in the face of common external and internal challenges. The outcome was the first viable regional organisation in the history of Southeast Asia: ASEAN. On the other hand, regionalism reflected, and contributed to, the ideological polarisation of Southeast Asia. The latter, in turn, generated an intense and wide-ranging pattern of regional conflict which engulfed the region for much of the 1970s and 80s.

ASA and Maphilindo

At the beginning of the 1960s, the prospects for a viable regional organisation in Southeast Asia looked bleak. Referring to Southeast Asia as the "Balkans of Asia", an American scholar, Albert Ravenholt observed that "increasingly, these eight newly-independent nations [Singapore was yet to be separated from Malaysia] and Thailand are drifting into the grip of petty nationalisms and jealousies, complete with border disputes and rivalries among their leaders."[1] Moreover, the continued dependence of regional countries on extra-regional powers for protection against internal as well as external threats also served to undermine early attempts at regional organisation. The strong security links of Thailand and the Philippines with the US, and that of Malaysia and Singapore with Britain, made the idea of regional cooperation less urgent.[2] The membership of the Philippines and Thailand in the Southeast Asia Treaty Organization also created a schism in the strategic perspectives between these two states and Indonesia, which had been a strong advocate of non-alignment, and which, even with the advent of a pro-Western regime, opposed any security role for outside powers in the region.

Against this backdrop, the establishment of the Association of Southeast Asia (ASA) in 1961 with the membership of Malaya, Thailand, and the Philippines was an unlikely development. The idea of ASA was initially proposed by Tunku Abdul Rahman soon after Malaya became independent in 1957. Rahman envisaged a regional grouping to fight communist subversion by targetting what he deduced to be its major cause: poverty. At a meeting with Philippine President Garcia in January 1959, the two had agreed on a Southeast Asian Friendship and Economic Treaty as the core of a regional association. The objectives of the proposed group, as revealed in portions of the Tunku's message to Sukarno, dated October 28, 1959, were:

> to encourage closer relations among the countries of Southeast Asia by discussion, conferences, or consultation, and to achieve agreement freely. It is hoped by this method that countries will be able to understand each other more deeply. It is also the objective of this association to study ways and means of helping one another—particularly in economic, social, and cultural and scientific fields .... You will understand that because of historical circumstances, the economic growth of most of the countries in Southeast Asia in this century has been influenced by relations with countries outside the region. Because of this, the feeling of "one region" has been stunted, ... and because of these historical circumstances, we have looked for help and examples from the outside and seldom look to ourselves ...[3]

The Tunku's idea received support from the then Thai Foreign Minister Thanat Khoman, who wanted a broad, inclusive grouping with the exception of North Vietnam. The Thais also prepared a "Preliminary Working Paper on Cooperation in Southeast Asia,"[4] which emphasized the need for an organisation with minimal administrative machinery. Although the Tunku attempted to convince other regional leaders of his idea, Indonesia remained suspicious of the organisation, viewing it as a front for SEATO. However, though the idea of a broader grouping failed, ASA was set up with the three members in 1961.

ASA's goals were modest. In the economic arena, it agreed to consider streamlining customs procedures and administration in each member country, to exchange information on imports and exports of manufactured goods in each country, and to consider the possibility of creating and developing wider intra-regional markets for the export commodities

80 THE QUEST FOR IDENTITY: INTERNATIONAL RELATIONS OF SOUTHEAST ASIA

of ASA countries. Another stated objective, classified under social and cultural cooperation, was the "promotion of Southeast Asian studies".[5]

The Tunku described ASA as "an alliance of three friendly countries formed to build a happy region in South-East Asia".[6] The purpose of ASA was to "show the world that peoples of Asia can think and plan for themselves."[7] Of all the ASA members, it was the Tunku who focused most on the issue of regional identity:

> In the past—and this is one of the faults of our history—the countries of South-East Asia have been very individualist, very prone to go different ways and very disclined to co-operate with each other. In fact, those with more rather tended to look down on others with less, there was no desire to try and help one another."[8]

Replying to critics of ASA, including some of the neighbouring states in Southeast Asia, the Tunku stated:

> They [the critics] do not believe, as we do, that ASA is a practical idea of benefit to all. They say it is all up in the air, just so much talk and no substance. This is the sort of attitude some neighbours appear to adopt. This is a regional defect, a failure to realise the importance of regional co-operation. There is no reason at all why this state of affairs should continue. Whatever others may think, we three nations are determined to work closely together for the common good of all.[9]

Malaysia's approach to ASA provides a clear illustration of a mutually reinforcing relationship between nationalism and regionalism. Under the Tunku's stewardship, ASA reflected Malaysia's quest for using regionalism to advance its nationalist agenda. The idea of such a regional association had been conceived even when the Tunku was leading Malaya's transition to independence in the late 1950s. At this time, joining a regional association with countries which had already emerged as nation-states was a means of securing legitimacy for the Malaysian nation. It was also useful in mitigating opposition to the Malaysian concept and territorial claims on the Malaysian states from neighbours such as Indonesia and the Philippines.

The Philippines seemed more interested in the practical aspects of regional cooperation. Its Vice-President and Secretary of Foreign Affairs, Emmanuel Pelaez, saw the rationale for ASA to lie in the fact that "we are entering an era of international regional cooperation which, as the experience of other countries have already shown, opens the door to faster and greater economic progress". ASA, he contended, would help its members to achieve "better work opportunities and greater income", while at the same time "meeting the increasing challenge of economic blocs from other parts of the world." For this reason, he called for ASA to "fully explore and exploit the possibilities and potentialities of greater intra-regional trade."[10]

THE EVOLUTION OF REGIONAL ORGANISATION   *81*

Despite being an association of Southeast Asia, ASA's proponents saw themselves as part of a larger Asian cultural, political and economic context. For Thai Foreign Minister and a key architect of ASA, Thanat Khoman, ASA was rooted in "Asian Culture and traditions" (sic). Describing ASA as an example of "Asian mutual co-operation", he argued: "For Asian solidarity must be and will be forged by Asian hands and the fact that our three countries: the Federation of Malaya, the Philippines, and Thailand, have joined hands in accomplishing this far-reaching task cannot be a mere coincidence."[11] While ASA considered the possibility of establishing a "Southeast Asian Voting Group" in the IMF and World Bank, the "Asian" rather than "Southeast Asian" context of ASA was further reflected in its proposal for an "Organization for Asian Economic Cooperation". Moreover, ASA remained open to the membership of countries which would later be excluded from ASEAN. As one study of the grouping put it, "ASA has demonstrated that it is not inward-looking in nature by its declared willingness to include other Asian countries", including India, Ceylon and Pakistan.[12]

Khoman described the purpose of ASA as being "practical coopera-tion" rather than political cooperation. But the political nature of ASA was evident in his call for regional self-reliance. In his view, ASA reflected a faith "in our capability to shape and direct for ourselves the future destiny of our nations."[13] Moreover, ASA was clearly anti-communist in orientation, despite being a non-political group. The Malaysian Foreign Minister in 1963 stated that the members of ASA were determined to "make a success of this organisation" because ASA's commitment to improve the "lives of our peoples" was "the best possible way of preventing the communists from trying to destroy the lives and souls of our nations".[14]

Certainly, Sukarno had no doubts about ASA's political nature. The fact that its members were all pro-Western, with Thailand and the Philippines having defence treaties with the US and Malaysia with Britain, was sufficient to provoke his opposition, even though ASA did not have an explicit security focus. Indonesia criticised ASA as a "Western-inspired", anti-communist bloc.[15] ASA soon joined as an object of Indonesian ire the proposed Malaysian Federation, which also sparked opposition from the Philippines. The latter laid claim to the former British-controlled territory of North Borneo (Sabah) in June 1962, challenging its decision to join the Malaysian Federation. This and Indonesia's armed campaign to "crush" the newly-independent Malaysian state spelled doom for ASA. Despite its swift demise, ASA's creation was significant in that it was a local initiative geared to local Southeast Asian concerns. Given that the earlier efforts at the Asian Relations Conference in Delhi and Bandung had failed to set up a permanent organisation, ASA's existence, brief though it might have been, set an important precedent. Additionally, the organisation did produce some diplomatic results,

82   THE QUEST FOR IDENTITY: INTERNATIONAL RELATIONS OF SOUTHEAST ASIA

including Thanat Khoman's mediation between the Philippines and Malaysia. Ironically, as Bernard Gordon notes, the Sabah claim that had stood in the way of ASA had itself been a catalyst in Manila's interest in closer association with Indonesia in search of a regional grouping. This, in turn, helped the Philippines shift towards an Asian and Southeast Asian identity, thereby offsetting its image as an appendage of the US.[16]

Manila's attitude was evident in President Diasdado Macapagal's proposal for a new group, Maphilindo, a loose confederation of the three independent states of Malay stock (Indonesia, Malaysia and the Philippines). The idea of Maphilindo had been born amidst a growing crisis in the region resulting from several factors: Sukarno's nationalism, his opposition to the Malaysian Federation and the resulting policy of *Konfrontasi*, and the Philippines' claim to North Borneo. According to the "Macapagal Plan", the organisation aimed to "restore and strengthen the historic unity and common heritage among the Malay peoples, and draw them to closer political, economic, and cultural relations."[17]

Maphilindo may be regarded as one of the first attempts at finding "regional solutions to regional problems", since the impetus for its creation came as a result of British refusal to discuss with Manila its claim to Sabah. That led to the hosting in Manila on 31 July 1963 of a "Summit Conference" among Sukarno, Macapagal and Tunku Abdul Rahman, where the three leaders tried to find a formula to settle the controversy arising from the impending formation of Malaysia. The formula agreed upon was Malaya's promise to seek British agreement for a UN team to determine whether the recently-held elections in Sarawak and North Borneo had enabled their people to express a choice on joining the federation of Malaysia. The agreement ultimately failed because the Tunku, pressed by the British timetable for withdrawing sovereignty, announced that the federation of Malaysia would become a reality on 16 September 1964, two days after the UN had said it would release the findings of its survey (which would confirm that the people of Sarawak and North Borneo had agreed to join the Malaysian Federation of their free will). This announce-ment was seen by Indonesia and the Philippines as unduly hasty and a breach of the agreement, and led both countries to announce their rejection of the Malaysian Federation.

Despite its failure, Maphilindo underscored the potential uses of culture in advancing the political and strategic objectives of Southeast Asian nations. In pushing for Maphilindo, one of President Macapagal's aims was also to prevent Indonesia from falling into the communist bloc by ensuring its integration into the "greater Malayan family".[18] Thus, a limited and culture-specific regional framework was seen as important for Philippine security objectives. Moreover, Maphilindo was important for the Philippines' own regional identification. It signaled Manila's realisation that the Philippines could not live alone in the region. The US

THE EVOLUTION OF REGIONAL ORGANISATION   83

defence umbrella was an important but insufficient basis for security. Regional identification was necessary.

Maphilindo was dismissed by one study as a "hardly more than a slogan and sentiment".[19] But even as that, it was a forerunner of some of the key principles of ASEAN. Its three member countries pledged not to let foreign military bases on their soil be used to "subvert the national independence" of any member. This was not an outright call for the removal of foreign bases, but implied a political intent to restrict the use of British bases in Singapore and American bases in the Philippines, although the Filipino side might also been seeking to preclude the establishment of Soviet bases in Indonesia. They also undertook not to use "collective defense to serve the interests of any among the big powers."[20] Second, it also brought about a declaratory commitment to the principle of consultation, or *musyawarah*, as the basis for settling differences among the members. This would be integral to ASEAN's approach to regional cooperation.

The Establishment of ASEAN: Motivating Factors

ASEAN was created in Bangkok on 8 August 1967 with Thailand, Malaysia, Indonesia, Singapore and the Philippines as its founding members. ASEAN members have subsequently claimed that its founders had actually envisaged a regional grouping of ten countries (Indonesia, Malaysia, Thailand, Myanmar, Laos, Cambodia, Vietnam, Singapore, the Philippines and Brunei). Historical evidence suggests that assertions to this effect are misleading. The vision of Southeast Asia's regional space held by ASEAN's founders was much more uncertain than the ASEAN-10 concept suggests. ASEAN's founding statement, the Bangkok Declaration of 1967, left membership in the organisation open to "all States in the South-East Asian region subscribing to the ... aims, principles and purposes" of ASEAN". But it did not provide a definite sense of where to draw the boundaries of the region itself.[21] Reinforcing this uncertainty is the fact that while signing the Bangkok Declaration, the foreign ministers of the five original members decided to "open the doors" of ASEAN to Burma, Cambodia, Laos, Ceylon (Sri Lanka), and both North and South Vietnam.[22] Ceylon did not take up the offer (ironically, its subsequent application to join ASEAN was rejected by the latter on the grounds that it did not belong to Southeast Asia) and as it happened, Burma and Cambodia refused to join ASEAN.

The invitation to join ASEAN clashed with Sihanouk's policy of neutrality. Having broken ties with the US and warmed up to the Chinese, Sihanouk was not about to join a grouping which he saw as being patently pro-Western and anti-Chinese. Moreover his choice on this matter was limited by the fear of upsetting Vietnam, which had already indicated its

84 THE QUEST FOR IDENTITY: INTERNATIONAL RELATIONS OF SOUTHEAST ASIA

hostility towards the ASEAN concept. A visit by Adam Malik to Sihanouk to discuss the proposed regional organisation failed to persuade the latter, as it did in the case of Burma which Malik also visited. The official reason for Burma's rejection of ASEAN was the presence of US military bases in the Philippines.[23] Like Cambodia, the Burmese government too viewed the proposed regional organisation to be an anti-Chinese front. Participation in ASEAN detracted from Burma's non-aligned and isolationist stance in international affairs, as articulated by strongman Ne Win in his highly idiosyncratic approach to foreign policy.[24]

The declared objectives of the association were not only to "accelerate the economic growth, social progress and cultural development in the region", but also to "promote regional peace and stability". ASEAN disavowed a security focus, but Thanat Khoman coined a term "collective political defence" to describe one of its goals.[25] The relative importance of "peace and stability" objectives in the formation of ASEAN was later stressed by Adam Malik, a founder of ASEAN:

> Although from the outset ASEAN was conceived as an organisation for economic, social and cultural cooperation, and although considerations in these fields were no doubt central, it was the fact that there was a convergence in the political outlook of the five prospective member-nations, both with regard to national priority objectives as on the question of how best to secure these objectives in the emergent strategic configuration of East Asia, which provided the main stimulus to join together in ASEAN...Whether consciously or unconsciously, considerations of national and regional security also figured largely in the minds of the founders of the ASEAN.[26]

ASEAN's formation reflected several changes in the regional climate. A major impetus came from regime change in Indonesia. The downfall of President Sukarno and the advent of a new regime with vastly different priorities in domestic and foreign policy spheres created a similar political outlook between the five governments "which had been involved in confrontation, whether as adversaries or as conciliators".[27] The New Order regime of Suharto in Indonesia became an enthusiastic proponent of ASEAN. Its motives were three-fold. First, Jakarta saw a regional group like ASEAN as convincing proof of its final abandonment of *Konfrontasi*, which had never been very popular within the military that wielded real power in the new regime. Second, Indonesia's new regime also saw regionalism as a vital adjunct to its national development plan, the essential part of its efforts to ensure domestic stability and establish the legitimacy of the New Order. Third, Jakarta saw ASEAN as having the potential "to serve as a forum for the expression of Indonesia's leadership in Southeast Asia", with the express approval and participation of its neighbours.[28]

THE EVOLUTION OF REGIONAL ORGANISATION   **85**

This had special relevance for Singapore. While Singapore's separation from the Malaysian Federation in 1965 left an air of considerable bitterness in bilateral relations between the two countries, its ties with Indonesia were even more problematic.[29] Feeling acutely vulnerable for its smallness, the island republic was profoundly suspicious of Indonesia's intentions towards its smaller neighbours. Even after the latter abandoned *Konfrontasi*, Singapore's relations with both Malaysia and Indonesia would be described as being marked by "an acute sense of vulnerability ... as the government of a conspicuously Chinese Republic, which was alarmed by the effusive expression of Malay blood-brotherhood which had attended the end of confrontation".[30]

Against this backdrop, developing a positive regional role for Indonesia "was a key purpose behind its neighbours' interest in ASEAN". As one Indonesian scholar puts it:

> Indonesia's membership within ASEAN would reduce the possibility of threat to their security posed by their giant neighbour...Indonesia would appear to be placed in what amounted to a "hostage" position, albeit in a golden cage. For the new leadership in Jakarta, ... it was within ASEAN that Indonesia might be provided with an opportunity to realise its ambitions, if any, to occupy a position of primacy or *primus inter pares* without recourse to a policy of confrontation ..."[31].

Apart from the need to mollify the regional power, each member had its own needs for viewing ASEAN in a positive light. Singapore, in particular, could use its participation in ASEAN "to gain acceptance as being part of Southeast Asia and playing a bigger role by being able to influence other like-minded countries on issues of mutual interest".[32] Along with Indonesia and Singapore, Thailand, Malaysia and the Philippines recognised ASEAN's potential as a forum for peaceful settlement of inter-regional disputes by helping to "foster and strengthen mutual trust and understanding amongst" its members.[33] To this end, the value of ASEAN also lay in the creation of a set of norms to govern relations among the member countries. The basic norms were spelt out by the Bangkok Declaration itself, which urged members to observe also "the rule of the law" in their relationships with one another.

Another major factor contributing to ASEAN's formation was the changing patterns of great power rivalry. Towards the end of the 1960s, the Sino-Soviet rift and competition for influence in Southeast Asia was assuming prominence over traditional Cold War patterns. The prospect of China emerging as the dominant force in the region and, as Lee Kuan Yew was to put it later, the related prospect of Southeast Asia becoming "to her what the Caribbean is to America or Eastern Europe to the USSR"[34] was one aspect of ASEAN members' collective apprehensions. Sino-Soviet competition, featuring both the Soviet quest for regional influence through establishment of links in Indochina and advancement of proposals regarding an "Asian Collective Security Arrangement", and Chinese warnings concerning Soviet "hegemonism", made the ASEAN countries realise the need for a united response to the new form of great power rivalry.[35] At the same time, the relaxation of tensions between the US and the Soviet Union on the one hand, and the US and China on the other, aroused a different kind of concern. ASEAN members were fearful that such great power compromises would leave their security interests ignored or undermined. Malaysia's Prime Minister, Hussein Onn, was to put it succinctly on the eve of the Bali summit when he noted that the big powers "...can create tension in any area...especially, when they try to settle their differences and impose their ideologies forcefully in other countries ... there is a Malay saying that when two elephants fight, the mouse deer wedged in between will suffer."[36]

It should be noted that the regionalism of Southeast Asia at this time reflected developments in regionalism in other parts of the world. The latter was marked by a shift from continental or macro-regional to micro-regional or subregional groupings. The credibility of the three larger regional organisations, the Organization of American States (OAS), the Arab League and the Organization of African Unity (OAU) had eroded in the 1970s.[37] This was due to several factors, including a lack of resources and inability to deal with internal conflicts, which accounted for a large percentage of conflicts in the developing world.[38] Neither were these organisations able to limit superpower meddling and intervention in regional affairs. Their decline gave impetus to more compact subregional frameworks for conflict mediation and management, which enjoyed the benefits of greater homogeneity.[39] In the economic sphere, subregionalism was also becoming prominent during the 1960s and 1970s. Several subregional groups had emerged seeking to emulate the European Economic Community (EEC) (later European Union), such as the Central American Common Market and the East African Community.

But the creation of ASEAN was not simply a reflection of these global trends. It was largely the product of local circumstances. The immediate motivating factors behind ASEAN had to do, firstly, with a common desire for collective diplomatic clout against external powers. ASEAN was expected to enhance the bargaining power of its small and weak members in their dealings with the great powers. ASEAN might not enable its member states to prevent the great powers from interfering in the affairs of the region, but it could, as Prime Minister Lee Kuan Yew of Singapore pointed out, help them to "have their interests taken into consideration when the great powers make their compromises".[40] Adam Malik, the Indonesian Foreign Minister made the same point:

Southeast Asia is one region in which the presence and interests of most major powers converge, politically as well as physically. The frequency and intensity of policy interactions among them, as well as their dominant influence on the countries in the region, cannot but have a direct bearing on political realities. In the face of this, the smaller nations of the region have no hope of ever making any impact on this pattern of dominant influence of the big powers, unless they act collectively and until they develop the capacity to forge among themselves an area of internal cohesion, stability and common purpose.

Thus regional cooperation within ASEAN also came to represent the conscious effort by its member countries to try to re-assert their position and contribute their own concepts and goals within the on-going process of stabilization of a new power equilibrium in the region.[41]

The establishment of ASEAN also reflected shared threat perceptions among its members. To be sure, there was limited agreement on external threats.[42] China's potential to pose a long-term security threat to Southeast Asia was viewed with considerably more seriousness by Indonesia and Malaysia than its other ASEAN partners. Thailand and Singapore, for their part, were less optimistic about Vietnam's post-war intentions towards its ASEAN neighbours than Indonesia. But the ASEAN leaders agreed more on the nature of their internal enemy and were strongly united by a "common interest in preventing radical internal political change".[43] This was partly the basis of their response to the communist victories in Indochina, which were feared for their demonstrative effect on the incipient "national liberation movements" within their own territories. Thus, the similarities of their domestic political orientation and a common fear of communist-led national liberation movements in Vietnam, Laos and Cambodia provided an important glue for ASEAN.[44] In this context, an early feature of relations among the ASEAN states was joint security measures undertaken on a bilateral basis but reinforced by ASEAN's collective political and ideological concern against communism[45].

Bilateral cooperation to combat insurgent activity along their common border areas had already developed between Malaysia and Indonesia and Malaysia and Thailand, even before the formation of ASEAN. Such an arrangement between Thailand and Malaysia had been initiated in 1959. A joint border committee was established in 1965 to oversee this effort. A similar agreement to control border movement had been signed between Indonesia and the Philippines in January 1964. After the end of hostilities between Indonesia and Malaysia, the two countries had signed an agreement in March 1967 which covered cooperation between their air, naval and land forces to curb communist insurgency, piracy and smuggling along the common border. The establishment of ASEAN would not only

88   THE QUEST FOR IDENTITY: INTERNATIONAL RELATIONS OF SOUTHEAST ASIA

reflect the members' shared concern over domestic insurgencies, but also provide further boost to bilateral security measures among them.

While superpower aid in general was a major factor in the ideological polarisation of Southeast Asia, in the case of the pro-Western ASEAN members, it also contributed to their economic growth and hence regime security, which in turn had become a fundamental basis of ASEAN's approach to regional order.[46] In this context, the Vietnam War helped economies of the ASEAN members in the 1960s and 70s. The case of Thailand and Singapore is particularly illustrative. The US had begun to funnel aid into Thailand from the mid-1950s onwards, and as the Vietnam War gathered momentum in the 1960s, American aid increased. By 1975 the US had spent nearly $3.5 billion in military and economic aid in Thailand.[47] The economic infrastructure was greatly improved, especially the highway system and key ports and airports, and the Thai bureaucracy, which had a long tradition of being at the centre of power in the country, was expanded and strengthened.[48]

The war helped Singapore, which separated from Malaysia to become an independent state in 1965. It became the regional petroleum-refining centre providing petroleum products for the American military campaign in Indochina. Its traditional entrepôt trade rapidly increased as US spending generated greater regional prosperity. Singapore also became a destination for US servicemen on leave in the region. The income generated for the Singapore economy by these developments helped the government to put in place its economic and social infrastructure programmes and to pursue an export-oriented development strategy.[49] Thus, while the US withdrawal from Indochina encouraged regional cooperation among those who had relied on its security umbrella, US wartime aid and spending helped to foster domestic economic conditions conducive to the kind of ideologically-moderate and free-market oriented regionalism that ASEAN represented. In addition, the US, as Owen puts it, "subsidized right-wing movements throughout the region", supporting coups in Indonesia (1965), Thailand (1976) and the imposition of martial law in the Philippines.[50] In the meantime, Chinese and Soviet aid was confined mainly to Indochina (although some failed overtures were made toward Burma and Indonesia, the two annually gave about $90 million to North Vietnam during 1955–65, and $400 million a year during the 1965–75 period[51]). This, while bringing the Indochinese countries closer together, sustained the ideological polarisation of Southeast Asia which ASEAN itself reflected.

Finally, growing economic policy convergence also contributed to the emergence of ASEAN. The evolution of post-war economies of the ASEAN member countries had gone through three phases.[52] The first was the rehabilitation and reconstruction of a primary-producing export economy created during the colonial era. This was followed by the advent

THE EVOLUTION OF REGIONAL ORGANISATION *89*

of import-substitution industrialisation (ISI), motivated and accompanied in many cases by economic nationalism. The third stage, export-oriented industrialisation (EOI), became the dominant feature of the international political economy of Southeast Asia from the late 1970s onwards, although Singapore had been the Southeast Asian pioneer of this strategy since the mid-1960s.

As noted in Chapter 2, by the late 1960s, Southeast Asian countries were experiencing differing economic growth rates. Singapore, Malaysia, and Thailand showed the best economic performance. Indonesia too from 1966 attracted growing foreign investment and began to improve education and living conditions. But the Philippines experienced economic stagnation, so much so that it became the rationale for President Marcos' decision to impose martial law in 1972 to regain public confidence. The economic conditions of the Indochinese countries were severely affected by war, while the socialist methods of Burma ("Burmese way to Socialism") plunged the country into prolonged and deep stagnation under the Ne Win regime.

While the differing economic predicament and policies of Southeast Asian countries were to some degree reflected with the ASEAN grouping, it was, as Owen points out, "not the differences of policy within this bloc that are striking, but the broad similarities".[53] While in the 1960s, nationalism might have aggravated economic competition, by the 1960s and 70s, a certain amount of homogenisation was taking place among the capitalist countries of the region. These economies had begun from a similar position of "uneven development, limited national integration and plural societies".[54] More importantly, they had reacted to this predicament in ways similar to one another. All had emphasised rapid urban-industrial development and maintained a relatively high degree of openness to the world economy. Consequently, through institutions such as the World Bank and the IMF, these economies were also highly receptive to ideas about economic liberalisation and export-led development. Moreover, the lack of adequate indigenous capital that characterised the capitalist economies of the region led them to seek and forge a close alliance between the state, foreign corporations and domestic capitalists. This created a common pattern of economic development.

In the 1960s, the ISI strategies being pursued by the Philippines, Thailand and Malaysia were producing less encouraging results. Indonesia, where they were still in the early stages, was an exception. But structural changes in the global economy would offer new incentives to the ASEAN countries to shift towards export-led development strategies.[55]

As the ASEAN members were beginning to pursue similar development strategies, there emerged a certain ideological community among them, which provided an important political foundation for ASEAN.

With the war in Indochina having prompted its members to lay urgent emphasis on economic growth within the free-market model, Ghazalie Shafie of Malaysia would proclaim that:

> The concept of free enterprise as they apply [sic] in the ASEAN region is the philosophical basis of ASEAN. The appreciation of this is vital in the understanding of ASEAN and its sense of direction. The countries of the ASEAN region had come together to protect the system of free enterprise as a counterpoise against communism on the one hand and monopolistic capitalism on the other ... When the leaders of Malaysia, Indonesia, Philippines, Singapore and Thailand got together in Bangkok in 1967 to officiate at the establishment of the Association of Southeast Asian Nations, they were in fact making a commitment to jointly strengthen and promote the system of free enterprise in their countries in the belief that together they could harness the strength of that system to bring about the kind of national and regional resilience that would serve as a bulwark against communism.[56]

The leaders of ASEAN countries recognised the root causes of communism to lie in domestic economic and social conditions. The most serious of these conditions were poverty and social inequalities which were then endemic features of all ASEAN societies.[57] As such, the long-term answer to the communist threat lay not in its military suppression, but in the achievement of rapid economic development which could diffuse the fundamental sources of socio-political discontent. As one study described it, economic growth would not only eradicate poverty, but also lead to greater equity. The use of advanced technology to sustain the process of urban industrial development would lead to the accumulation of wealth. This could then have a "trickle down effect", producing automatic adjustments to the distribution of wealth in the society as a whole. Thus:

> Development strategies generally chosen by non-Communist Southeast Asian governments are aimed at bringing about rapid economic growth with focus on urban-based industrial promotion and utilization of advanced technology in an atmosphere of free enterprise. The underlying assumption is that sooner or later there will be "trickle down effects" and any mal-adjustments in terms of distribution will automatically be corrected. In that eventuality equity in terms of equal shares will not be achieved, but everyone's demands and requirements will be `satisfied' and there will be further incentive to work for another round of growth and trickle-down effects.[58]

General acceptance of these ideas, coupled with persistent concern over the common internal enemy, fostered a common understanding of how to promote regional economic security. While rejecting a military role for ASEAN, its members hoped that political cooperation would create an atmosphere of stability which in turn would facilitate economic growth. As Carlos Romulo, the foreign minister of the Philippines, put it:

The main enemy we have is subversion, and the only way to counteract subversion is to improve the lot of the masses, to give them social justice, to have economic development. That is why the main thrust of ASEAN is economic development.[59]

In stressing the importance of economic regionalism, President Marcos went as far as to speak of "estimates" made by ASEAN leaders according to which the ASEAN countries could, by working jointly for "anywhere between five to seven years" achieve the necessary economic conditions to eliminate the threat of subversion, whereas it "could take two decades" to achieve this goal if the members were to work for such development individually.[60] At this stage, no one thought ASEAN would follow the model of west European economic integration. However, its founders believed that the Association could make a contribution to the national economic development by ensuring domestic tranquility in member states through its non-interference doctrine. Moreover, ASEAN's prospective economic security role was seen to lie not in creating regional wealth and equity through economic integration, but in fostering a climate free from inter-state tensions in which its members could devote their resources to national economic development. As Lee Kuan Yew put it, "each ASEAN country has to ensure sufficient economic growth and social justice that will make insurgency unattractive and unlikely to succeed".[61] In addition, by limiting interference of members in each other's affairs, and thereby contributing to an atmosphere of stability, ASEAN could affect the flow of foreign investment into the region, which in turn was viewed to be the key to fostering rapid economic growth.

Dimensions of ASEAN Regionalism

The new regional organisation in Southeast Asia almost suffered a hasty demise. This had to do with a sudden escalation of the Sabah dispute. Just as it had in the case of ASA and Maphilindo, the Philippines claim to Sabah threatened the early years of ASEAN's development. Between April 1968 and December 1969, relations between Malaysia and the Philippines worsened considerably over the issue, although Sabah was a state now firmly within the Malaysian Federation. Though the origin of the dispute dated back to 1961, the spark for the renewal of the bilateral crisis was reports appearing in the Manila press in March 1968 that a secret army was being trained on the island of Corregidor in preparation for an impending invasion of Sabah. While the government of the Philippines denied its involvement in any such plan, its reaction to the so-called "Corregidor affair" showed a renewed pursuit of its claim on Sabah. The affair not only plunged Manila's relationship with Kuala Lumpur into a crisis situation, but also threatened the very survival of ASEAN, barely six months after its creation in August 1967.

At first, other ASEAN members carefully avoided publicly voicing any views on the dispute that might be construed by the disputants as an indication of partiality. Their neutrality deprived Manila of the kind of international diplomatic support it needed to effectively pursue its claim. It might also have discouraged further action by President Marcos in escalating the dispute.

Although Thailand and Indonesia offered their good offices in urging the two sides to reach a negotiated settlement, both shied away from directly mediating in the dispute. Initially, the rest of the ASEAN members tried to keep the Sabah issue separate from ASEAN, hoping that this would limit the dispute's damaging effects on the fledgling organisation. But as bilateral talks between Malaysia and the Philippines in June 1967 failed, followed by the severance of their diplomatic relations and Malaysia's refusal to take part in any further ASEAN meetings where the Philippines might raise the Sabah issue, the link between ASEAN and the Sabah dispute could no longer be avoided.

In a bid to contain the crisis, ASEAN Foreign Ministers met in Jakarta in August and in Bangkok in December 1968 to persuade the two sides to minimise their public airing of the dispute and accept a "cooling off period". Statements by Thailand and Indonesia urged restraint on both sides for the sake of ASEAN. Until their suspension, various ASEAN ad hoc and standing committees provided crucial channels of communication between the two sides when none other existed. In March 1969, Manila agreed not to raise the Sabah issue at future ASEAN meetings, thereby indicating a new flexibility and meeting a key Malaysian demand. It was an ASEAN committee meeting in Indonesia in May 1969 which brought the two countries together for the first time in eight months (excluding the ad hoc December 1968 Foreign Ministers meeting). The softening of Manila's stand was partly due to the ASEAN factor, since the hitherto suspension of all ASEAN meetings had deprived Manila of a major channel to pursue its claim and threatened its relations with other ASEAN members—Indonesia, Thailand and Singapore.

At an ASEAN Foreign Ministers' meeting in December 1969, Malaysia and the Philippines agreed to resume diplomatic relations, thereby effectively putting the issue on the back-burner. This episode gave ASEAN a new confidence and sense of purpose. The avoidance of any further escalation of the Sabah dispute was all the more significant because it took place at a time when the degree of economic interdependence within the region was not significant enough to act as an incentive against inter-state tensions. In the words of the joint communique of the December ASEAN Foreign Ministers' meeting, the resumption of diplomatic ties was possible "because of the great value Malaysia and the Philippines placed on ASEAN".

THE EVOLUTION OF REGIONAL ORGANISATION 93

To be sure, ASEAN did not, and could not *resolve* the Sabah dispute, which continued to elude a decisive settlement. Neither did ASEAN play the role of conflict mediator/manager in a formal and legalistic sense. But ASEAN members, through direct and indirect measures of restraint, pressure, diplomacy, communication and trade-offs, did succeed in preventing any further escalation of the crisis that might have led to armed hostilities and destroyed the organisation.[62]

After surviving the intra-mural dispute over Sabah, ASEAN faced the challenge of responding to the changing pattern of great power rivalry in the region. The first major initiative considered by the Association was a Malaysian proposal for the neutralisation of Southeast Asia. This proposal reflected Malaysia's disenchantment with external security guarantees, aggravated by the British withdrawal. The implementation of neutralisation required the imposition of reciprocal obligations on the regional countries as well as those external powers who were to guarantee the neutral status of the region. The former were required to abstain from military alliances with the great powers and prevent the establishment of foreign military bases on their soil, while the latter were asked to "refrain from forging alliances with the neutralised states, stationing armed forces on their territory, and using their presence to subvert or interfere in any other way with other countries".[63]

But the neutralisation proposal ran counter to Indonesia's foreign policy beliefs. Because neutralisation was to be secured through guarantees from the major powers, Jakarta saw this as giving the latter an undue say in the maintenance of regional order. Indonesia's reservations led to revisions to the neutralisation proposal. The new framework, the idea of a Zone of Peace, Freedom and Neutrality (ZOPFAN) in Southeast Asia, adopted by the foreign ministers of ASEAN countries meeting in Kuala Lumpur in November 1971, gave greater emphasis to Indonesia's preferred approach in which the regional countries themselves would have the principal responsibility for ensuring regional security. No guarantees from outside powers were to be sought. The ZOPFAN concept also emphasised the need for the regional countries to "respect one another's sovereignty and territorial integrity, and not participate in activities likely to directly or indirectly threaten the security of another".[64]

It also encouraged ASEAN members to stay away from alliances with foreign powers, refrain from inviting or giving consent to intervention by external powers in the domestic affairs of the regional states, abstain from involvement in any conflict of powers outside the zone, and ensure the eventual removal of foreign military bases in the territory of zonal states.[65]

But the implementation of the ZOPFAN concept was plagued by intra-mural disagreements. The view of Thailand, Singapore and the Philippines regarding the need for a US presence in the region was at variance with the professed principles and objectives of ZOPFAN, which were strongly espoused by Indonesia and Malaysia. Singapore, reflecting its support for a strong US presence in the region, warned that the ZOPFAN concept made the continuation of the US presence all the more necessary since there was no certainty that all the other great powers would abide by the restraints required upon their geopolitical behaviour by ZOPFAN. As Lee Kuan Yew put it, "in the event of one or more great powers not respecting, it may be useful that there would be some [US] naval and air base facilities so that some balance can be maintained".[66]

Apart from difficulties encountered in securing the implementation of ZOPFAN, ASEAN also faced problems in moving towards greater security and defence cooperation. The US withdrawal from Indochina and the communist takeover of South Vietnam, Cambodia and Laos provided the impetus to the historic first ASEAN summit at Bali in February 1976, which in turn gave ASEAN's latent security objectives their most serious public expression. On the eve of the Bali summit, the threat of insurgency and subversion had pushed the ASEAN members towards regular exchanges of intelligence, both on a bilateral and multilateral basis. In the course of preparations towards the first ASEAN summit, there were indications that sections within the Indonesian leadership were willing to propose multilateral defence cooperation within ASEAN. An Indonesian study paper circulated prior to the summit was believed to have suggested the formation of a "joint council" for defence cooperation and holding joint military exercises among the ASEAN states.[67] However, deliberations over security issues at the pre-summit meeting of ASEAN foreign ministers in Pattaya indicated, as Carlos Romulo put it, a "general view...that security considerations should not be institutionalised on an ASEAN basis". At the Pattaya meeting "complete agreement was reached on the desirability of continued" bilateral cooperation, "some of which ante-date the association".[68]

The Bali summit confirmed ASEAN's rejection of a military pact. The Prime Minister of Malaysia, Hussein Onn, stated just after the Bali summit:

> It is obvious that the ASEAN members do not wish to change the character of ASEAN from a socio-economic organisation into a security alliance as this would only create misunderstanding in the region and undermine the positive achievements of ASEAN in promoting peace and stability through co-operation in the socio-economic and related fields.[69]

In the Declaration of ASEAN Concord signed at the Bali summit, the ASEAN leaders expressed their approval of "continuation of co-operation on a non-ASEAN basis between the member states in security matters in accordance with their mutual needs and interests", a clear reference to the border and intelligence cooperation arrangements that had already developed among ASEAN states on a bilateral basis. While ASEAN states did not fully agree on the role of great powers in their security environment, and while progress towards ZOPFAN was decidedly slow, they were united in asserting the need for self-reliance in countering their domestic security problems. Moreover, through collective diplomatic efforts, they hoped to reduce, if not eliminate, their dependence on external security guarantees.

At Bali, ASEAN stressed the need to manage great power competition and intervention through the ZOPFAN framework, which would render the external security links of individual members some-what non-provocative (to adversaries like Vietnam and China). The Treaty of Amity and Cooperation signed at the Bali summit outlined the norms that were to form the basis of ASEAN's code of inter-state behaviour. These norms included: (1) "Mutual respect for the independence, sovereignty, territorial integrity of all nations"; (2) "The right of every state to lead its national existence free from external interference, subversion and coercion"; (3) "Non-interference in the internal affairs of one another"; (4) "Settlement of differences and disputes by peaceful means"; and (5) "Renunciation of the threat of use of force".[70]

In the aftermath of the Bali summit, ASEAN policy-makers continued to reject the idea of multilateral security and defence cooperation. At the annual ASEAN foreign ministers' conference in Singapore in July 1977, the representatives from Malaysia and Indonesia issued a joint statement proclaiming that the main threat to the region was the possibility of increased subversive activities which could be handled on a national and bilateral basis.[71] The Thai foreign minister declared that military alliances were "obsolete" and stressed that ASEAN had "nothing to do with military cooperation".[72] This position was reaffirmed at the Kuala Lumpur summit held later that year where the leaders were believed to have consulted closely on the threat posed by subversive activities, but rejected any change to ASEAN's position on, and preference for, security bi-lateralism.[73] Bilateral cooperation against border insurgencies that had developed between Malaysia and Indonesia and Malaysia and Thailand was considered to be acceptable model for security cooperation which would be sufficient to deal with the threat at hand.

These arrangements had increased in scope after the formation of ASEAN. In 1969, Malaysia and Thailand announced an agreement permitting "hot pursuit" of insurgents by the security forces of both sides into each other's territory. While joint operations were initially carried out by police, from 1970, regular troops were deployed alongside the police. Similar joint operations against communist insurgents along the Kalimantan border were conducted in 1971 by Indonesia and Malaysia.

96 THE QUEST FOR IDENTITY: INTERNATIONAL RELATIONS OF SOUTHEAST ASIA

ASEAN's rejection of multilateral defence cooperation was largely motivated by a desire to prevent comparisons with SEATO. This was especially important in view of Vietnam's increasingly shrill accusations at the time that "ASEAN will become another SEATO and Japan and the U.S. may use ASEAN as an organisation to expand their influence in Southeast Asia ..."[74] Indonesia, which prided itself as the only genuine non-aligned country in ASEAN, opposed any ASEAN military pact which smacked of dependence on Western security guarantees. As Adam Malik put it, "Pacts are of no value and don't really add strength to a region".[75] Carlos Romulo, the foreign minister of the Philippines agreed with this view: "We did not phase out SEATO in order to set up another one."[76] A military role for ASEAN was deemed both unnecessary and inappropriate as the ASEAN states were concerned primarily with security issues within their own borders which could be best dealt with through non-military means.

ASEAN was more open to multilateral economic cooperation. But two Asian-wide multilateral economic institutions were already in existence. These were the Economic and Social Commission for Asia and the Pacific (ESCAP), and the Asian Development Bank (the latter was set up in 1966).[77] They provided concepts and resources for development efforts of the ASEAN members within the framework of the global financial institutions. Prospects for economic cooperation within the ASEAN framework had to be seen in the context of a number of similarities and differences among the members. First, in terms of the level of development, its members remained a diverse lot. According to a 1975 World Bank report, the Philippines and Thailand were classified as "very poor" (with a per capita GNP of less than US$520), while Indonesia was among the "poorest" nations (with a per capita GNP of less than US$265). Singapore and Malaysia were well above these categories, with per capita GNPs of US$2450 and US$760 respectively. But in terms of growth rates, the ASEAN economies could all be classified as middle-income less developed economies. During the 1960–70 period, Indonesia's real growth rate averaged 3.9%, Malaysia's 5.8%, the Philippines' 5.1%, Singapore's 9.4% and Thailand's 8.0%. The average annual growth rate for all five countries was estimated at 5.6%. The growth rates for the 1970–77 period were more impressive: Indonesia 7.7%, Malaysia 7.5%, the Philippines 6.2%, Singapore 8.9% and Thailand 6.6%, for an total ASEAN average of 7.1%.[78]

As noted in the previous chapter the ASEAN members differed in terms of their openness to foreign investment. During the 1971–77 period, Singapore and Malaysia were most accessible to FDI. In the Philippines, the low level of FDI reflected the strength of economic nationalism, while in Thailand, political uncertainty and instability as well as the communist victories in Indochina accounted for a declining level of FDI. For example, during 1976, Indonesia's ratio of FDI to total capital was .17% (this may

THE EVOLUTION OF REGIONAL ORGANISATION **97**

not reflect the trend for the 1971–77 period, because the figure was .32% in 1971 and .74%, in 1975), Malaysia's .69%, Philippines' .11%, Singapore's .77% and Thailand's .15% (down from .41% in 1971).[79]

With the exception of Singapore, primary commodities accounted for the larger share of exports of ASEAN members, reflecting the colonial pattern of development despite policies to change the export structure. But, for all ASEAN economies, foreign trade formed a major part of national economic activities. Malaysia's ratio of foreign trade to Gross Domestic Product was over 90% during each of the three years 1974, 1975 and 1976. The figure from Indonesia ranged from 31% in 1971 to 50% in 1974. Indonesia's ratio hit 50% in 1974 and was never less than 31% (1971). For the Philippines, the ratio was 38% in 1971 and 42% in 1976, with a peak of 48% in 1974. For Thailand, the ratio was 38% in 1971, 45% in 1976, with a peak of 48% in 1974.[80]

By the early and mid 1970s, ASEAN members had emerged as middle-level developing economies with rapid growth rates. All were highly export-dependent and therefore their fortunes were closely linked to the international economic situation. At the same time, their economies were competitive, rather than complementary, thereby rendering the common dependence on foreign trade a divisive factor as each country turned away from the region to external trading partners and sought separate bilateral trade and economic ties. This meant low levels of intra-ASEAN trade. Indeed, total intra-ASEAN trade in 1975 was estimated at 15% of the total trade of its five members.[81]

Against this backdrop, ASEAN's initial efforts at economic co-operation involved a modest programme of trade liberalisation. This was centered on the scheme called ASEAN Preferential Trading Arrangements, whose basic agreement was signed in 1977. The PTA provided for a number of measures to liberalise and increase intra-ASEAN trade including long-term quantity contracts, liberalisation of non-tariff measures on a preferential basis, exchange of tariff preferences, preferential terms for financing of imports, and preference for ASEAN products in procurement by government bodies. Yet the impact of the PTA remained limited, even though intra-ASEAN trade as a proportion of total ASEAN trade rose from 13.5% in 1973 to a peak of 20% in 1983 (it fell to 16% in 1985). Much of the total intra-ASEAN trade volume would be accounted for by bilateral trade between Singapore and Malaysia and Malaysia and Indonesia. In addition, about 65% of intra-ASEAN trade was fuel trade (mineral fuels, lubricants and related materials).[82] Thus, the increase in intra-ASEAN trade in the early 1980s was due largely to increase in fuel prices, rather than to increased trade in industrial products.

ASEAN's avoidance of EU-style regional economic integration had much to do with the national development strategies of its members. Heavily dependent on access to international capital and markets, the

98 THE QUEST FOR IDENTITY: INTERNATIONAL RELATIONS OF SOUTHEAST ASIA

ASEAN states were wary of the harmful effects of inward-looking regional integration approaches. The perceived dangers of such integration were highlighted in a 1980s report on ASEAN economic cooperation:

> ASEAN countries owe their economic prosperity to trade and investment links with the outside world. Measures in the name of regional integration that discriminates against more efficient producers can undermine this. ASEAN must continue to maintain its outward-looking orientation and remain competitive in world markets.[83]

To this end, ASEAN's economic cooperation was geared to expanding and maintaining access to international markets and capital. Its role in collective external bargaining took precedence over the goal of intra-regional trade liberalisations. Beginning in the early 1970s, the collective external bargaining role of ASEAN featured negotiating favourable commodity prices.[84] A major example was bargaining with Japan over natural rubber. Japan had been accused of producing and dumping synthetic rubber in the international market, thereby undercutting ASEAN producers of the commodity. ASEAN's efforts were successful in winning major concessions from Japan. Another aim of collective bargaining was to secure greater market access for ASEAN products. The highlight of this effort was ASEAN's success in expanding the coverage of its exports in the EC's generalised system of preferences. Finally, ASEAN sought to develop a united position at multilateral trade negotiations, starting with the coordination of positions at the Tokyo Round of GATT talks. This was followed by similar coordination at the Uruguay Round, which as will be seen in Chapter 5, played an important part in ASEAN's growing attention to economic regionalism.[85]

Conclusion

Some Southeast Asian scholars have discerned important similarities between nation-building and region-building in Southeast Asia. "The search for national solidarity and unity", wrote a Filipino scholar, Alejandro Melchor, "... is replicated, albeit on a broader scale and less urgent, but equally persistent, in the relations among nations of Southeast Asia."[86] Later, Russell Fifield, an American observer investigating Southeast Asia's claim to be a region, pointed out that the development and acceptance of the regional concept of Southeast Asia was akin to the development of nationalism, especially the way Benedict Anderson had studied the process. Anderson had argued that the idea of nationalism was, among other things, "learned" by the indigenous elite while receiving their education in the West.[87] Fifield found that like concepts such as nationalism, Marxism, and social humanism, the idea of regionalism was "brought to Southeast Asia by the indigenous upper class" who often received their education in the capitals of the colonial powers.[88]

In this context, one may note the essentially elite-driven nature of ASEAN regionalism. Moreover, like nationalism, ASEAN regionalism came to represent an imagined community underpinned by its own organising myths and principles. From the very outset, its leaders recognised the importance of regional identity-building. While the first ASEAN declaration (the Bangkok Declaration of 1967) had assured its members that the grouping would "preserve their national identities", S. Rajaratnam, the then Foreign Minister of Singapore and a founding father of ASEAN, argued that this objective should be reconciled with the development of a "regional existence". In his view, the success of ASEAN depended on "a new way of thinking about our problems". Since ASEAN member states had been used to viewing [intra-mural] problems from the perspective of their national interests or existence, the shift to a "regional existence means painful adjustments to those practices and thinking in our respective countries."[89]

The leaders of ASEAN also saw their organisation as a framework for providing "regional solutions to regional problems". This hope was articulated by Adam Malik, Indonesia's foreign minister and another founding father of ASEAN, in 1975. As Malik put it, "regional problems, i.e. those having a direct bearing upon the region concerned, should be accepted as being of primary concern to that region itself. Mutual consultations and cooperation among the countries of the region in facing these problems may...lead to the point where the views of the region are accorded the primacy they deserve in the search for solution."[90]

This quest for regional autonomy was initially shaped by a concern, prevalent in the Cold War milieu, that regional conflicts not managed at the regional level would invite intervention by outside powers, which in turn would aggravate existing intra-regional tensions and polarisation. To this end, ASEAN regionalism championed the principles of mutual non-interference, non-intervention, and non-use of force. Through ZOPFAN, ASEAN emphasised its concern with the danger of great power rivalry and the need for greater security self-reliance as the basis of a common regional identity.

Yet, the identity-building process undertaken by ASEAN was rudely and severely jolted by developments in Southeast Asia's international relations towards the end of the 1970s. Vietnam's invasion of Cambodia marked an end to prospects for a single Southeast Asian regional entity based on an inclusive form of regionalism. The ensuing ASEAN-Indochina rivalry, featuring ASEAN's campaign to drive Vietnam out of Cambodia, led to the further polarisation of Southeast Asia—a division which would persist through the 1980s.

Notes

1 A. Ravenholt (1964) "Maphilindo: Dream or Achievable Reality", New York: American University Field Staff Reports, Southeast Asia Series, Vol.xii, no.1, 1964, p.2.

2 A. Jorgensen-Dahl (1982) *Regional Organization and Order in Southeast Asia*, op. cit., p.229.

3 B.K. Gordon (1966) *Dimensions of Conflict in Southeast Asia*, op.cit., p.170.

4 Ibid., p.167.

5 Association of Southeast Asia, *Report of the Special Session of Foreign Ministers of ASA* (Kuala Lumpur/Cameron Highlands, Federation of Malaya, April 1962), p.13.

6 Ibid., Annex A, p.21.

7 Ibid., p.22.

8 Ibid., p.24.

9 Ibid.

10 Speech before the Special Session of Foreign Ministers of ASA, Annex B of Ibid, pp.27–28.

11 Ibid., p.33.

12 H. Kitamura and A.N. Bhagat (1969)"Aspects of Regional Harmonization of National Development Plans", in T. Morgan and N. Spoelstra, eds. (1969) *Economic Intereependence in Southeast Asia*, Madison: University of Wisconsin Press, p.53.

13 Ibid., pp.32–33.

14 Cited in E. Young (1981) *Development Cooperation in ASEAN: Balancing Free Trade and Regional Planning*, Ph.D. Dissertation, The University of Michigan, Ann Arbor, 1981, p.90.

15 Ibid., p.91.

16 B.K. Gordon (1966), *Dimensions of Conflict in Southeast Asia*, op.cit., p.21.

17 Ibid., p.191.

18 A. Ravenholt (1964) "Maphilindo: Dream or Achievable Reality", op.cit., pp.8–9.

19 "Introduction", in T. Morgan and N. Spoelstra, eds. (1969) *Economic_Intereependence in Southeast Asia*, op.cit., p.10.

20 Ibid.

21 *The ASEAN Declaration*, op.cit., p.2.

22 R. Gill (1987) *ASEAN: Coming of Age*, Singapore: Sterling Corporate Services, p.15.

23 T.H. Daw (1988) *Common Vision: Burma's Regional Outlook*, Occasional Paper Washington, D.C.: Institute for the Study of Diplomacy.

24 I am grateful to Tin Maung Maung Than for offering helpful views on Burma's reasons for not joining ASEAN in 1967.

25 C.M. Turnbull (1992), "Regionalism and Nationalism", in Nicholas Tarling, ed. (1992) *The Cambridge History of Southeast Asia*, Volume 2, "The Nineteenth and Twentieth Centuries", Cambridge: Cambridge University Pressp, p.616.

26 A. Malik (1975) Regional Cooperation in International Politics, in *Regionalism in Southeast Asia*, Jakarta: Yayasan Proklamasi, Centre for Strategic and International Studies, pp.161–62.

[27] M. Leifer, (1983) *Indonesia's Foreign Policy*, London: George Allen and Unwin, p.120

[28] F. Weinstein (1969) *Indonesia Abandons Confrontation*, Interim Report Series, Modern Indonesia Project, Southeast Asia Program, Department of Asian Studies, Cornell University, 1969, pp.87–88.

[29] T.S. Lau (1980) "The Role of Singapore in Southeast Asia", *World Review*, Vol. 19, No. 3 (August 1980), p.35.

[30] M. Leifer, *Indonesia's Foreign Policy*, op.cit., p.123.

[31] J. Soedjati Djiwandono (1983) "The Political and Security Aspects of ASEAN: Its Principal Achievements", *Indonesian Quarterly*, Vol 11 (July 1983), p.20.

[35] C.M. Seah (1979) *Singapore's Position in ASEAN Cooperation*, Occasional Paper No. 38, Department of Political Science, National University of Singapore, p.18.

[33] Statement by President Suharto at the opening of the Seventh ASEAN Ministerial Meeting in Jakarta.

[34] K.Y. Lee quoted in *The Straits Times*, 11 May 1975.

[35] T. Phanit, *Regional Integration Attempts in Southeast Asia: A Study of ASEAN's Problems and Progress*, op.cit., pp.218–22.

[36] *The Straits Times*, 7 February 1976.

[37] E.B. Haas, "Regime Decay: Conflict Management and International Organizations", *International Organization*, vol. 37 (Spring 1983), pp.189–256; E.B. Haas, *Why We Still Need the United Nations: The Collective Management of International Conflict* (Berkeley: University of California, Institute of International Relations, 1986); M.W. Zacher, *International Conflicts and Collective Security, 1946–1977* (New York: Praeger, 1979).

[38] L.B. Miller, "Regional Organization and the Regulation of Internal Conflict", *World Politics*, Vol. 19, No. 4 (July 1967), pp.582–600.

[39] See A. Jorgensen-Dahl, *Regional Organisation and Order in Southeast Asia* (London: Macmillan, 1982); M.Z. Ispahani, "Alone Together: Regional Security Arrangements in Southern Africa and the Arabian Gulf", *International Security*, vol.8, no.4 (Spring 1984),pp.152–175; E. Peterson, *The Gulf Cooperation Council Search for Unity in a Dynamic Region* (Boulder, C.O: Westview Press, 1988).

[40] *The Sunday Times* (Singapore), 18 March 1978.

[41] A. Malik, "Regional Cooperation in International Politics", op. cit., pp.162–63.

[42] For a comprehensive study of external threat perceptions of the ASEAN countries see, R.O. Tillman (1987) *Southeast Asia and the Enemy Beyond: ASEAN Perceptions of External Threats*, Boulder, Colorado: Westview Press.

[43] M. Leifer (1978) "The Paradox of ASEAN: A Security Organization Without the Structure of an Alliance", *The Round Table*, Vol. 68, No. 271 (July 1978), p.268.

[44] M. Zarkovic (1977) The Revival of ASEAN, *Review of International Affairs*, 5 October 1977, pp.29–31.

[45] For discussion of these arrangements, see: R.D. Palmer (1987) *Building ASEAN: 20 Years of Southeast Asian Cooperation*, The Washington Papers, No. 127, New York: Praeger for the Centre for Strategic and International Studies, pp.116–127; H.M. Federspiel and K.E. Rafferty (1969) *Prospects for Regional Military Cooperation in Southeast Asia*, McLean, Virginia: Research Analysis Corporation, pp. 67-69; S. Simon (1978), The ASEAN States: Obstacles to Security Cooperation, *Orbis*, Vol. 22, No. 2 Summer 1978, pp.415–34; "A New Era of Cooperation", *Asian Defence Journal* (March/ April 1977), pp.14–20; "Operation Cooperation: The Malaysian-Thai Joint Border Operations", *Asian Defence Journal* (October 1977), pp.18–21.

46 This section draws heavily from A. Acharya and R. Stubbs (1995) "The Perils of Prosperity? Security and Economic Growth in the ASEAN Region", in J. Davis, ed., *Security Issues in the Post-Cold War World*. London: Edward Elgar, pp.99–112.

47 J.L.S. Girling (1981) *Thailand: Society and Politics*, Ithaca: Cornell University Press, pp.235–36. See also Economist Intelligence Unit, *The Economic Effects of the Vietnam War in east and Southeast Asia*, QER Special No.3, London: Economist Intelligence Unit, November, 1968.

48 See D.E. Nuechterlein (1967) "Thailand: Another Vietnam?" *Asian Survey*, February 1967; J.A. Caldwell (1974) *American Economic Aid to Thailand*, Lexington, Mass.: D.C. Heath; and R.J. Muscat (1990) *Thailand and the United States: Development, Security and Foreign Aid*, New York: Columbia University Press.

49 R. Stubbs, "Geopolitics and the Political Economy of Southeast Asia," *International Journal* vol.44, Summer 1989, pp.529–60.

50 N. Owen, "Economic and Social Change", in Nicholas Tarling, ed. (1992) *The Cambridge History of Southeast Asia*, Volume 2, "The Nineteenth and Twentieth Centuries", Cambridge: Cambridge University Press, p.479.

51 Ibid., p.474.

52 Ibid.

53 Ibid., p.149.

54 C. Dixon (1991) *South East Asia in the World-Economy: A Regional Geography*, London: Cambridge University Press, p.150.

55 R. Robison, R. Higgott and K. Hewison (1987) "Crisis in economic strategy in the 1980s: the factors at work', in R. Robison, R. Higgot and K. Hewison, eds. (1987) *South East Asia in the 1980s: the politics of economic crisis*, Allen and Unwin, Sydney: 1-15.

56 M. Ghazali bin Shafie (1982) "Confrontation Leads to ASEAN", *Asian Defence Journal*, February 1982, p.31.

57 Malaysian Prime Minister Hussein Onn, cited in *New Straits Times*, 5 August 1977 For a discussion of the similarities and differences in the perceptions of ASEAN leaders of the time in relation to internal threats, see, E.D. Solidum (1974) *Towards a Southeast Asian Community*, Quezon City: University of the Philippines Press, pp.103–110.

58 S. Paribatra and C. Samudavanija (1986) "Internal Dimensions of Security in Southeast Asia", in M. Ayoob, ed. (1986) *Regional Security in the Third World*, London: Croom Helm, 1986, p.67.

59 *The Straits Times*, 3 August 1977.

60 *The Straits Times*, 9 July 1977.

61 *The Straits Times*, 24 April 1975.

62 The discussion of ASEAN's role in the Sabah dispute draws heavily from A. Jorgensen-Dahl (1982) *Regional Organization and Order in Southeast Asia*, op.cit.; and T.S. Lau, *Conflict-Resolution in ASEAN: The Sabah Issue*, Department of Political Science, University of Singapore, undated. *New Directions in the International Relations of Southeast Asia*, op.cit.

63 N. Sopiee (1975) "The `Neutralisation of Southeast Asia", in H. Bull, ed. (1975) *Asia and the Western Pacific: Towards a New International Order*, Melbourne and Sydney: Thomas Nelson, p.144.

64 M. Ghazalie bin Shafie (1971) "The Neutralisation of Southeast Asia", *Pacific Community*, October 1971, p.115.

THE EVOLUTION OF REGIONAL ORGANISATION *103*

[65] H. Hanggi (1991) *ASEAN and the ZOPFAN Concept*, Singapore: Institute of Southeast Asian Studies, p.25.

[66] *The Straits Times*, 6 February 1976.

[67] F. Frost (1980) "The Origins and Evolution of ASEAN", *World Review*, Vol 19, No. 3 August 1980, p.10; T. Huxley (1986) *The ASEAN States' Defence Policies, 1975–81: Military Response to Indochina?*, Working Paper No.88 , Canberra: Australian National University, Strategic and Defence Studies Centre, p.52. See also *The Straits Times*, 10 February 1976. An indication of Indonesia's interest in greater ASEAN military cooperation was·the composition of the Indonesian delegation to the pre-summit meeting of ASEAN foreign ministers in Pattaya. It included at least four senior military and intelligence officers. Also important was the timing of a strong statement by Indonesian foreign minister Adam Malik on the Chinese threat to the region. Just prior to the Pattaya meeting, Malik criticised the complacency that he sensed in the attitude of his ASEAN partners, especially Thailand, towards China. His statement was seen as an attempt to put defence and security at the top of the Bali summit agenda. *The Straits Times*, 22 December 1975; *The Straits Times*, 7 February 1976; *The Straits Times*, 10 February 1976; *The Straits Times*, 12 February 1976.

[68] *The Straits Times*, 12 February 1976.

[69] *New Straits Times*, 1 April 1976.

[70] T. Thongswasdi (1979) *ASEAN After the Vietnam War: Stability and Development through Regional Cooperation,* Ph.D. Dissertation, Claremont Graduate School, 1979, p.123.

[71] *The Straits Times*, 6 July 1977.

[72] Ibid.

[73] *Manila Journal*, 21–27 August 1977.

[74] Cited in *The Straits Times*, 12 February 1976.

[75] *The Straits Times*, 22 August 1974.

[76] *The Straits Times*, 22 December 1975.

[77] J. Walton, "Economics", in M. Halib and T. Huxley, eds. (996) *An Introduction to Southeast Asian Studies*, London: I.B. Tauris, p.192.

[78] M.L. Syriyamongkol, *The Politics of Economic Cooperation in the Association of Southeast Asian Nations* Ph.D. Dissertation, University of Illinois at Urbana-Champaign, 1982, p.55.

[79] Ibid., p.78.

[80] Ibid., p.64.

[81] Ibid., p.68.

[82] M. Hadi Soesastro (1990) "Prospects for Pacific-Asian Regional Trade Structures", in R. Scalapino et. al., eds. (1990) *Regional Dynamics: Security, Political and Economic Issues in the Asia-Pacific Region*, Jakarta: Centre for Strategic and International Studies, p.391.

[83] "Summary Record: New Directions For ASEAN Economic Cooperation", in Proceedings of the Second ASEAN Roundtable, Kuala Lumpur, Institute of Strategic and International Studies, 20–21 July 1987, p.8.

[84] Apart from trade liberalisation and collective bargaining ASEAN's economic regionalism during the 1970s included measures to promote industrial development and energy and food security. ASEAN industrial development cooperation had three main aspects. The first was ASEAN Industrial Projects, launched in 1978. These included an Ammonia-urea project in Indonesia, an urea project in Malaysia, a rock

salt soda ash project in Thailand, a copper fabrication plant in the Philippines and a Hepatitis B vaccine project in Singapore. The second was the ASEAN Industrial Complementation Scheme, whose Basic Agreement was signed in June 1981. The Scheme was aimed at promoting industrial development in the region by permitting the private sector to agree in advance to industrial specialisation, thereby eliminating "unnecessary competition among ASEAN countries". It provided for vertical and horizontal specialisation. But the number of industrial projects suitable for component production was limited and getting ASEAN members to agree on a scheme proved to be difficult. Hence the rationale for the third element in ASEAN industrial cooperation, called the ASEAN Industrial Joint Venture Scheme. Launched in 1980, this scheme aimed at encouraging private sector participation in intra-ASEAN industrial cooperation. AIJV schemes required participation by only two private sector partners.

In addition, ASEAN economic cooperation included food and energy security programmes. In 1977, ASEAN members agreed to an ASEAN emergency petroleum sharing scheme comprising the national oil corporations of the member countries. An ASEAN Food Security Reserve System was set up in 1979 to provide mutual support in the time of emergencies as well as an early warning system for such emergencies. An ASEAN Emergency Rice Reserve of 50,000 tons was one offshoot of this.

Chng M.K., "ASEAN Economic Cooperation: The Current Status", *Southeast Asian Affairs 1985* (Singapore: Institute of Southeast Asian Studies, 1985), pp.31–53, M.L. Suriyamongkol (1988) *Politics of ASEAN Economic Co-operation*, Singapore: Oxford University Press. For a review of the main literature on ASEAN economic cooperation, see: H.C. Rieger (1989) "Regional Economic Cooperation in the Asia-Pacific Region", *Asia-Pacific Economic Literature*, vol.3, no.2, September 1989, pp.5–33.

[85] For an overview of ASEAN's role in GATT, see M. Hadi Soesastro (1987) "ASEAN's Participation in GATT", *Indonesian Quarterly*, vol. 15, no.1, January 1987, pp.107–27

[86] A. Melchor Jr. (1975) "Security Issues in Southeast Asia", op.cit., p.46.

[87] B. Anderson (1983) *Imagined Communities: Reflections on the Origin and Spread of Nationalism*, London: Verso.

[88] R. Fifield, 'Southeast Asia' and 'ASEAN' as Regional Concepts, op.cit., p.128.

[89] Cited in C.P. Luhulima (1995) *ASEAN's Security Framework*, CAPA Reports no.22, San Fransisco: Center for Asia Pacific Affairs, The Asia Foundation, p.1.

[90] A. Malik (1975) "Regional Cooperation in International Politics", in *Regionalism in Southeast Asia* (Jakarta: CSIS, 1975), p.160.

CHAPTER 4

Southeast Asia Divided: Polarisation and Reconciliation

Introduction

The period from 1979 to 1991 may be regarded as a distinctive phase in modern Southeast Asian history. It began with the most serious challenges to peace and stability in the region since the end of the Vietnam War— the Vietnamese invasion of Cambodia in December 1978. The ensuing crisis saw the polarisation of Southeast Asia into two antagonistic political groups, one represented by ASEAN, the other by the three Indochinese states spearheaded by Vietnam. As the rivalry between the two groups intensified, ASEAN's concept of regionalism was opposed by that of Vietnam, which held Indochina to be a single strategic unit. The regional conflict in Southeast Asia reflected changes in the international security environment, especially the collapse of the superpower *detente* and the advent of the "second Cold War". Renewed superpower tensions fuelled the stalemate in the Cambodia conflict and were manifested in heightened US-Soviet strategic rivalry, part of which was played out in the form of naval competition in the Pacific. Sino-Soviet and Sino-Vietnamese ties too plunged to new lows during the period, with China putting military pressure on Vietnam on their common border and providing military support to the Cambodian rebels so as to impose a heavy cost on Hanoi's occupation of Cambodia.

But the crisis in regional relations was also in many respects a blessing in disguise, not only for ASEAN, but arguably for the whole region of Southeast Asia. For it provided the ASEAN grouping a new sense of unity and purpose, brought international recognition and support for its diplomatic and political role in finding a solution to the Third Indochina War, and strengthened the recognition among the ASEAN regimes that economic development was the best guarantee of their political legitimacy and national stability. While the accelerated pace of economic liberalisation and globalisation in the non-communist part of Southeast Asia owed to a variety of factors, such as the southward movement of Japanese capital in the wake of the 1985 Plaza Accord, and the spread of post-Fordist transnational production, it was also a response by the ASEAN govern-ments to the insecurity and vulnerability in the wake of the ideological polarisation of the region. In the end, what began as a period of crisis and conflict turned out to be a period of remarkable transformation in Southeast Asia's economic and strategic landscape, one that paved the way for a more united and resilient region by the early 1990s.

Vietnam and ASEAN

The US withdrawal from Indochina and the communist takeover in Vietnam, Laos and Cambodia entrenched the polarisation of Southeast Asia into two ideologically hostile blocs. The communist takeovers were unexpectedly swift. The Khmer Rouge was the first, seizing Phnom Penh in mid-April 1975. Less than two weeks passed before Saigon fell as the result of a final attack by Hanoi. In Vientiene, the Pathet Lao took over in November 1975 as the existing coalition government collapsed and t he king abdicated. From this point onwards, this intra-regional divide became the principal determinant of international relations of Southeast Asia, outweighing even the traditionally decisive impact of the Cold War.

The communist takeovers in Indochina were received by the ASEAN states with a mix of both anxiety and hope. Their impact on regional stability had to be seen against the backdrop of the effects of the Sino-Soviet split. The Sino-US rapprochement of 1972 changed the political context of Sino-Vietnamese relations. Hanoi felt betrayed by Beijing and suspected a Sino-US deal at the expense of Vietnam's interests. Despite the fact that China had provided massive support to Vietnam's war effort, it showed no interest in helping its reunification effort. Part of the reason may have been its traditional fear of a strong united Vietnam. Cooperation among communists in the two countries dated back to the Comintern days of the early 1920s. China had helped Ho Chi Minh launch the communist organisation, and until Ho's death in 1969, China remained a close ally. But international developments, such as the Sino-Soviet split, changes in Sino-US relations, and domestic developments in Vietnam, especially reunification, changed all that.

Fears of communist domination in the region undermined hopes raised by the *detente* at the global level. The formation and early life of ASEAN was greeted with considerable suspicion by Vietnam, despite the fact that ASEAN had carefully avoided intra-mural military cooperation precisely for fear of provoking Hanoi. The reason for the communist states in the region viewing ASEAN as a pro-Western and anti-communist front is not hard to understand. Not only were ASEAN members engaged in the suppression of communist insurgencies backed by China and the Soviet Union, and maintained security links with the Western countries, they also received substantial economic aid from the West. Vietnam saw ASEAN as a Western tool replacing SEATO but serving essentially the same function of imposing Western capitalist political and economic domination. ASEAN feared the emergence of a unified Indochina federation under Vietnamese hegemony. To be sure, Vietnam, Cambodia and Laos proclaimed a "militant solidarity", but no political integration ensued.

There was little evidence that post-reunification Vietnam saw its destiny to lie within the Southeast Asian community of nations. Hanoi seemed to make greater efforts to project its image as a non-aligned nation within the developing world. But Hanoi also during the 1976–77 period began a diplomatic effort to underscore its independence from socialist powers. This meant distancing itself from China and identifying itself as a Southeast Asian nation. Indeed, Southeast Asia did figure in Vietnam's own perception of its place in the world; Party leader Le Duan on 15 May 1975 proclaimed the nation's intention to turn itself "into a civilised, prosperous and powerful country, an inviolable bastion of national independence, democracy and socialism in Indochina and South East Asia".[1] During 1976–77, Hanoi began adopting a softer stance towards ASEAN, despite continuing to criticise it for its anti-communist under-pinnings and the development of bilateral defence ties among ASEAN members.

As Vietnam seemed to concentrate on reunification and reconstruction, in September 1975, Premier Pham Van Dong offered an olive branch to ASEAN, declaring a commitment to peaceful reconstruction, and acknowledging that this would require building good relations with other countries in Southeast Asia. He affirmed his nation's commitment to non-interference and mutual respect. After the reunified state, the Socialist Republic of Vietnam, was established in July 1976, Hanoi expected normal ties and aid from the US under the 1973 Paris Agreement. While undertaking collectivisation and a change from capitalist to socialist mode in the south and promoting socialist ideology and culture at home, Vietnam was seeking external aid to support its economic and political programme. It joined the World Bank, IMF and ADB, and developed trade relations with India, Sweden, Singapore, Japan and Australia. During this period it seemed as though Hanoi was more interested in rebuilding its economy than in fostering the spread of communism.

But despite its conciliatory tone towards ASEAN, Hanoi's own vision of regional order clashed with that of ASEAN. Spcifically, Hanoi's relations with Laos and Cambodia, both of whom fell under communist rule, rekindled fears in ASEAN of Hanoi's old plan for an Indochina federation. The Vietnamese Communist Party had begun life as the Communist Party of Indochina with the goal of achieving power not just in Vietnam but also in the entire Indochina area. Ho Chi Minh in his role as Comintern representative before the Second World War, was tasked with revolution not just in Indochina, but in the entire Southeast Asian region, and Hanoi had supported, albeit in a minor way, communist insurgencies in Malaysia, Burma, and Thailand.[2] Although this goal had been abandoned as an immediate objective after the end of the Second World War (to be revived again in 1951 and abandoned reluctantly after 1954), it now seemed to be on Hanoi's foreign policy agenda.

The conception of Indochina as a region was based not just on common colonial legacy, but also ideology and geopolitics. There were several ways this could be achieved. An extreme form would be formal integration, which seemed remote. A different form would be a gradual move towards a loose federation in which Laos and Cambodia would retain their own ethnic governments under Vietnamese dominance. The regime in Laos was more receptive to this idea than that in Cambodia, though some sections of its leadership seemed favourably disposed for ideological and practical reasons. A realisation of this idea would have meant a form of regionalism different from that represented by ASEAN. In it, Vietnam would have been the dominant power, without having to accept any norms of self-restraint towards its lesser partners, while ASEAN was based on the understanding that the leading member, Indonesia, would not seek regional hegemony and exercise restraint towards its smaller neighbours.

But Hanoi's vision of Indochina faltered amidst diverging political conditions in Laos and Cambodia. The ruling communist regime in Laos, despite its collectivisation programme and re-education camps, sought to develop a more moderate version of communist rule than Vietnam by tolerating Buddhism and accepting foreign aid. While Laos's foreign policy was staunchly pro-Vietnamese, it did not want to be seen as a Vietnamese puppet. Cambodia was a different case. Under the brutal Khmer Rouge, it experienced far more domestic turmoil than Vietnam and Laos. The regime ordered mass evacuation of the capital to the countryside and sought to bring about the rapid transformation of society and economy by forcible restructuring toward communal living. This process was accompanied by mass killings of intellectuals, peasants and former leaders, the abolishment of private property, banning of the Buddhist church, and abolition of the use of money. King Norodom Sihanouk was put under house arrest and later exiled to Beijing with a new constitution establishing a Democratic Kampuchea in January 1976. The party then turned upon itself to weed out disloyal elements. In total, more than a million Cambodians died. While the domestic violence continued, the Khmer Rouge pursued a much more nationalist and thus anti-Vietnamese posture. As its conflict with Vietnam escalated, it moved closer to Beijing, seeking economic and military support, thereby ensuring that Vietnam's vision of an alternative regional order centred on Indochina could only be realised by overthrowing the Khmer Rouge regime militarily.

In the meantime, Hanoi's policy towards ASEAN remained ambiguous. On the one hand, it sought improvement in bilateral ties. But its support for ASEAN was more qualified. Vietnamese Foreign Minister, Nguyen Duy Trinh, during a tour of all ASEAN members (except Singapore) between 20 December 1977 to 12 January 1978, called for Southeast Asia to achieve "peace, independence, and neutrality" which echoed ASEAN's official doctrine of "peace, freedom, and neutrality". But his deputy, Vo Dong Giang, suggested during a visit to Kuala Lumpur that ASEAN ought to be wound up as it was "American-backed" and be replaced with a new regional body which Hanoi would join.[3] Later, in June 1978, Hanoi proposed the creation of a Zone of Peace, Independence and Neutrality, but faced with suspicion from ASEAN, was willing to revert to the original term "freedom" instead of "independence". This failed to assuage the fears of some ASEAN members, such as Singapore, who suspected Soviet prodding behind Vietnam's shift.

Hanoi's hesitant wooing of ASEAN reflected its concern over the developing relationship between Cambodia and China, as Hanoi's own ties with the Khmer Rouge deteriorated. It is also noteworthy that the Khmer Rouge regime rejected regionalism. While stating that it was not opposed to ASEAN or its ZOPFAN proposal, it proclaimed its intention to "avoid leaning towards or associating with any bloc or join any regional grouping".[4] By 1978, the earlier hopes created by Vietnam's peace offensive towards ASEAN had died down.

The communist victory in Vietnam was not seen by its ASEAN neighbours as a direct military threat. In fact, few ASEAN policy-makers believed that either China or Vietnam could pose a direct military threat to non-communist Southeast Asia. The threat of Chinese aggression, in particular, appeared remote with the advent of the Sino-Soviet rift and the Sino-US rapprochement. Vietnam after 1975 was a different story, but even in this case there were few apprehensions that the Vietnamese hostility to ASEAN could take the form of a military attack. In the immediate aftermath of the fall of Saigon, and until its military intervention in Cambodia, such a possibility could hardly have been likely. This was not just because a war-weary Vietnam needed to pay urgent attention to the formidable task of reconstruction. To pose a military threat, Hanoi would have required strong external assistance from either China or the Soviet Union, or both, and each of these powers were then seeking better ties with the US. At a meeting of ASEAN foreign ministers in Singapore in July 1977, the then foreign minister of Thailand, Dr Upadit Pachariyangkun, described the prospect of any ASEAN member being threatened by external aggression as "obsolete". Rather, "We are more preoccupied with the possibility of increased subversive activities which get aid from outside...I am sure that there will be no external aggression, not even from North Vietnam".[5] Even in the aftermath of Vietnam's invasion of Kampuchea (the official name of Cambodia under the Khmer Rouge), the possibility of a direct Vietnamese attack on any ASEAN member was not credible for a number of reasons. Not only was Vietnam preoccupied with the pacification of Kampuchea as well as with the maintenance of its military and political presence in Laos, it also lacked any significant power projection capability. Moreover, in so far as the prospect of an attack on Thailand was concerned, Vietnam did not host an exile Thai faction which could be used to justify a direct military attack on that state (as was the case with Kampuchea).[6]

Neither did the communist victories in Indochina signal an intensified Vietnamese campaign to export its communist revolution as predicted by the "domino theory". This theory was met with considerable skepticism in ASEAN. As a Malaysian newspaper editorialised: "The domino theory is a cold-war relic. If the non-communist [Southeast Asian] states are toppled, they will almost certainly be toppled from within."[7] While the possibility of Vietnamese-backed communist subversion was noted by ASEAN leaders, who also expressed concern that weapons left by the US in Vietnam could find their way to insurgents in their countries, they regarded the communist threat in the ASEAN context as more likely to be internally inspired. ASEAN leaders were all too aware that the communist insurgencies and subversion they were facing or might have to face in the future were rooted, first and foremost, in the internal contradictions of their societies. The origin of these insurgencies predated the fall of Saigon. As noted in Chapter 2, they had established themselves internally by exploiting the nationalist campaign against colonial and external powers.

Thus, President Marcos of the Philippines predicted that the danger from within would continue to be the main security problem for the ASEAN states.[8] He also warned that if external powers, including the superpowers, were to destabilise the ASEAN states, the only way they would succeed was by taking advantage of the internal vulnerabilities of the latter:

> "[The threat of great power rivalry]... is not an open threat of aggression. It is exploitation of internal weaknesses, and exploitation of internal contradictions-lack of economic development and/or the lack of an even spread of the benefits of economic development, leading to guerrilla insurgency"[9].

Nowhere was the emphasis on internal stability in ASEAN's collective security perceptions better illustrated than in Indonesia's concepts of "national resilience" and "regional resilience", phrases that were to become something of a rallying slogan for all the ASEAN regimes. According to the Indonesian view, domestic stability in the individual ASEAN states was an indispensable prerequisite for regional security and regional collaboration. The concept of national resilience emphasised the non-military, internal dimensions of security; it was "an inward-looking concept, based on the proposition that national security lies not in military alliances or under the military umbrella of any great power, but in self-reliance deriving from domestic factors such as economic and social development, political stability and a sense of nationalism".[10] On the face of it, the emphasis on national security and nationalism would seem to go against the spirit of regionalism. But the Indonesian view was exactly the opposite; as a prominent Indonesian scholar on regional security put it: "if each member nation can accomplish an overall national development and overcome internal threats, regional resilience will automatically result much in the same way as a chain derives its overall strength from the strength of its constituent parts".[11] The underlying assumption was that with their houses in order, ASEAN countries would find it easier to settle their disputes and devise collective plans to promote long-term stability and security in the region.

The foregoing analysis suggests that communist victories in Indochina in 1975 did not by itself plunge Southeast Asia into intra-regional turmoil and competition. Preoccupied with internal problems, both Vietnam and ASEAN entertained hopes for accommodating each other's security interests and concerns. The ASEAN members seemed prepared to live with Vietnam if Hanoi expressed a commitment to regional peace and stability and accepted the principle of non-interference. Indonesia and Malaysia seemed most willing to cooperate with Hanoi in developing a framework of political accommodation that might have led to the admission of the Indochinese states into ASEAN. But any hope for such an outcome was dashed by Vietnam's invasion of Cambodia in December 1978.

ASEAN and the Cambodia Conflict

Vietnam's move into Cambodia was the culmination of deteriorating relations between the two communist governments. Soon after seizing power in Phnom Penh, the Pol Pot regime not only launched a brutal domestic programme of building a rural utopia, including wholesale expulsion of residents of the capital to the country-side, it also carried out increasingly violent incursions into Vietnamese territory. In retaliation, Vietnam's leadership extended support to a break-away faction of the Khmer Rouge led by Heng Samrin and Hun Sen. Invading Vietnamese forces toppled the Pol Pot regime and installed Heng Samrin as the leader of Cambodia, thereby plunging Southeast Asia into a new crisis with profound international implications.

Vietnam tried unsuccessfully to convince the international community that what was going on in Cambodia was essentially a domestic power struggle between rival Cambodian factions in which the genocidal Pol Pot regime had been justly overthrown by a Cambodian "salvation" front. It also hinted that its actions in support of the Heng Samrin regime were a defensive move to counter the threat of Chinese expansionism given Beijing's strong backing for Pol Pot. Hanoi refused to accept that it was a direct party to the Cambodia conflict. The question of the withdrawal of its troops could only be decided by the Heng Samrin regime as the sole legitimate government of Cambodia. The domestic situation in Cambodia, i.e. the replacement of the Pol Pot regime by Heng Samrin, was "irreversible".[12] While Vietnam was willing to discuss ASEAN's security concerns arising from the crisis in Cambodia proposing, among other things, the creation of a demilitarised zone on the Thai-Cambodian border to be supervised by a joint commission, and expressing willingness to sign non-aggression treaties with Thailand and other ASEAN countries, it rejected the idea of an international conference on Cambodia as put forward by ASEAN which would include all the belligerent sides. Instead, Hanoi tried to persuade Thailand to accept a limited withdrawal of its forces to be decided by Hanoi and Phnom Penh.

The Vietnamese invasion swept away any incipient idea on the part of ASEAN to develop accommodation with Hanoi. ASEAN claimed that Hanoi's move decisively rebuffed its overtures for peaceful co-existence with communist Indochina which might have created a place for the latter within the regional grouping. Furthermore, Hanoi's move showed contempt for the cardinal principles of non-interference and non-use of force in inter-state relations. Hardline elements in ASEAN states argued that the invasion of Cambodia showed Hanoi's aspiration for regional hegemony, beginning with the strategic domination of Indochina and extending into other parts of Southeast Asia through use of subversion and intimidation. ASEAN was presented with another security challenge from Vietnam when Hanoi nationalised private trade in March 1978, severely affecting its ethnic Chinese community. This led to an exodus of ethnic Chinese, the so-called "boat people", into the ASEAN states, creating a new source of tension between ASEAN and Vietnam.

The Vietnamese invasion dashed hopes that the US disengagement from Indochina would usher in an era of relative peace and stability in the Southeast Asian region. It also marked the beginning of a period of heightened great power rivalry with the Sino-Vietnamese confrontation aggravating the existing Sino-Soviet rivalry. Ironically, Vietnam, which had been dismissive of ASEAN's desire to limit the role of external powers in Southeast Asian security, was the main victim of renewed great power interventionism, as it faced considerable military pressure from China. Military tensions between China and Vietnam had already escalated over their territorial dispute over the South China Sea islands, especially after Chinese forces seized the Paracels in January 1974 and began extending China's claims to the Spratly islands claimed by Vietnam. But these tensions were nothing compared to the aftermath of Vietnam's invasion of Cambodia. In March 1979, China launched an attack into the northern border zone of Vietnam, ostensibly to "teach Hanoi a lesson", but the attack proved costly for Beijing. While it failed to force Vietnam's hand

and produced no change in the political situation in Cambodia, it also had the effect of forcing Vietnam deeper into the Soviet orbit.

The Soviet Union had given considerable military aid to Hanoi during the last stages of Vietnam War. Moscow, sensing Washington's China card, courted Hanoi as a counter. Its interests coincided with Vietnam's own enmity with China. The strategic relationship between the two countries had already grown closer following the December 1975 visit by Vietnam's leader Le Duan to Moscow, followed by a bilateral economic agreement in 1976, Vietnam's incorporation into the Council for Mutual Economic Assistance (COMECON) in June 1978 and, in November that year, a 25-year Treaty of Friendship and Cooperation. The fact that Vietnam had invaded Cambodia, a month after signing the Treaty, gave Beijing a confirmation of Soviet hegemonism through collusion with Vietnam. Beijing blamed the Vietnamese invasion on the massive Soviet backing for Hanoi. The presence of Vietnamese forces in Cambodia was listed by China as one of the principal obstacles to normalising ties with Moscow in future "normalisation" talks between the Soviet Union and China. China would reiterate its demand that Moscow discipline Hanoi over Cambodia as a precondition for improved relations. But little progress was achieved. As a result, Beijing continued to pursue a "counter-hegemony" platform, aimed at resisting Soviet geopolitical moves in the region. As part of this policy, Beijing continued to improve its ties with the US, maintained strong support for ASEAN's hardline stance against Vietnam, and cultivated influence with ASEAN by extending a commitment to discontinue its support for communist insurgencies in Southeast Asia.

Apart from renewing the spectre of great power rivalry, the Third Indochina War also raised the possibility of a wider intra-regional military confrontation. The Vietnamese military presence in Cambodia and the spillover of its military raids into Thai territory led Thailand to perceive a direct military threat from the instability in Indochina. Presenting itself as a "frontline state", Thailand turned to China and the US for military assistance. This included acquisition of Chinese arms for the Thai military and the reaffirmation of the Thai-US security alliance. In addition, Thailand secured assurances of military support from some of the ASEAN partners, such as Singapore and Malaysia, although this fell short of a formal ASEAN military alliance. Intra-ASEAN political differences and suspicions aside, ASEAN remained reluctant to develop military ties for fear of aggravating Hanoi's hostility. This in turn served to highlight ASEAN's continued dependence on external security guarantees, despite the professed goal of self-reliance in the wake of the British and American withdrawal from the region.

ASEAN's immediate priority in responding to the Vietnamese invasion was to deny Vietnam a *fait accompli* in Cambodia. This meant denying recognition and legitimacy to the Heng Samrin government while mobilising support for Pol Pot's Democratic Kampuchea that had been overthrown by Hanoi, and ensuring Hanoi's international isolation both diplomatically and economically.[13] ASEAN focused its diplomatic energies at the UN, mobilising international censure of Hanoi. But ASEAN's diplomacy suffered from internal divisions, with Indonesia and Malaysia showing a greater willingness (as evident by the so-called Kuantan principle jointly enunciated by their leaders in March 1980) to recognise Vietnam's security interests in Indochina if Hanoi was to reduce its strategic links with and dependence on the Soviet Union.[14] The position of Malaysia and Indonesia reflected a growing concern that the Cambodian conflict, if unresolved, would become a grave threat to the security of all regional states. For both Jakarta and Kuala Lumpur, it was China which posed the real long-term threat to Southeast Asia and Vietnam could be a bulwark against Chinese expansionism. If ASEAN went along with China's "bleed Vietnam" policy, this would not only lead to a more entrenched Soviet-Vietnam strategic alliance, including the acquisition by the latter of military bases in Cam Ranh Bay, but would also contribute to a dangerous degree of Chinese influence in the region.[15] This view conflicted with the position of Singapore and Thailand, which remained concerned with Vietnam as the main threat to regional peace and security.

It was not the differences within ASEAN or between ASEAN and Vietnam which alone undermined early attempts at finding a diplomatic solution to the Third Indochina War. Sharp differences between ASEAN and China surfaced at the International Conference on Kampuchea (ICK) held under the auspices of the UN in 1981. Boycotted by Hanoi and the Soviet Union, the ICK saw a clash between China and ASEAN over how to handle the Khmer Rouge. ASEAN pushed for a formula which would ensure the total withdrawal of Vietnamese forces from Cambodia, disarm all Cambodian factions and give all factions representation in an interim government. This would prevent the return of the Khmer Rouge to power. But China, backed by the US, rejected the ASEAN proposal on the grounds that it would give the Vietnamese aggressor and the resistance factions equal status. The resulting failure of the ICK was a major blow to the Cambodian peace process, creating a diplomatic stalemate which had already taken root over the refusal of the Indochinese states to accept ASEAN's position on the conflict.

The stalemate in the Cambodia conflict was also fuelled by geo-political rivalry among the great powers. Since the Soviet invasion of Afghanistan in December 1979, US-Soviet relations had reached a new low, making it difficult for any dialogue on resolving regional conflicts. While, in contrast to its massive support for the Afghan resistance, Washington provided no overt military assistance to the Cambodian resistance, it did encourage support from China and ASEAN for the resistance factions. The US remained largely inactive in the Cambodian peace process, lending support to ASEAN's diplomatic efforts while at the same time siding with China's "bleed Vietnam" policy, to the discomfort of Indonesia and Malaysia.

Thanks to military assistance from China and ASEAN to the Cambodian resistance factions, the stalemate in the Cambodian peace process was both matched and conditioned by the stalemate on the battlefield.[16] Hanoi's failure to pacify Cambodia was amply evident by the mid-1980s. Frustrated by its inability to decimate the forces of the regime it had toppled, estimated to be some 60,000 in 1980, Hanoi only succeeded in forcing the resistance to retreat to the Thai-Cambodia border, areas from where they were able to reorganise and fight back with the help of massive Chinese aid, Thai willingness to grant sanctuaries, and political and material support from the ASEAN states. The Khmer Rouge was joined by two non-communist resistance armies: the Khmer People's National Liberation Front (KPNLF) and Armee National Sihanoukist (ANS). Their emergence forced Hanoi to switch to a regular pattern of cross-border dry season offensives into Thailand, which produced, in January 1984, direct engagements between Thai and Vietnamese forces. The Vietnamese dry season offensive during 1984–85 wiped out almost every resistance camp inside Cambodia and sent about 200,000 civilians flee to refugee camps in Thailand. But while damaging the resistance, Vietnam failed to destroy it. The inefficiency of the forces of the Heng Samrin regime and the creation of a resistance coalition called Coalition Government of Democratic Kampuchea (CGDK) served to reinforce the stalemate on the battlefront. At the same time, the resistance was not capable of inflicting a military defeat on Vietnam or toppling the Vietnamese-installed regime in Phnom Penh thanks to internal divisions within the factions (especially the KPNLF which had received a large chunk of the aid from ASEAN). Nonetheless, the resistance was able to thwart Hanoi's desire to consolidate the rule of the Heng Samrin regime. The stalemate was reflected in the fact that the dry season of 1987 passed without military engagements.

The polarisation of Southeast Asia that accompanied the Third Indochina War was not confined to the political and strategic sphere. It was also reflected in the economic arena. The economic development policies among the region's capitalist countries, all of which belonged to ASEAN, presented a marked contrast to those of the socialist segment. With communist Indochina now excluded from trading opportunities with both the United States and ASEAN, Vietnam, despite its own poverty, played the role of regional hegemon. It developed special ties with Laos after 1975 and Cambodia after 1979 and even made interest-free loans to Laos in 1975. However, its greater size and better educational and economic facilities were not enough to underwrite such a role and Vietnam became increasingly dependent upon the USSR to supply it with several crucial import items such as oil, iron, steel, chemical fertilizer and cotton.[17]

In contrast, revolution and war in Indochina served to improve the economic positioning of the ASEAN economies vis-à-vis the world economy. Prompted by the Vietnamese invasion of Cambodia, and the subsequent fears in the region of Vietnamese expansionism, and spurred on by the US, Japan increased its aid to the ASEAN members. For example, during the height of the Cambodian conflict from 1982 to 1986, the four largest ASEAN states—Indonesia, Malaysia, the Philippines and Thailand —together received nearly $1 billion in development assistance from the Japanese.[18] For the government of Japan this was the best way of ensuring that a region which was increasingly vital to Japanese companies seeking lower-cost sites for producing manufacturing goods for export to the US and Europe, and which sat astride key sealanes linking Japan to Europe and the Middle East, was kept relatively stable. Hence, once again security issues paved the way for the injection of capital into the ASEAN region which in turn promoted economic growth.

In contrast to Indochina and Burma, the ASEAN states were committed to economic liberalisation and structural change, facilitated by a conscious integration into the new international division of labour. Moreover, the Third Indochina War created a more favourable external climate for the economic development of ASEAN states. Although mostly an urban phenomenon, in the early seventies the progressive integration of Malaysia and Thailand into the world economy enhanced their economic development prospects. In Indonesia and the Philippines economic development was still stalled, however, though under both the Suharto and Marcos governments' internationalisation programs were instituted and economic collapse avoided.[19] Overall, the impressive economic growth rates — at times reaching well over 9 percent per year in Thailand, Singapore and Malaysia — of the ASEAN members could be attributed in good part to the impact that security issues had on the region's economies. The Korean War, the Vietnam War and the Vietnamese occupation of Cambodia all produced much-needed external funds which helped to create greater prosperity in ASEAN countries. In addition, the communist threat helped ASEAN regimes to justify strong domestic institutions to which their citizens were generally willing to cede considerable authority for the sake of security and stability.[20]

At the larger international level, the Third Indochina War became a flashpoint of the "New Cold War" between the US and the Soviet Union. That had resulted from the breakdown of the *détente* following the Soviet invasion of Afghanistan and what the US perceived to be Soviet geopolitical gains throughout the Third World, including Southeast Asia, where the Soviet-Vietnamese alliance had seemed to Washington to indicate a general expansion of Soviet geopolitical interest in the region.

These fears, shared by some of Washington's allies in Southeast Asia (especially Singapore) were aggravated by the build-up of the Soviet naval fleet in the Pacific. The Soviet move, which involved the acquiring bases in Cam Ranh Bay, was seen by the pro-Western countries of the region as dramatically enhancing its power projection capabilities in Southeast Asia, posing a threat to the security of the sealanes.[21]

The advent of the Reagan administration in 1981 saw a major intensification of US against Soviet gains in the Third World by imposing a heavy political, economic and military burden on Moscow. Instead of providing a focus for mutual dialogue, regional conflicts such as Cambodia were cited by the administration as a major factor in the deterioration of East-West relations and as justification for a massive American military modernisation program. The administration's attitude towards the Cambodia conflict was shaped by its overall policy framework towards regional conflicts, called the "Reagan Doctrine". Cambodia, which the administration held to be a direct result of Moscow's military and economic backing for Vietnam, was included among the targets of the Reagan Doctrine, which aimed to achieve a "roll-back" of Soviet geopolitical advances by supporting directly or indirectly (as in the case of Cambodia) guerrilla groups resisting Soviet-backed regimes.

Despite Washington's fear of a Soviet geopolitical offensive, Moscow's influence in Southeast Asia remained quite limited. Moscow had earlier courted the region with a plan for a Collective Security System for Asia, first proposed by General Secretary Leonid Brezhnev in 1969. However, this proposal had received a cold response from the ASEAN states, largely due to their perception that Moscow's real objective was to isolate the US, China and the Western European powers from the region. Even later Soviet proposals, such as those made by Mikhail Gorbachev in the late 1980s concerning regional security, were not very enthusiastically received by ASEAN members because of the larger issue of Soviet refusal to push Vietnam into withdrawing from Cambodia. As long as their suspicion of Soviet motives in Indochina remained, the ASEAN states did not embrace any Soviet initiatives for regional cooperation too warmly.

While the Third Indochina War aggravated the security dilemma in Southeast Asia and further undermined ASEAN's professed security framework (especially ZOPFAN), it also had a dramatic impact in giving a more substantive meaning to ASEAN political and security cooperation. Moreover, it helped propel ASEAN from being a relatively unknown grouping, to the centre stage of international diplomacy in search of a political solution to the Cambodia conflict.

Towards Regional Reconciliation

By the mid-1980s, the military and diplomatic situation in the Cambodia conflict showed little sign of leading to victory for either of the contending parties. On the one hand, Hanoi's goal of making the rule of Heng Samrin's PRK "irreversible", and thereby extending its influence over Indochina, had not been fulfilled. On the other hand the efforts by the anti-Vietnamese coalition, which consisted of the CGDK, China and ASEAN with backing from Western countries, to put pressure on Vietnam both politically (through condemnation and isolation) and militarily (through backing for the military efforts of the CGDK) had not succeeded in securing a Vietnamese roll-back. In fact, the "bleed Vietnam" strategy might have been counter-productive. As the *Strategic Survey* published by the London-based International Institute for Strategic Studies pointed out: "The strategy of diplomatic isolation and support for the Khmer resistance's guerrilla campaign of attrition, which ASEAN, China and the West pursued, far from forcing concessions from her [Vietnam], only reinforced her intrasigence and her insistence that the situation in Kampuchea was both "irreversible" and an "internal" matter".[22]

After some time, the rival Khmer factions and their principal external backers, China and Vietnam, came increasingly to the realisation that their objectives could not be achieved by military means within acceptable costs. Moreover, at least for three major players in the conflict, namely Vietnam, the Soviet Union and ASEAN, the costs of the stalemate seemed to be higher than the cost of a political settlement. For Vietnam, whose intervention had been the key issue in the conflict, the cost of the conflict in human, political and economic terms was high. In July 1988, the Vice-commander of Vietnamese troops in Cambodia estimated that about 55,000 Vietnamese troops and civilians had perished. The conflict not only deprived Vietnam access to international capital and aid urgently needed for economic development, it also increased Vietnamese dependence on the Soviet Union. Vietnam also remained politically isolated, as reflected in increasing majorities supporting the annual ASEAN-sponsored resolution in the UN General Assembly condemning its invasion of Cambodia.

For the Soviet Union, the Cambodia stalemate imposed major costs in political as well as economic terms. The massive amount of economic and military aid to Hanoi, estimated at between 4 to 6 billion US dollars a year,[23] without which the latter's campaign in Cambodia could not have been sustained, was an increasingly unacceptable burden on an ailing Soviet economy. Politically, Soviet support for Hanoi's Cambodia venture had obstructed the process of normalisation of its ties with China and the prospect of superpower rapprochement. Moscow's role in bringing about a settlement to the Cambodia conflict was sure to help its standing within the Asia-Pacific region, especially in the eyes of the ASEAN countries with which Moscow was actively seeking closer economic ties. On the other hand, possible "losses" for the Soviet Union from a Cambodia settlement,

SOUTHEAST ASIA DIVIDED: POLARISATION AND RECONCILIATION **119**

which might make Vietnam less dependent on Moscow and affect Soviet access to military installations at Cam Ranh Bay, would not be critical. Towards the end of the 1980s, Moscow had begun to withdraw its forces from Vietnam as part of Gorbachev's overall force reduction programme. As diplomacy replaced a strong regional military presence as the chief instrument of Moscow's policy towards the Asia Pacific, the fear of losing these bases did not deter Moscow from applying pressure on Hanoi to adopt a more flexible stand on the Cambodia problem.

Gorbachev's famous speech at Vladivostock on 28 July 1986[24] heralded a new era in Soviet strategic thinking on the Asia Pacific region and indicated an eagerness to win recognition as a peaceful player in the region. Although the Soviet leader offered no concessions on the Cambodia conflict, he signaled the Soviet desire to disengage in Afghanistan and make concessions on its border dispute with China, the other "obstacles" to a Sino-Soviet rapprochement. With Vladivostock marking the beginning of a thaw in Sino-Soviet rivalry, the stakes and interests of external powers in the Cambodia conflict were dramatically altered. The Soviet desire to extricate itself from regional hotspots reduced its support for Vietnam's continuing occupation of Cambodia and forced Hanoi's decision to withdraw its troops from Cambodia. The Sino-Soviet rapprochement also lessened Beijing's interest in using its support for the Cambodian resistance factions to bleed the Soviet Union.

For ASEAN, a stalemate in the Cambodia conflict had been a mixed blessing at best. The Cambodia problem clearly helped ASEAN's unity and its international reputation initially. But as the stalemate continued, ASEAN began counting its costs. It severely tested ASEAN's unity, and brought to the surface the differing intra-mural perceptions of China and Vietnam. The stalemate sustained Chinese influence over the security concerns of the grouping, a factor especially unwelcome to Indonesia and Malaysia.

The changing international political climate and the interest and role of a group of mediators were major factors in generating hopes for a breakthrough in Paris. The evolving Reagan-Gorbachev *détente* created hope for mutual restraint and understanding on regional disputes in the Third World, including Cambodia. The activism and success of the UN in mediating regional disputes had further contributed to a positive international climate for an agreement on the Cambodia problem. A similar interest on the part of a number of so-called "middle powers", such as Australia, France, Japan, Canada and India, and their willingness to contribute to the reconstruction of the war-devastated country, were additional factors that created hopes for a settlement in Cambodia.

As the conflict entered the second half of the 1980s, a realisation that the stalemate on the battlefield could not be broken without a dramatic increase in military operations and its attendant risks, contributed to

120   THE QUEST FOR IDENTITY: INTERNATIONAL RELATIONS OF SOUTHEAST ASIA

a greater willingness among the major parties to search for compromises in the diplomatic arena. The possibility of such a negotiated settlement, as seen earlier, had been marred by lack of agreement on an appropriate negotiating forum. While ASEAN had tried to "internationalise" the conflict, Hanoi preferred a "regional" dialogue. With the evident failure of the ICK, however, another international gathering to discuss the conflict seemed unrealistic. In addition, although ASEAN's efforts to keep the issue alive at the UN by sponsoring an annual resolution in the General Assembly condemning the Vietnamese invasion were successful in isolating Hanoi, they had made little difference to the task of conflict-resolution. Thus, it was logical that ideas to channel the peace process through more limited, "regional" forums were soon advocated, with Indonesia, as ASEAN's officially-designated interlocutor with Hanoi on the Cambodia issue, playing a key role in organizing them.

The regional peace process took shape in the form of two Jakarta Informal Meetings (JIM I in July 1988 and JIM II in February 1989). These meetings marked a high point in ASEAN diplomacy, particularly for Indonesia. While not producing a decisive outcome, the JIM process helped to narrow the differences among the Cambodian factions and the external powers on the crucial issue of power-sharing in post-conflict Cambodia.

The final stages of the Cambodia conflict were dominated by the two sittings of the Paris Peace Conference. Here, the five permanent members of the UN Security Council (P5) as well as Australia, took centre-stage, to some extent at ASEAN's expense. While the first sitting of the conference in 1989 did not resolve the issue of power-sharing among the Cambodian factions and had to be postponed, the second sitting in 1991 resulted in a diplomatic settlement leading to the signing of the Final Act of the Paris Conference on 23 October 1991.[25]

The Paris Agreement was not without limitations. While it marked an end to the so-called "external aspects" of the conflict, i.e. the competitive intervention of China and Vietnam with Soviet backing, its provisions for bringing peace within Cambodia by resolving the issue of power-sharing among the Khmer factions was left uncertain and at the hands of a United Nations authority.[26] But in so far as ASEAN was concerned, the accord was a cause for celebration for two reasons. First, the peace settlement conformed to terms set by ASEAN from the very outset, including the reversal of Vietnamese occupation and the replacement of the regime installed by its invasion. Vietnam had to abandon its desire to impose its security framework on Indochina. Secondly, the accord was seen by the international community as a vindication of ASEAN's diplomatic efforts, notwithstanding the fact that ASEAN's role in the final stages of the process had been over-shadowed by the role of the permanent members of the UN Security Council.

ASEAN also gained new momentum in realising its vision of regional order in Southeast Asia. The positive turn in the Cambodian peace process was accompanied by movement towards bridging the ideological divide of Southeast Asia. The transformation of ASEAN-Vietnam relations had begun as a slow and tortuous process.[27] It was driven by a thaw in Thai-Vietnamese rivalry, which in turn was helped by domestic changes in both countries. Domestic reform in Vietnam aimed at transforming its socialist economy into a market economy. The Vietnamese Communist Party's adoption in 1986 of the policy of "rennovation" or *doi moi* signaled Hanoi's realisation that its occupation of Cambodia entailed severe economic costs that it could no longer afford. Managing the economic crisis at home to ensure regime survival became a more important concern for Hanoi than maintaining its occupation of Cambodia ostensibly to counter external threats to national security.[28] "Renovation" was adopted by the 6th National Congress of the Vietnamese Communist Party and strengthened by a Conference of the Politburo in May 1989 and the 7th National Congress of the Party in June 1991.

Initially, the ASEAN states had ignored the implications of Vietnamese reform for ASEAN-Indochina relations, choosing instead to focus on Hanoi's continued occupation of Cambodia. But the advent of a new Thai government under Prime Minister Chatichai Choonhavan in August 1988 produced a major shift in Thailand's hitherto hardline policy towards Hanoi. Chatichai recognised the opportunities offered by Vietnam's efforts to create a "market mechanism economy", and declared that Thai policy would now aim at "turning the Indochinese battlefields to marketplaces". Initially, Thai economic and political initiatives that flowed from Chatichai's new policy served to undermine ASEAN's consensual diplomacy on Cambodia led by Indonesia.[29] In particular, Bangkok's move to invite Prime Minister Hun Sen in January 1989 caused discomfort and apprehension in other ASEAN capitals, especially Singapore and Indonesia. Yet, the shift in Thai policy, followed by steady progress in the Cambodia peace process, led to a common ASEAN interest in bringing Vietnam into its fold. By 1988, the Vietnamese inclusion within ASEAN had already been foreseen by Malaysia and Indonesia. As Malaysian Prime Minister Mahathir had put it, "if Vietnam subscribes to the ideas of ASEAN, the system of government it practices should not be something that stands in the way of becoming a member of ASEAN".[31]

Continued emphasis on economic reform increased Hanoi's stakes in improved relations with ASEAN. ASEAN membership, it calculated, would create the necessary external political environment for economic growth, help it to normalise ties with the West, attract foreign technology and investment, and reduce dependence on the Soviet Union.[32] ASEAN had the potential to be Vietnam's "bridge" to the West.[33] For ASEAN, Vietnam's transition to a capitalist economy provided significant economic opportunities at a time when the latter's traditional Western markets were turning protectionist. Thus, Chatichai's policy of turning the Indochinese "battlefields to marketplaces" was vindicated as ASEAN governments moved to develop significant trade and investment linkages with Vietnam.

On 5 April 1989, Hanoi surprised the international community by announcing that it would pull out its troops from Cambodia by September 1989 irrespective of the result of the forthcoming peace talks. While ASEAN members, including Thailand, waited for proof of Hanoi's good intentions,[34] there was no question that the Vietnamese move would remove two of ASEAN's most serious concerns about its occupation of Cambodia: (1) Vietnam as a security threat to Thailand, and (2) Vietnam's domination of Indochina as a single strategic unit. Thus, it was not surprising that the announcement of the Vietnamese withdrawal produced speculation about Vietnam eventually becoming a partner of ASEAN through functional cooperation as well as acquiring formal membership in ASEAN.[35] But ASEAN became a victim of its own success in keeping international interest in the conflict alive, because towards the final stages of the peace process, its own diplomacy was overwhelmed by the role of great powers. Thus, by seeking closer relations with Indochina, ASEAN tried to regain some initiative on issues of regional order in the post-Cambodia context.

Another factor conducive to improved ASEAN-Vietnam relations was the changing relationship among the principal great powers involved in Southeast Asian security. Among these changes was the normalisation of Sino-Soviet relations. This meant that Vietnam could no longer count on Soviet backing against China with which it had a major territorial dispute. Vietnamese insecurity was further compounded by the Soviet military retreat from Asia and the cessation of Soviet aid to Vietnam. To compound matters, the prospective withdrawal of the US from the Philippines, and the general cutbacks in superpower military presence in the Asia Pacific, contributed to a greater sense of vulnerability on the part of ASEAN as well as Vietnam vis-à-vis China, which seemed the likely candidate to step into the vacuum created the end of the Cold War. Such insecurity, in turn, initially led Hanoi to seek accommodation with Beijing, but Beijing soon made it clear that any improved relations would be on its own terms, and hence, not entirely satisfactory to Hanoi. Thus, better relations with ASEAN could, from Hanoi's perspective, offset some of the vulnerabilities arising from the changing great power relationship in the Asia Pacific. ASEAN could be a valuable political ally, if not a strategic and economic partner of enough consequence to offset the loss of the Soviet Union as a donor and security guarantor.

The ASEAN-Vietnam rapprochement was visible in both economic and political arenas. Between 1987 (when the liberalisation of Vietnam's economy began) and 1990, the total volume of official trade (exports and imports) between ASEAN and Vietnam increased almost six-fold from US$58.2 million to US$337.2 million.[36] Vietnam became an increasingly attractive target for investments by the ASEAN states as the latter came to recognise the economic potential of Vietnam with its rich natural and human resource base.[37] ASEAN-Vietnam political accommodation also received a boost in November 1990 when Indonesian President Suharto became the highest-ranking ASEAN leader to visit Hanoi since the Vietnamese invasion of Cambodia. Despite warnings from Singapore against "undue haste" in helping Vietnam,[38] opposition within ASEAN to reconciliation with Vietnam became progressively muted. As a sign of changing times, between October 1991 and March 1992, Vo Van Kiet, Chairman of the Council of Ministers of Vietnam, visited all six ASEAN countries. While in Singapore in October 1991, Vo listened to Singapore's Prime Minister Goh Chok Tong speak of his hope for "a more relaxed strategic environment in Southeast Asia as Vietnam's economy and policies become more compatible with the ASEAN countries."[39] Not long afterwards, in January 1992, Thai Prime Minister Anand Panyarachun arrived in Hanoi for the first visit by a Thai head of government since the establishment of diplomatic relations between Thailand and Vietnam in 1975. And in April 1992, Mahathir Mohamad became the first ever Malaysian Prime Minister to visit Hanoi.

An important development in the political arena was the seeming convergence of Vietnam's security philosophy with ASEAN's. Hanoi not only abandoned its past policy of seeking close ties with one great power (the Soviet Union) to oppose another (first the US, and later China) and its neighbouring states (ASEAN). Its new security policy sought "appropriately balanced relationships with great powers outside the region, with a view to resolving disputes for influence between them over the region".[40] This conformed to ASEAN's philosophy of regional autonomy and marked the end of Hanoi's opposition to regional cooperation within the ASEAN framework.

East Asian Regionalisation and Southeast Asian Regionalism

While ASEAN was working hard to achieve greater regional autonomy in the political and security sphere, in the economic arena, its members were actively pursuing policies of greater integration into the global and capitalist system as well as the regional economy of Eastern Asia. The outward-looking economic focus of ASEAN members could be explained by several factors. During the 1970s and 80s, the ASEAN countries were reaping the benefits of export-led industrialisation strategies, with average annual growth rates during the 1965–70 and 1980–90 periods reaching 7.0% and 5.5% for Indonesia, 7.4% and 5.2% for Malaysia, 5.7% and 0.9%

for the Philippines, 10.0% and 6.4% for Singapore and 7.3% and 7.6% for Thailand.[41] From 1965 to 1986 when the Third World almost doubled its share of world foreign direct investment (FDI), the ASEAN states were a major receptacle of this trend in international investment.[42] Although Singapore and Malaysia were the major beneficiaries, the ASEAN states as a whole increased their share of Third World FDI from 10.2% in 1973 to 16.9% in 1986.[43] In total, the market economies of Southeast Asia received investments worth US $38 billion during the 1980s.[44]

Even more important, the ASEAN countries became major targets of the southward movement of Japanese capital. This followed an agreement among the Finance Ministers of the Group of Seven (G-7) industrialised nations in 1985 which gave their central banks the responsibility of raising the value of the yen against the dollar. The agreement, called the Plaza Accord, resulted in a rapid appreciation of the yen. Japanese corporations, already facing high costs at home, were now endowed with vastly increased capital assets. They began relocating to lower-cost countries, initially to South Korea and Taiwan but, later, as the currencies of these countries also appreciated, to Southeast Asia. For Japanese investors, Southeast Asia had the advantages of geographical proximity, reasonably good infrastructure, a cheap but relatively skilled workforce, relative political stability and strong bureaucracy, and policies of economic liberalisation, including the the relatively "open" stance of Southeast Asian governments towards trade, foreign investment and the operations of multinational corporations.[45] Added to these were Southeast Asia's resource endowment and the market potential of a population of over 300 million.[46] During the 1985–89 period, Japan's FDI grew at an average annual rate of 62%.[47] The main beneficiaries of the massive flow of Japanese investment were four Southeast Asian countries, Malaysia, Singapore, Indonesia and Thailand. Between 1987 and 1991, Japanese FDI in ASEAN amounted to US$16.7 billion. Its FDI in Thailand rose from US$250 million in 1987 to US$1.3 billion in 1989, while in Singapore the figure was from US$302 million in 1986 to US$1.9 billion in 1989.[48] Another US$15 billion of Japanese FDI flowed to Southeast Asia between 1990 and 1993, compared to US$10 billion from the US.[49] Taiwan (often for political reasons) and South Korea also directed major portions of their investment towards Southeast Asia. These investment flows and the ensuing trade linkages among these countries contributed to the growing regionalisation of production among the East Asian economies.[50]

This pattern of regionalisation covered both inter-industry and intra-industry or intra-firm trade. In the early 1990s, the regionalisation of East Asian economies was often described in terms of a three-tier production structure. In this structure, Japan exported the most technologically advanced products, followed by the NICs (Singapore, Hongkong, South Korea and Taiwan) exporting skilled labour-intensive products and then by the ASEAN-4 (Malaysia, Indonesia, Thailand and the Philippines) and China exporting labour-intensive products. But this missed the extent of intra-firm trade, i.e. trade taking place within multinational corporations operating in East Asia. According to one estimate, the rise in the index of intra-industry trade during the 1979–88 period was 91% for the Philippines, 90% for Indonesia, 85% for Thailand, and 64% for Malaysia.[51]

The question now emerges whether the regionalisation of East Asian economies helped shape a new regionalism and regional identity.[52] The trade and investment linkages among Japan, Taiwan, South Korea on the one hand and the ASEAN economies on the other implied a trend toward greater East Asian, rather than *Southeast Asian* integration. It is interesting to note that the percentage of intra-ASEAN trade actually declined during the 1980s. But the regionalisation of East Asian economies contributed to pressures for regional trade liberalistaion among the ASEAN countries in several ways. One of the main consequences of the inflow of Japanese investment was the emergence of a series of production networks of parts and component producers linked to assembly plants, especially in the auto and electrical sectors. As a result, Japan wanted to be able to move components from country to country without facing intra-ASEAN trade barriers. As such, Tokyo began urging the ASEAN states to move towards greater trade liberalisation, often using its Official Development Assistance (ODA) and other means to this end. Moreover, Northeast Asian investments in Southeast Asia had a major impact in altering the composition of intra-ASEAN trade which created a new rationale for ASEAN economic cooperation. While in 1980 the percentage of manufactured goods accounted for 28.2% of total intra-ASEAN trade, in 1990, the figure was 61.3%. Much of the increase was due to the activities of multinational corporations in spreading their production bases to several countries in ASEAN. This led the ASEAN governments to realise that an ASEAN trade arrangement would present the ASEAN region as a single investment area to outside investors and thereby make it much more attractive to the latter by offering incentives which no country could individually offer.[53]

While the regionalisation of East Asian economies did create new incentives for greater ASEAN regionalism, it also posed questions as to whether Southeast Asia was following the "Japan model" or an "East Asian" model of economic development. The idea of a "Japan model" and "East Asian model" of development had emerged when political economists challenged neo-classical assumptions about the invisible hand of the marketplace that underplayed the role of the government while stressing the role of "vigorous, competitive and enterpreneural private business".[54] Chalmers Johnson, for example, outlined a "four-fold structural model of East Asian high-growth systems". The model consisted of the following elements: "stable rule by a political-bureaucratic elite not acceding to political demands that would undermine economic growth;

cooperation between public and private sectors under the overall guidance of a pilot planning agency; heavy and continuing investment in education for everyone, combined with policies to ensure the equitable distribution of the wealth created by high-speed growth; and a government that understands the need to use and respect methods of economic intervention based on the price mechanism."[55]

While the question of whether the Southeast Asian economies fitted into this pattern or not would become a matter of intense debate, Singapore and Malaysia consciously evoked Japan as a role model for their own development. Mahathir's "Look East" policy followed Singapore's "Learn from Japan" campaign in late 1970s. At the same time, Southeast Asia's position as an integral part of the East Asian regional political economy was popularised by the somewhat loose and rhetorical notion of "flying geese". The analogy was linked to the Japanese "wild flying geese pattern" in which the leader of the inverse V formation of geese is periodically replaced by a newcomer. In this sense, some Southeast Asian countries, especially Thailand, Malaysia and Indonesia, would represent the next "geese" by picking up the light manufacturing industries (e.g., textiles, food-processing, and simpler electronics) which had been shed by the original NICs (South Korea, Taiwan, Hong Kong and Singapore). Thus, Southeast Asia would be progressively integrated into the process of technological diffusion emanating from Japan.

On the other hand, the validity of models assuming similarities between Southeast Asian and Northeast Asian development could be questioned on the basis of major differences in economic situation and development policy.[56] While some aspects of the Japanese model of industrialisation were to be found in other East Asian, including Southeast Asian, countries, including emphasis on universal primary education, high savings rates, institutional and anti-monopoly reforms by the government to promote competition within the private sector, other factors remained peculiar to Japan. This included Japan's restrictions on private foreign investment (not found in Southeast Asia) and its guarantee of life-time employment. Moreover, the economies of the Southeast Asian countries, including Indonesia, Malaysia, Thailand and the Philippines (called the near-NICs) shared a number of characteristics that differed from those of the original NICs. These differences included a shortage of qualified technical, professional and managerial manpower in the former, owing partly to rigid social structures, religious influences and greater rural poverty. In addition, the Southeast Asian near-NICs showed greater differential in wages between different categories of the workforce and a greater incidence of individualism among the workers. While their domestic savings were high, they was less stable than the original NICs due to commodity price fluctuations on which the economies of the former were much more dependent. In the Southeast Asian near-NICs, pervasive government intervention had the effect of reducing innovation and risk-taking in the private sector. Against this backdrop, one could speak of not one, but several growth and industrialisation models in East Asia; R. Hirono identified three: the Japanese, the newly industrialising and the near-industrialising country models, while insisting that the performance of more advanced countries could not be copied by the less advanced countries.[57]

The fact that the near-NICs of Southeast Asia could not be regarded simply as the latest "geese" could also be seen from the fact that the growth of their manufacturing sectors did not build on an experience of successful import-substituting industrialization. Instead, in many cases, exporting industries were "grafted" onto economies marked by small manufacturing sectors with a high incidence of rent-seeking behaviour. In addition, the Southeast Asian economies had a much higher degree of technological dependence than Korea and Taiwan and much greater dependence on transnational corporations and their subsidiaries for manufactured exports. Southeast Asia had experienced a technologyless industrialisation.[58] Overall, the second-generation NICs differed from the first considerably in terms of their initial conditions of development and their political institutions. This helped to establish claims that Southeast Asia's economic growth was linked to its subregional circumstances, despite economic globalisation and integration with the Northeast Asian economies.

The "ASEAN Way"

While the extent to which the political economy of ASEAN was organised distinctively from that of Northeast Asia could be a matter of debate, there was little question as to the distinctive nature of the diplomatic style and pattern of elite socialisation prevailing within ASEAN. In a variety of ways, ASEAN was able to reinforce its claim as a cohesive regional grouping which had developed a special and successful approach to peace, stability and development. Part of this was articulated in relation to the ideological and economic currents sweeping the communist societies of Indochina. Before the eyes of the international community, ASEAN was able to con-trast Vietnamese "expansionism" with ASEAN's "good-neighbourliness" and desire for regional political stability (implying a territorial and political status quo in Southeast Asia), Vietnam's alliance with the Soviet Union with ASEAN's professed goal of a Zone of Peace, Freedom and Neutrality (ZOPFAN) in Southeast Asia, Vietnam's intense nationalism and ideological fervour with ASEAN's pragmatism and developmentalism, and Vietnam's military suppression of the Cambodian rebels with ASEAN's efforts for a political settlement of the conflict. Moreover, the ASEAN members pointed to the superiority of their model of economic development and political management vis-à-vis the Indochina model. By stressing its "free-market", "anti-communist" and "pro-Western" image, ASEAN gained for itself international goodwill as well as political and economic support from the West.

A more controversial claim made by ASEAN members concerned the so-called "ASEAN Way".[59] Presented by ASEAN leaders to be a distinctive approach to inter-state relations and regional cooperation, the ASEAN Way was supposed to consist of avoidance of formal mechanisms and legalistic procedures for decision-making, and reliance on *musyawarah* (consultation) and *mufakat* (consensus) to achieve collective goals.[60] Moreover, the ASEAN Way implied emphasis on quiet diplomacy and rejection of adversarial posturing in negotiations; a former Indonesian Foreign Minister described *musyawarah* as a setting in which negotiations take place "not as between opponents but as between friends and brothers".[61]

An important example of the ASEAN Way could be found in the provisions concerning dispute-settlement contained in ASEAN's Treaty of Amity and Cooperation. This Treaty (under Chapter IV, Articles 13 to 17) provided for an official dispute settlement mechanism, called a High Council, consisting of ministerial-level representatives from each member state. The role of the Council was to encourage direct negotiations between parties to a dispute and take appropriate measures such as good offices, mediation, inquiry or conciliation to facilitate a settlement. But the ASEAN members never chose to convene a meeting of the High Council, despite the existence of numerous intra-mural disputes. While some would see this as a sign of weakness,[62] ASEAN leaders found in it a vindication of the ASEAN Way. Thus, Noordin Sopiee, a Malaysian scholar, pointed to "the intangible but real 'spirit' of ASEAN, which has been effective in sublimating and diffusing conflicts as in actually resolving them."[63] The implication was that unlike other multilateral bodies, including European regional organisations, ASEAN's approach rested on an assumed capacity to manage disputes without resorting to formal, multilateral measures.

The ASEAN Way of informality was also reflected in its decision to keep its bureaucratic apparatus relatively small, although there was a proliferation of official ASEAN meetings (exceeding 300 a year in the 1990s). While legalistic procedures would be evident in some of the subsequent ASEAN initiatives (such as the Southeast Asia Nuclear Weapon Free Zone Treaty of 1995), the ASEAN brand of "soft regionalism", relying primarily on consultations and consensus remained the norm for much of its history. The Asian economic crisis in the late 1990s has led some ASEAN leaders to adopt a more institutionalised approach to cooperation, but any initiatives in this regard are unlikely to turn ASEAN into a European Union-style bureaucracy.

Conclusion

For Southeast Asia the end of the regional Cold War came with the Vietnamese withdrawal from Cambodia which culminated in the May 1993 Cambodian elections. It became obvious that Vietnam was no longer a significant security concern for the ASEAN states. In December 1989, an agreement was signed by the Malaysian government, the Thai government and the Communist Party of Malaysia (CPM), which ended the over forty-year guerilla struggle to overthrow the Malayan/ Malaysian government. This preceded the collapse of the Communist Party of Thailand, followed by the decline of the Communist New People's Army in the Philippines. Thus ended the threat of communist subversion in the region which itself had contributed to the intra-regional polarisation of Southeast Asia. These developments secured for Southeast Asia a greater and more positive international recognition than was the case during the 1970s, which had been dominated by the Vietnam War and myriad internal revolts. While the decade of the 1980s had begun with Southeast Asia projecting the image of a region divided, the rhetorical quest for "One Southeast Asia" became the organising slogan for the region in the 1990s.

Notes

[1] Cited in The Parliament of the Commonwealth of Australia, Joint Committee on Foreign Affairs and Defence, *Power in Indochina Since 1975*. Canberra: Australian Government Publishing Service, 1981, p.64.

[2] A.W. Cameron (1976) *Indochina: Prospects After 'the End'* , Washington, D.C.: American Enterprise Institute for Public Policy Research, p.25.

[3] K.K. Nair (1984) *ASEAN-Indochina Relations Since 1975: The Politics of Accommodation*, Canberra Papers on Strategy and Defence No.30, Canberra: Australian National University, Strategic and Defence Studies Centre, pp.94–95.

[4] Ibid., p.94.

[5] *The Straits Times*, 6 July 1977.

[6] See S. Simon (1982) *ASEAN States and Regional Security* , Stanford, California: Hoover Instituion Press, p.53; T. Huxley (1986) Indochina as a Security concern of the ASEAN states 1975–81, Ph.D Dissertation, Australian National University, pp.130–188.

[7] *The New Straits Times*, 14 May 1975.

[8] *The Straits Times*, 18 February 1976.

[9] *The Straits Times*, 26 November 1975.

[10] D. Irvine (1982) "Making Haste Slowly: ASEAN From 1975", in Alison Broinowski, ed. (1982) *Understanding ASEAN*, London: Macmillan, p.40.

[11] J. Wanandi (1984) "Security Issues in the ASEAN Region", in K.D. Jackson and M. Hadi Soesastro, eds. (1984) *ASEAN Security and Economic Development*, Research Papers and Policy Studies No. 11, Berkeley: Institute of East Asian Studies, University of California, Berkeley, 1984, p.305.

130 THE QUEST FOR IDENTITY: INTERNATIONAL RELATIONS OF SOUTHEAST ASIA

[12] H. Singh (1999) "Understanding Conflict Resolution in Cambodia: A Neorealist Perspective", *Asian Journal of Political Science*. vol.7, no.1.

[13] H.C. Chan (1980) "The Interests and Role of ASEAN in the Indochina Conflict", paper presented to the International Conference on Indochina and Problems of Security and Stability in Southeast Asia" held at Chulalongkron University, Bangkok, 19–21 June 1980, p.12.

[14] J.M. van der Kroef (1981)"ASEAN, Hanoi, and the Kampuchean Conflict: Between Kuantan and a Third Alternative", *Asian Survey*, vol 21, no.5 (May 1981), pp.516–521.

[15] Ibid., pp.517–18.

[16] E. Becker (1987) "Stalemate in Cambodia", *Current History*, vol. 86, no. 519, April 1987, p.158.

[17] D.J. Steinberg, ed. (1987) *In Search of Southeast Asia A Modern History*, op.cit., p.449.

[18] Japanese Economic Institute, *JEI Reports*, various dates.

[19] L.W. Pye (1967) *Southeast Asia's Political Systems*, 2d ed. Englewood Cliffs, New Jersey: Prentice-Hall Inc., p.92.

[20] R. Stubbs (1994) "The Political Economy of the Asia-Pacific Region" in R. Stubbs and G.R.D. Underhill (1994) *Political Economy and the Changing Global Order*, London: Macmillan, pp.370–71.

[21] A. Acharya (1988) "The United States Versus the U.S.S.R. in the Pacific: Trends in the Military Balance", *Contemporary Southeast Asia*, Vol.9, No.4 , March 1988, pp.282–299.

[22] *Strategic Survey 1982–1983*, London: International Institute for Strategic Studies, 1983, p.95.

[23] G. Hervouet (1988) *The Return of Vietnam to the Interntional System*, Occasional Paper no.6, Ottawa: Canadian Institute for International Peace and Security, p.42.

[24] For details and implications of Gorbechev's Vladivostok speech, see A. Acharya (1987) "The Asia-Pacific Region: Cockpit for Superpower Rivalry", *The World Today*, Vol.43, Nos.8–9 August/September 1987, pp.155–159.

[25] The Final Act of the Paris Conference, signed on 23 October 1991, consists of three documents: (1) "An Agreement on a Comprehensive Political Settlement of the Cambodia Conflict"; (2) "An Agreement Concerning the Sovereignty, Independence, Territorial Integrity and Inviolability, Neutrality and National Unity of Cambodia"; and (3) "Declaration on the Rehabilitation and Reconstruction of Cambodia". The first document contained annexes on "the mandate for UNTAC, military matters, elections, repatriation of Cambodian refugees and displaced persons, and the principles for a new Cambodian constitution".

[26] See M. Leifer (1992) "Power-sharing and Peacemaking in Cambodia", *SAIS Review*, vol.12, no.1, Winter-Spring 1992, pp.139–153.

[27] H. Singh (1997) "Vietnam and ASEAN: The Politics of Accommodation" (1997), *Australian Journal of International Affairs*, vol.51, no.2. pp.215–29.

[28] C.A. Thayer (1992) "The Challenges Facing Vietnamese Communism", *Southeast Asian Affairs 1992*, Singapore: Institute of Southeast Asian Studies, p.352.

[29] For an excellent discussion of the implication of the Chatichai initiative, see: D. Weatherbee (1989) "ASEAN the big Loser in Thai Race for Profit in Indochina", *The Straits Times*, 5 May 1989.

[30] S. Rajaratnam (1989) "Riding the Vietnamese Tiger", *Contemporary Southeast Asia*, vol.10, no.4, March 1989.

SOUTHEAST ASIA DIVIDED: POLARISATION AND RECONCILIATION *131*

[31] *Bangkok Post,* 16 December 1988.

[32] *International Herald Tribune,* 21 March 1989. The Vietnamese desire to join ASEAN was clearly conveyed to visiting Philippine Foreign Secretary Raul Manglapus by Party Chairman Nguyen Van Linh and Foreign Minister Nguyen Co Thach in November 1988. *The Straits Times,* 18 April 1989.

[33] Cited in F. Frost (1991) "Vietnam and Asean: From Enmity to Cooperation", *Trends,* 29 December 1991, p.26.

[34] P. Srichratchanya (1989) "Wait and See", *Far Eastern Economic Review,* 11 May 1989, p.21.

[35] See M. Alagappa (1989) "Bringing Indochina into Asean", *Far Eastern Economic Review,* 29 June 1989, pp.21–22.

[36] International Monetary Fund, *Direction of Trade Statistics Yearbook* as reported in M. Than (1991) "ASEAN, Indochina and Myanmar: Towards Economic Cooperation", *ASEAN Economic Bulletin,* vol.8, no.2, November 1991, p.183.

[37] *Regional Outlook 1991 ,* Singapore: Institute of Southeast Asian Studies, p.58.

[38] "Sense of place, sense of time", *The Straits Times,* 23 November 1990.

[39] C.T. Goh (1991) "Towards a Positive Relationship With Vietnam", *Speeches* (Singapore: Ministry of Information and the Arts), vol.15, no.5, September–October 1991, p.9.

[40] Vietnamese Assistant Foreign Minister H.C. Tran, cited in Thu My (1992) "Rennovation in Vietnam and Its Effects on Peace, friendship and Cooperation in Southeast Asia", in D.Q. Nguen, ed., *Unity in Diversity: Cooperation Between Vietnam and Other Southeast Asian Countries,* Hanoi: Social Science Publishing House, 1992, pp.141–142.

[41] J. Bresnan (1994) *From Dominos to Dynamos,* New York: Council on Foreign Relations Press, p.19.

[42] C. Dixon (1991) *South East Asia in the World-Economy: A Regional Geography,* London: Cambridge University Press. pp.12–13.

[43] Ibid., p.12.

[44] *Far Eastern Economic Review,* 20 March 1993, p.24.

[45] R. Stubbs (1999), "Signing on to Liberalization: AFTA and the Politics of Regional Economic Cooperation", p.10.

[46] C. Dixon.(1991) *South East Asia in the World-Economy: A Regional Geography,* op.cit., p.4.

[47] P. Bowles (1997), "ASEAN, AFTA and the New Regionalism", *Pacific Affairs,* vol.70, no.2, Summer 1997, pp.219–233.

[48] R. Stubbs, "Signing on to Liberalization: AFTA and the Politics of Regional Economic Cooperation", op.cit., pp.10–11.

[49] M. Mason (1994) "Foreign Direct Investment in East Asia: Trends and Critical Issues, CFR Asia Project Working Paper, p.6.

[50] R. Stubbs (1999), "Regionalization and Globalization", in R. Stubbs and G.R.D. Underhill, eds., *Political Economy and the Changing Global Order,* 2nd edition. Toronto: Oxford University Press, p.222.

[51] P. Bowles (1997), "ASEAN, AFTA and the New Regionalism", op.cit., p.223.

[52] R. Stubbs, "Regionalization and Globalization", in R. Stubbs and G. Underhill, eds., *Political Economy and Global Order,* op.cit., p.222.

132   THE QUEST FOR IDENTITY: INTERNATIONAL RELATIONS OF SOUTHEAST ASIA

[53] P. Bowles, "ASEAN, AFTA and the New Regionalism", op.cit., p.223.

[54] S. Awanohara (1987) "'Look East' — The Japan Model", *Asian-Pacific Economic Literature*, vol.1, no.1, May 1987, pp.75–89.

[55] C. Johnson, "Political Institutions and Economic Performance: the Government-Business Relationship in Japan, South Korea, and Taiwan", in F.C. Deyo, ed. *The Political Economy of New Asian Industrialism*, Ithaca: Cornell University Press, p.145.

[56] For further discussion, see W. Hatch and K. Yamamura (1996) *Asia in Japan's Embrace: Building a Regional Production Alliance*, New York: Cambridge University Press.

[57] R. Hirono (1988) "Japan: Model for East Asia Industrialization", in H. Hughes, ed. (1988) *Achieving Industrialization in East Asia*, p.259.

[58] M. Bernard and J. Ravenhill (1995) "Beyond Product Cycles and Flying Geese: Regionalisation, Hierarchy and Industrialisation in East Asia", *World Politics*, vol.47, no.2, pp.171–209.

[59] For a more detailed discussion of the "ASEAN Way" and its role in building regional cooperation, see A. Acharya (1997) "Ideas, Identity, and Institution-Building: From the "ASEAN Way to the Asia-Pacific Way", *Pacific Review*, vol.10, no.3, 1997.

[60] J.N. Mak has identified some of the key features of the ASEAN process: (1) it is unstructured, with no clear format for decision-making or implementation; (2) it often lacks a formal agenda, issues are negotiated on an ad hoc basis "as and when they arise"; (3) it is an exercise in consensus-building; (4) decisions are made on the basis of unanimity; (5) decision-making can take a long time because of the need for consensus, there is no fixed time-table, negotiations may go on as long as it takes to reach a position acceptable to all parties; (6) it is closed, behind-the-scenes, lacking transparency." J.N. Mak (1995) "The ASEAN Process ("Way") of Multilateral Co-operation and Cooperative Security: The Road to a Regional Arms Register?", Paper Presented to the MIMA-SIPRI Workshop on An ASEAN Arms Register: Developing Transparency, Kuala Lumpur, 2–3 October 1995, p.6.

[61] Cited in A. Jorgensen-Dahl, (1982) *Regional Organisation and Order in Southeast Asia*, op.cit., p.166.

[62] M. Leifer (1992) "Debating Asian Security: Michael Leifer Responds to Geoffrey Wiseman", *Pacific Review*, vol.5, no.2, 1992, p.169.

[63] N. Sopiee, "ASEAN and Regional Security", op.cit., p.228.

CHAPTER 5

Managing "One Southeast Asia"

Introduction

The end of the Cold War brought fundamental changes to the international relations and regional identity of Southeast Asia. The image of a region divided, fuelled by the ASEAN-Vietnam conflict, was coming to an end, in parallel with breakthroughs in the Cambodian peace process in the late 1980s. ASEAN's vigorous diplomacy on Cambodia had not only earned it positive international recognition, but also contributed to the impression of Southeast Asia as a region able to provide indigenous solutions to regional problems. Regional cohesion and unity had been bolstered by the easing of intra-mural disputes within ASEAN. The ASEAN model or "ASEAN Way" was presented by leaders and commentators both inside and outside the region as an example of how a region can manage its problems and develop a positive identity in international relations. Both in terms of intra-regional interactions and extra-regional perceptions, Southeast Asia had become the symbol of a dynamic, prosperous and peaceful region.

Yet, the elements of integration and cohesion went hand in hand with the forces of conflict and fragmentation. Much of the latter stemmed from the need to adapt to external developments, such as the changing global economic and security order, including globalisation and strategic multi-polarity. There also emerged fresh challenges to intra-regional relations, including territorial and political disputes which had been dormant or sidelined during the Cold War years. The regional organisation, ASEAN, which had been widely praised for its contribution to stability and prosperity, was presented with a host of new problems, including those stemming from expansion of its membership to realise the aspirations of its founders regarding a united Southeast Asia. Buoyed by its Cambodia success, ASEAN also felt confident enough to assume a major role in developing cooperative security frameworks for the larger Asia Pacific region, partly in response to a perceived strategic void caused by superpower retrenchment and the anxieties linked to the rise of China. Finally, Southeast Asia's integration into the wider regional (East Asian) economy, which accelerated in the late 1980s and early 1990s, created its own host of problems. As the Asian economic crisis in the later part of the 1990s demonstrated, Southeast Asian states had to exist and interact within a larger context of globalisation which would redefine their quest for regional identity and autonomy.

Towards "One Southeast Asia"

Perhaps the most significant project undertaken by Southeast Asian countries following the end of the Cold War was the fulfillment of the "One Southeast Asia" concept. This was a conscious region-building exercise seeking to redefine the Southeast Asian political space. It was the logical extension of the political settlement of the Cambodia conflict following the Paris Agreement of 1991. As the then Thai Prime Minister Anand Panyarachun, contended, ASEAN was working "towards a new regional order that embraces all nations of South-east Asia in peace, progress and prosperity".[1] Foreign Minister Ali Alatas of Indonesia offered an even loftier vision:

> ... one quintessential dividend of peace in Cambodia to strive for would be the dawning of a new era in Southeast Asian history - an era in which for the first time Southeast Asia would be truly peaceful and truly free to deal with its problems in terms of its own aspirations rather than in terms of major-power rivalry and contention; an era marking the beginning of a new Southeast Asia, capable of addressing itself to the outside world with commensurate authenticity and able to arrange its internal relationships on the basis of genuine independence, equality and peaceful cooperation.[2]

At the first post-Cold War summit held in Singapore in 1992, ASEAN leaders declared that they "shall forge a closer relationship based on friendship and cooperation with the Indo-Chinese countries, following the settlement on Cambodia." As a first step, the Singapore Summit Declaration opened the door to all countries of Southeast Asia to sign the Treaty of Amity and Cooperation with Vietnam and Laos being the first signatories, to be followed by Cambodia once its internal political structure was settled through elections held under the UN.[3] By accepting the Indochinese states into the Treaty, ASEAN would commit them to a regional code of conduct, including norms such as pacific settlement of disputes, and non-interference in the internal affairs of each other.

ASEAN pursued the vision of "One Southeast Asia" as a matter of faith. Its realisation, argued Thai scholar Sukhumbhand Paribatra, would "enhance the region's security and well-being", and represent "the fulfillment of a dream to create a region-wide organisation, which had begun some three decades before ...."[4] Several non-governmental initiatives made the same point, including documents such as *Shared Destiny: Southeast Asia in the 21st Century*, issued in 1993, and *Southeast Asia Beyond the Year 2000: A Statement of Vision*, issued by prominent academics and think tanks in 1994. These attested to the fact, as Carolina Hernandez wrote, that "one Southeast Asia ... is a goal increasingly captivating the imagination and support of the region's political and other opinion leaders from academe, the media, the private sector, and other professionals."[5]

Vietnam became ASEAN's seventh member in July 1995. Laos and Myanmar (Burma) were admitted in 1997 while Cambodia's entry was delayed by ASEAN until April 1999 because of its domestic difficulties that followed the breakdown of the Hun Sen-Ranarridh coalition in 1997. The most significant new member was clearly Vietnam, whose entry was not only of profound symbolic value (in terms of ending the polarisation of Southeast Asia) but was also expected to strengthen ASEAN's collective political clout in dealing with the great powers. But the expansion of ASEAN would not be without costs and difficulties.

One key uncertainty was, and remains, whether the new members would be able to fit into the "ASEAN Way" of diplomacy and decision-making, based on the principles of consultation and consensus which the original members of ASEAN had developed over a long period during the Cold War. This was an important challenge due to additional bilateral disputes and problems, such as the Thai-Vietnamese, Vietnamese-Cambodian and Thai-Burmese disputes over territory and resources, that now became matters of concern for the organisation. That the new members would place the same degree of importance upon ASEAN's norms concerning non-use of force and pacific settlement of disputes could not be taken for granted.

Moreover, the entry of new members complicated ASEAN's relations with external powers. Vietnam's inclusion brought ASEAN's "'diplomatic border' right up to the frontier with China.[6] Capitalising on existing Malaysian and Indonesian suspicions of the growing Chinese naval power, Vietnam publicised the "common fear of Chinese policy in the South China Sea" that it shared with certain ASEAN members and sought ASEAN's support in its protest against Chinese oil exploration activities in its claimed territorial waters.[7] The anti-China stance that Vietnam provoked carried the potential to divide the organisation.

Myanmar's induction into the regional organisation at its July 1997 Annual Ministerial Meeting posed a more serious test for ASEAN than Vietnam's. It created considerable tension with the Western powers, especially the EU, while drawing condemnation from Southeast Asian non-governmental organisations as well. ASEAN refused to bow to international pressure to keep Myanmar out on the grounds that doing so would violate its principle of non-interference. Yet granting membership to Myanmar, while essential to the realisation of the ASEAN-10 concept, reinforced a negative image of ASEAN as a champion of authoritarianism.

The postponement of Cambodia's membership by ASEAN Foreign Ministers at a meeting on 10 July 1997 was also a test of ASEAN's non-interference doctrine. Since the decision to postpone was prompted by internal political developments in Cambodia, i.e., Cambodian leader Hun Sen's ouster of his co-Prime Minister Prince Norodom Ranarridh, it seemed like a departure from ASEAN's non-interference doctrine. Yet, as a signatory to the Paris Agreement on Cambodia of 1991, ASEAN did have a legal basis, indeed obligation, to respond to Cambodia's domestic developments that threatened to unravel the peace process. But the episode did underscore the complexities and pitfalls of bringing the "One Southeast Asia" concept to fruition, especially the burden it imposed on ASEAN in dealing with its weaker and politically less stable new member states.

The expansion of ASEAN also reshaped regional economic inter-dependence and integration. It increased the volume of both intra-regional trade and ASEAN's total trade. The participation of the new members in the ASEAN Free Trade Area (AFTA) was expected to increase ASEAN's collective competitiveness and expand the appeal of ASEAN's internal market to foreign investors, and prevent the diversion of investment to other areas such as China and India. For existing members, the liberalisation programmes pursued by the new membership provided important new markets in the event of increasing protectionism in the West. They also offered access to a cheaper source of raw materials and production locations. The new members also stood to benefit economically, ending their economic isolation, expanding the potential for sub-regional cooperation, increasing investment in manufacturing and infrastructure, and sustaining the momentum of current attempts at economic reform. On the negative side, expansion widened economic disparities within ASEAN, creating the basis for polarisation and friction between richer older members and the poorer new ones.

Overall, ASEAN's expansion was celebrated as a political victory for those seeking the unity and integrity of Southeast Asia as a region. In the words of Ali Alatas, the Indonesian foreign minister at the time when ASEAN-10 became a reality, expansion would "increase our ability to deal with these problems now that we are together, not divided nations of seven plus three."[8] But a less sanguine view of ASEAN's expansion was offered by a Thai newspaper, the *Bangkok Post*: "There is also the distinct possibility that the happy 10 will become something of a dysfunctional family unless the more progressive members grasp the formidable challenges that the three newcomers... present."[9] An expanded ASEAN made it more difficult for the group to achieve consensus on key issues, which in turn con-strained its ability to provide leadership and direction to the new members. It threatened to thereby dilute ASEAN's unity and consultative decision-making style and thereby reduce the credibility of the organisation in the eyes of the international community.

Apart from burdens imposed by membership expansion, Southeast Asian regionalism faced a host of new challenges in the 1990s. One set of challenges had to do with the danger of intra-regional conflict. As noted in Chapter 4, some of the sources of regional tension of the Cold War period, such as the spillover effect of communist insurgency in Thailand

and Malaysia, had declined by the early 1990s. The decline of communist insurgency had also occurred in the Philippines and Indonesia. This, in turn, contributed to the ASEAN states' confidence in normalising ties with Vietnam, thereby reviving the prospects for regional unity, and vindicated the ASEAN states' approach to economic development and regional order, thereby giving ASEAN increased clout. On the other hand, the collapse of communist insurgency removed a major basis of ASEAN solidarity, since a common fear of this danger had served as a catalyst for ASEAN's formation and continued survival in the 1960s and 70s. Moreover, the transboundary spillover effect of ethnic separatist movements, including those in the southern Philippines, Aceh and southern Thailand, remained as a source of inter-state tension. For example, the exodus of refugees from Aceh to Malaysia soured Indonesia-Malaysia relations in the 1990s, while Manila's worry that the Moro separatists in Mindanao were receiving support from the Malaysian state of Sabah led Philippine politicians to take a hardline stand on formal renunciation of the Philippine claim to Sabah.

Intra-ASEAN relations were marked by a number of bilateral disputes, such as between Malaysia and Singapore over the Pedra Branca island, between Malaysia and Indonesia over Sipadan and Ligitan islands in the Sulawesi Sea, between Thailand and Malaysia over border-crossing rights, and between Malaysia and Brunei over the Limbang territory. Disputes in the maritime sphere were another source of regional discord. Thanks largely to the Law of the Sea Convention, such disputes had proliferated during the 1980s. In 1989, of the 15 maritime boundaries in the South China Sea (excluding the Gulf of Thailand), 12 were in dispute, two had been agreed (one partially) and one resolved through a joint exploitation agreement. Six of these boundary disputes were between then ASEAN member countries, with Malaysia having disputes with every other ASEAN country.[10] A different category of intra-regional conflict that acquired a new importance in the post-Cold War era was the Spratly Islands dispute involving China, Vietnam, Taiwan, Malaysia, Brunei and the Philippines.[11] This dispute was seen as having the potential to become the next regional "flashpoint of conflict" in Southeast Asia after Cambodia.[12] Overall, as the Governor of Indonesia's Defence Institute warned, Southeast Asia had the potential to become the theatre of "prolonged, low-intensity conflicts without directly involving strong nations" that would replace larger conflicts fuelled by superpower rivalry during the Cold War.[13]

A related challenge to regional order was the military modernisation programmes undertaken by Southeast Asian states.[14] Despite the improved security climate brought about by the end of the Cold War and the peace agreement on Cambodia, Southeast Asia witnessed a large-scale arms build-up. Defence expenditures increased significantly in all the

ASEAN states,[15] who also modernised their armed forces by purchasing sophisticated weapons systems, especially combat aircraft, naval platforms and missiles, in order to enhance their capacity for inter-state conventional warfare.[16] The regional military build-up could not be simply regarded as a full-blown "arms race" driven by interactive rivalry. A number of other factors had contributed to it. The end of the Cold War had left the major defence manufacturers of the world with large quantities of weapons which had to be exported to save jobs. Their consequent scramble for new markets presented the increasingly prosperous ASEAN states with an opportunity to indulge in post-Cold War bargain-hunting. Other considerations behind the military build-up included the perceived need for greater self-reliance in the wake of superpower retrenchment from the region, anxieties about rivalry among extra-regional actors, such as China, Japan and India, domestic inter-service rivalry, the prestige value of sophisticated weapons, and the technological spin-offs of advanced weapon acquisitions. Yet, whatever their cause, the increases in defence spending and arms purchases raised questions about the future of regional unity and order, especially at a time when ASEAN was making strong assertions about its contribution to peaceful relations in the region.

Apart from these somewhat more conventional challenges, Southeast Asian regionalism was also faced with relatively new sets of issue-areas with significant implications for regional cohesion. Foremost among them were human rights, democracy and the environment. The early 1990s saw human rights and democracy gaining a new salience as a result of the changing international environment, especially with the greater emphasis on human rights and democracy in the policy agenda of Western governments. The anti-communist thrust of Western policy, which tolerated blatant human rights abuses by pro-Western Asian governments in the past had ended. Lee Kuan Yew lamented that with the end of the Cold War, US policies toward China, Japan and the countries of East Asia were no longer "guided by strategic and economic considerations as they used to be". Instead, "issues of human rights and democracy have become an obsession with the US media, Congress and the administration."[17] In general, Southeast Asian governments faced increasing pressure from the West over the their human rights records. Violent military suppression of political protesters in Thailand in 1992 and East Timor separatists in 1991 attracted a great deal of negative international publicity. Other ASEAN countries, especially Malaysia and Singapore, were criticised by international human rights watchdogs for their internal security detention laws and lack of democratic freedoms. Faced with the loss of jobs to foreign competition (especially East Asian), trade unions and human rights groups in the US increasingly demanded linking trade privileges for countries such as Malaysia with their allowance of workers' rights.

Initially, it appeared that Southeast Asian governments, especially the ASEAN members, would be capable of presenting a collective front before the West on human rights and democracy. There were two broad areas of relative agreement in their perspectives. The first focused on cultural relativism, which argued that human rights should "vary because of differences in socio-economic and cultural backgrounds".[18] In 1993, prior to the Vienna World Conference on Human Rights, ASEAN worked with other like-minded Asian countries (including China) to draft a declaration which stated that human rights "must be considered in the context of a dynamic and evolving process of international norm-setting, bearing in mind the significance of national and regional particularities and various historical, cultural and religious backgrounds."[19] To strengthen the case for relativism, Southeast Asian elites also presented a communitarian view of governance. Ali Alatas, speaking at the Vienna UN World Conference on Human Rights, argued that Indonesia and the developing world have to maintain a balance between an "individualistic approach" to human rights and the interests of the society as a whole. Singapore invoked the Confucian principle of "community over self".[20]

The second point of commonality amongst ASEAN states was the view that political freedom should not be stressed over economic and social rights. ASEAN Foreign Ministers, meeting in Singapore in July 1993, issued a statement contending that:

> ... human rights are interrelated and indivisible comprising civil, political, economic, social and cultural rights. These rights are of equal importance. They should be addressed in a balanced and integrated manner and protected and promoted with due regard for specific cultural, social, economic and political circumstances...the promotion and protection of human rights should not be politicised.[21]

ASEAN's stance of cultural relativism came under criticism from both Western and local sources. Critics saw it as a justification for authoritarian political control. Moreover, the definition of what constituted cultural standards for defining human rights was not uniform between or within regional societies. Singapore's invoking of Confucian values could not be shared by Islamic Malaysia or Catholic Philippines or Buddhist Thailand. Nor do values converge within individual ASEAN states. In multi-ethnic ASEAN states, any attempt by the ruling elite to articulate a "national" position on human rights would be contested by other groups —especially religious and ethnic minorities. Thus, it would be spurious to talk about a Southeast Asian position on human rights when individual countries could not overcome inter-ethnic competition within their own territories.[22]

Moreover, despite the talk about "Asian values" and the "ASEAN Way", even the elites in ASEAN could not necessarily share the same view on human rights and democracy. As Carolina Hernandez argued, differences among the ASEAN states on human rights questions arose because their governments:

> follow different paths (1) in the way they interpret human rights and democracy, (2) in their assumption of international legal obligations as indicated by their acceptance of international human rights norms embodied in various international human rights documents, (3) in the manner in which they have organized their domestic constitutional, legal and judicial systems as they relate to human rights concerns, and (4) in the degree of political openness of their societies ...[23]

As with human rights, authoritarian Southeast Asian governments were initially alarmed by what they saw as Western efforts to promote democracy in the region. Dismissing the suitability of Western-style democracy for the region, they argued that external pressures, including economic sanctions, would not be effective in bringing about democratic change. They also warned that the West's democratic zeal risked undermining the foundations of regional order based on the inviolability of state sovereignty. It went against one of the most vaunted ASEAN norms: the doctrine of non-interference in the internal affairs of members. With the possible exception of its unprecedented collective support for the democratic Aquino regime, ASEAN, instead of promoting democratic norms, had regarded the internal political structure of a country as being irrelevant to its regional framework.

In the case of Myanmar, ASEAN was instrumental in resisting Western calls for sanctions against the military regime and pushing for a policy of "constructive engagement".[24] Similarly, Vietnam was allowed to join ASEAN despite its communist political structure. These confirmed the nature of Southeast Asian regionalism as an elite-driven process in which human rights and democracy did not figure. Despite its claim to be based on broad historical, cultural and societal ties, the drive for regionalism to a large extent reflected the need of the post-colonial elite to ensure regime survival. The definition of what constituted the region, and who was to be included and excluded were determined by the political and security interests of states, with non-state actors playing a rather marginal role.

But this situation began to change somewhat towards the late 1990s, when non-governmental organisations (NGOs) increasingly made their presence felt over a host of issues including development, environment and human rights issues, thereby developing a parallel track of regionalism. In the 1990s, Southeast Asian governments faced increasing demands for respect for human rights from these NGOs (especially in Thailand, Malaysia, Indonesia and the Philippines).[25] Despite scant resources and government suppression, these groups were encouraged by the favourable international climate for their cause. Their perspectives contrasted sharply with those of the Southeast Asian elites and provided an alternative channel for the development of human rights norms. The NGO community became especially active in the Philippines and Thailand, and in Indonesia after the fall of Suharto.

While the development of human rights NGOs in Southeast Asia owed partly to financial support from Western donor countries, these groups did have strong domestic roots.[26] Some of the larger human rights NGOs in the region developed in response to political crackdowns by their own governments without being prompted by West. This was the case of the emergence of NGOs in the Philippines after the declaration of martial law in 1972, the establishment of the Legal Aid Institute (later called The Indonesian Legal Aid Foundation) in Indonesia in 1971, and the emergence of Thai human rights groups after the coup of 1973.

Apart from action within the domestic sphere, there were some examples of concerted international action by Southeast Asian human rights NGOs. An example of this was the Bangkok NGO Declaration of March 1993, which was a clear rejection of the stand adopted by regional governments. The meeting revealed strong coordination among Southeast Asian NGOs (especially Thai, Malaysian, Filipino and Indonesian), as well as between South and Southeast Asian NGOs. Subsequently, Southeast Asian human rights activists tried unsuccessfully to submit their recommendations to the ASEAN foreign ministers during the inaugural ARF meeting in July 1994. Consequently, they accused the ASEAN foreign ministers of adopting "double standards by only showing concern for problems outside the region such as Bosnia and Rwanda while not demonstrating similar concern for problems that exist within the region, especially in Burma and East Timor." Exiled East Timorese leader Jose Ramos-Horta stated that "while ASEAN can be proud of its contribution to the resolution of the Cambodian conflict, it cannot be proud of its role on East Timor or on Burma". Regional NGOs also pointed out that while the ASEAN foreign ministers were rejecting Western policies linking workers' rights, labour standards and environmental issues with trade as a new type of protectionism, "the ASEAN governments should primarily be held responsible for continued violations of workers' rights, the undermining of labour standards and degradation of the environment in their respective countries."[27]

The wider transboundary focus of human rights NGOs became more pronounced in the case of Thai groups that had "gone regional" and organised joint meetings with Indonesian human rights NGOs. This development prompted one observer to note that "official solidarity [among the ASEAN members] is mirrored by a greater sense of regionalism among non-governmental activists".[28]

While the development of human rights NGOs in Southeast Asia remains limited, the emergence of an NGO perspective on human rights already has important implications for the regional identity and international politics of Southeast Asia. Among other things, it ensures that the demand for human rights extends to and becomes more vocal in every Southeast Asian country. It refutes the government view that human rights is an externally-imposed subject from the liberal West. It creates a more receptive audience for Western human rights policies. And finally, the pressure from NGOs forced Southeast Asian govern-ments to respond and exercise greater sensitivity toward human rights, such as Indonesia's creation of a national human rights commission in June 1993. The campaign of NGOs to oppose ASEAN's policy of "constructive en-gagement" towards the military regime in Myanmar, and to seek self-determination in East Timor marked the beginning of a "bottom-up" vision of regionalism, and a more inclusive approach to defining Southeast Asia's regional identity and role in the international system.

Like human rights and democracy, environmental issues became prominent in the policy agendas of Southeast Asian governments and an important factor behind perceptions of regional interdependence and unity. Nothing highlighted this more than the Indonesian forest fires of 1997. The fires reflected the scale of deforestation in Southeast Asia. According to the United Nations Food and Agriculture Organization (FAO), the rate of deforestation in Southeast Asia accelerated during the 1980s, doubling between 1976–80 and 1986–90.[29] Another estimate found a drop of approximately 17% in the region's forest cover between the late 1960s and the late 80s. The countries where deforestation had been most rapid between 1970 and 1990 were Vietnam (68.8% 124, 820km+), the Philippines (56.0% 83, 980km+) and Thailand (41.7% 106, 900km+). However Indonesia (17.1% 243, 769km+) had lost the most rainforest in gross terms. Thailand and the Philippines, threatened with the near extinction of their existing reserves, banned logging in 1989.[30] With more than 10% of the world's rainforests, and 40% of Asia's, Indonesia increasingly became the main source of tropical timber in the region. Each year, according to the international environmental organisation Earth Action, the nation had been destroying a forested area larger than Lebanon, reflecting its role as one of the world's largest exporters of wood products.[31]

Fires on the islands of Sumatra and Kalimantan had been a severe problem for many years,[32] leading to the loss of vast tracts of virgin rainforest which according to one estimate would take up to 500 years to recover. (Independent reports confirmed losses of between 750,000 ha to 1.7 million ha of forest due to the 1997 fires.[33]) Of greater significance to the other ASEAN members in underscoring the transnational aspect of environmental degradation was the haze that covered much of Indonesia

MANAGING "ONE SOUTHEAST ASIA" 143

and neighbouring Singapore and Malaysia. An estimate in 1997 suggested that the health of over 40,000 people across the region had been affected by the haze.[34] The Economy and Environment Programme for Southeast Asia (EEPSEA) put the economic cost of 1997's haze at US$1.4 billion. Private estimates put the total cost of the forest fires and the ensuing haze to the Southeast Asian region at US$5-6billion.[35]

Not surprisingly, therefore, the haze drew the ire of Singapore and Malaysia, prompting an apology from President Suharto. It also ensured that environmental issues would come into the agenda of regional inter-governmental cooperation. Regional efforts to help Indonesia cope with the haze problem included the institutionalisation of a new ministerial meeting on the haze in November 1997, the implementation of a regional haze action plan and the establishment of a new haze task force coordination unit at the ASEAN Secretariat. But the result of cooperation has not been encouraging, suggesting inadequate political will and collective capacity for regional disaster management.

Southeast Asia and Asia Pacific Security Cooperation

One post-Cold War development with important implications for Southeast Asian regionalism and regional identity was the emergence of Asia Pacific multilateral institutions in the security and economic sphere. While the "One Southeast Asia" concept was motivated by a desire to enhance regional cohesion and clout, Southeast Asia's participation in these wider regional groupings was conditioned by the need to preserve regional identity in the face of apparently overpowering extra-regional security and political challenges.

The development of security multilateralism in the Asia Pacific region was shaped by trends in the international system that accompanied the end of the Cold War.[36] The post-Cold War milieu, some Southeast Asian analysts feared, would see an unleashing of conflicts which had been effectively frozen or "suppressed" during the colonial era and the subsequent period of superpower rivalry.[37] A major determinant of the early post-Cold War international environment had to do with the reduction in superpower forces in the Asia Pacific region. The withdrawal of the Soviet presence in Cam Ranh Bay, Vietnam was followed by the removal of the US bases in the Philippines. At its peak in the mid-1980s, the Soviet presence in Cam Ranh Bay had aroused strong concerns in ASEAN, which feared the threat it could pose to the security of sealanes and the impetus it might give to Vietnamese designs in Southeast Asia. But by January 1990, the Soviets had reportedly withdrawn most of their forces at Cam Ranh Bay.[38] The Soviet withdrawal caused concern that it would reduce the stakes of the US in its Philippines bases and precipitate a reduction in the American military presence in the Pacific that ASEAN considered vital to regional stability. And for at least some ASEAN states, particularly Malaysia, the Soviet withdrawal from Vietnam removed a useful counterweight to China's regional ambitions.

Adding to the concern were uncertainties about the American military presence in the Pacific in general, and in the Philippines bases in particular. Despite repeated US statements that any cutbacks in its military presence would not be substantial, the initial US plan to reduce its military presence in Japan, South Korea and the Philippines by 15%, became a source of ASEAN's security concern.[39] All ASEAN member states acknowledged the role of the US as a stabilising force in the region. Even Indonesia and Malaysia, the staunchest supporters of ASEAN's ZOPFAN concept, conceded the need for a US presence in the region.[40]

Although there was no regional consensus as to the nature of the threat posed by developments in great power relations, it was clear that the rise of China evoked the most immediate concern in Southeast Asia in the post-Cold War era. Sino-ASEAN relations had improved dramatically during the Cambodia conflict. Not only was ASEAN able to secure a Chinese pledge to cease its support for communist insurgencies in the region, but China was also seen as a potential guarantor of ASEAN's security against the Vietnamese threat. Thailand became a de facto ally of Beijing, developing a substantial arms transfer relationship. The end of the Cold War and the Cambodian conflict coincided with the growing military and economic power of China. The end of the Sino-Soviet conflict and Soviet force withdrawals from their common border enabled Beijing to devote more resources and attention to contingencies in the South China Sea.[41] While watching these developments about China with concern, the ASEAN countries also continued to maintain a very ambivalent attitude towards Japan, although, as Lee Kuan Yew said, in ASEAN, "fear of Japan's re-militarisation [was] more emotional than rational."[42] Any prospect of a unilateral Japanese security posture was viewed with grave suspicion. Japan's role in UN peacekeeping operations through the use of noncombatant soldiers could be tolerated.[43] But increased US pressure on Tokyo to enhance its maritime defence capabilities in the late 1980s caused discomfort in Southeast Asia, where some also feared that a major US military withdrawal from the region would prompt Japanese remilitarisation.[44] And concerns persisted in ASEAN capitals about further US force reductions in the region, despite assurances by US officials to the contrary. In addition, ASEAN governments feared that the retreat of the US, by prompting Japan to become a more self-reliant military power, could provoke China to increase its own military capability, thereby creating a new security dilemma in Asia.

The shift from superpower to regional power rivalry formed the core of security concerns in Southeast Asia. By seeking to balance each other, regional powers might engage in a competition that would make a multipolar regional order much less stable than the Cold War system. Regional order could also be challenged by rivalry between the US and two of the leading regional powers: China and Japan. The prospective escalation of the US-Japan trade dispute threatening the fate of the US-Japan security relationship constituted the worst-case scenario. The state of Sino-US relations was another key factor in Southeast Asian security. The growing friction between the US and China over human rights and Washington's threat of economic sanctions against China was seen by Lee Kuan Yew as having "serious long-term consequences for Asia-Pacific peace and stability."[45]

It is against the backdrop of these concerns and uncertainties that ASEAN began to develop new frameworks and responses in the political and security sphere. While the project to complete "One Southeast Asia" proceeded, ASEAN governments also felt that Southeast Asian-specific solutions would not suffice, given the seriousness of the challenges facing them on the security front. They would also need to address these challenges at the wider Asia Pacific level. This would be a major departure from ASEAN's security approach, which had during the Cold War focused essentially on the sub-regional environment of Southeast Asia. Then the ASEAN framework had professed the need for regional autonomy with a strong suspicion of externally-inspired solutions to regional problems. Now, ASEAN's approach to regional security came to embrace a wider concept of "region" than in the previous era. Southeast Asia could no longer hope to insulate itself from the impact of security trends in the wider Asia Pacific region set in motion by new patterns of interaction among the US, China, Japan and Russia.

This realisation also necessitated a rethinking of the ZOPFAN concept. ZOPFAN had already proved to be an impracticable concept because some ASEAN members, especially Singapore and Thailand, saw it as detrimental to regional stability given the need for the region to retain the "balancing wheel" role of the US to ensure its security and economic progress. [46] Now, in the post-Cold War context, the relevance of ZOPFAN was even further undermined. Although ASEAN members maintained a declaratory commitment to ZOPFAN, even its staunchest supporters conceded that the ideal required reassessment and adjustment in view of the changing regional strategic environment.[47] Frameworks of security that were more inclusionary of regional and extra-regional powers had to be given due consideration.

Adding pressure towards such rethinking were proposals for "common security" and "cooperative security" advanced by other Asia Pacific nations.[48] These proposals initiated by Russia, Australia and Canada, called for the creation of a regional security institution to facilitate confidence-building and conflict resolution within the region. Security multilateralism was viewed by these proponents as a more desirable

146 THE QUEST FOR IDENTITY: INTERNATIONAL RELATIONS OF SOUTHEAST ASIA

alternative to deterrence-based security underpinned by US military alliances. The very fact that the region's former adversaries, such as the ASEAN states and Vietnam, Russia and Japan, and China and Russia, had been searching for a common ground in which to bury the Cold War hatchet, further encouraged ideas concerning multilateral approaches to security issues.

ASEAN's initial response to these proposals was marked by some apprehension and skepticism. ASEAN leaders argued that the Asia Pacific theatre was too complex and diverse to allow for European-style multi-lateral security cooperation. Moreover, the fact that almost all the proposals for regional security cooperation came from "outside" powers and that some of these were based on European models of security cooperation aroused suspicions in ASEAN, which had hitherto believed that regional order must be based on indigenous conceptions of security without any kind of influence or interference by countries outside of the region.

But ASEAN could not ignore the growing call for multilateralism. Lest the outside powers seize the initiative, ASEAN had to come up with an "indigenous" framework that would enable it to play a central role in developing any multilateral framework for regional security. In this sense, ASEAN was faced with an opportunity to project its subregional experience in security cooperation into a larger regional arena and thereby enhance its relevance and role as a regional institution in the post-Cold War era. Against this backdrop, on 28 January 1992, at the end of the fourth summit meeting held in Singapore, ASEAN leaders agreed to "promote external dialogues on enhancing security as well as intra-ASEAN dialogues on ASEAN security cooperation".[49] They expressed support for informal and consultative mechanisms within the existing ASEAN framework, especially through the annual meeting between ASEAN foreign ministers and their dialogue partners (called the ASEAN Post-Ministerial Conferences). This move, which ensured that ASEAN would remain at the centre of the evolving security apparatus in the Asia Pacific, culminated in the formation of the ASEAN Regional Forum in 1994.

The ARF began life with 18 members: Brunei, Malaysia, Indonesia, Thailand, Singapore, the Philippines, Vietnam, Laos, the US, Canada, South Korea, Australia, Japan, New Zealand, the European Union, Russia, China and Papua New Guinea (Cambodia joined a year later, while India and Myanmar were accepted as members in 1996). The ARF was not only the first truly "multilateral" security forum covering the wider Asia Pacific region, it was also the only "regional" security framework in the world in which all the great powers (including the US, Russia, Japan, China, India, as well as Britain, France and Germany as part of the European Union delegation) were represented.

The founding statement of the ARF defined its goals as the creation of a "more predictable and constructive pattern of relations for the Asia

Pacific region."[50] The key principle underlying the ARF was the notion of "cooperative security", defined by Gareth Evans, the then foreign minister of Australia, as an effort to build "security with others rather than against them."[51] Through the ARF, ASEAN sought to influence and manage regional order in five ways. The first was to offset the strategic uncertainties of the post-Cold War period. A multilateral security forum could help to avoid misperceptions and generate new ideas about, and approaches to, regional order. The second was to "engage" China in a system of regional order to dilute the threat to regional stability posed by its unprecedented economic growth and military build-up. This strategy was seen as being preferable to the alternative of "containment" which ASEAN members saw as an impractical and dangerous strategic option. Thirdly, the ARF could be a useful device to ensure the continued engagement of the US in the region's security affairs. This in turn would preclude the emergence of an independent Japanese security role, a development which ASEAN viewed as highly destabilising. The fourth goal that ASEAN sought to pursue through the ARF was to ensure that intra-regional conflicts, such as the territorial dispute in the South China Sea, could be managed peacefully through multilateral norms and principles. To this end, the ARF sought to develop measures of confidence-building and preventive diplomacy to constrain the use of force in inter-state relations. Finally, the ARF provided ASEAN, a coalition of small powers, with a measure of influence over great power geopolitics in the region. Acting collectively through a multilateral forum, ASEAN could shape the development of a set of ideas and principles which might persuade the region's major powers to view diplomacy and "rules of acceptable conduct", rather than arms races and alliances, as the principal means of preserving regional equilibrium.

Since its inception, the ARF has been characterised by two broad features: incrementalism and soft institutionalism. Incrementalism, implying a step-by-step approach to security collaboration, is evident from a document entitled "The ASEAN Regional Forum: A Concept Paper" developed by ASEAN in 1995. The paper envisages three stages of security cooperation: confidence-building, preventive diplomacy, and conflict resolution.[52] The initial measures of confidence-building selected by the ARF include annual exchange of information on defence postures on a voluntary basis, increased dialogues on security issues on a bilateral, sub-regional and regional basis, forging of senior-level contacts and exchanges among military institutions, and participation of the ARF members in the UN Conventional Arms Register. Though limited, the ARF's confidence-building initiatives are an important step towards greater regional security cooperation. The outlook for preventive diplomacy, however, is more constrained due to concerns by some members (especially China) that it would violate the principle of non-interference in the internal affairs of states.

148 THE QUEST FOR IDENTITY: INTERNATIONAL RELATIONS OF SOUTHEAST ASIA

ASEAN's involvement in the ARF is marked by a number of problems. Under its guidance, the ARF has adopted an evolutionary and non-legalistic approach to security cooperation. Critics of the ARF argue that it will remain essentially a "talk shop", rather than an instrument of collective action in regional conflicts. ASEAN's style and leadership of the ARF does not sit well with the some of the Western members who would like the ARF to develop quickly and adopt concrete measures.[53] They doubt whether the so-called "ASEAN Way" of consultations and consensus-building will be effective in the Asia Pacific context. Finally, by getting too closely involved in a wider regional cooperation framework, ASEAN might have risked the dilution of its own quest for a Southeast Asian autonomy and identity. Its leadership role in the ARF challenges the conception of Southeast Asia as a distinctive security region.

Southeast Asia and Asia Pacific Economic Cooperation

As in the security arena, the development of Asia Pacific multilateralism in the economic arena also poses a challenge to Southeast Asia's regional identity. In the late 1980s and early 1990s, ASEAN took steps to develop a free trade area. This was in marked contrast to its lackadaisical attitude towards regional economic cooperation in the 1960s and 70s. That attitude, as Stubbs points out, had to do with a concern with sovereignty as well as the domestic economic conditions in the member states. Until the late 1980s, the most populous ASEAN countries, Indonesia, Thailand, the Philippines and Malaysia had remained heavily reliant on raw material exports and import substitution strategies. Indonesia's oil boom of the 1970s discouraged export promotion strategies. In Malaysia, the advent of the New Economic Policy (NEP) aimed at giving indigenous Malays a greater share of the national wealth, resulted in massive government inter-vention, especially in creating import-substituting heavy industries. These conditions lessened the urgency of intra-regional trade liberalisation, which is more commonly associated with economies geared towards export promotion. Moreover, the level of intra-ASEAN trade had remained fairly low due to colonial linkages and the impact of the Vietnam War. As the 1990s approached, ASEAN members' trade with US, West Europe and Japan was considerably higher than intra-ASEAN trade.[54]

A number of developments led to a shift in the attitude of the ASEAN states towards trade liberalistaion. The first had to do with changes in the international poltical economy in the 1980s, especially the global economic downturn in the early 1980s, rising protectionism in the US, the international debt crisis and the consequent reduction in flow of Northern capital to the South, and the economic recession in the ASEAN countries in the early 1980s. These developments made the ASEAN

Table 5.1: Intra-ASEAN Exports as a Percentage of Total Value of Exports, 1970-87

	Year	Brunei	Indonesia	Malaysia	Philippines	Singapore	Thailand	Total
Brunei	1970	-	0	82.2	0	1.0	0	83.2
	1976	-	0	6.3	1.7	1.7	0	9.7
	1982	-	0	0.03	2.2	0.4	0.5	3.1
	1987	-	0.03	0.6	2.6	6.6	12.3	21.6
Indonesia	1970	0	-	3.2	2.3	15.5	0	21.0
	1976	0	-	0.3	1.1	7.5	0.02	8.9
	1982	0	-	0.3	1.0	5.2	0.02	6.52
	1987	0.05	-	0.6	0.4	6.1	0.6	7.8
Malaysia	1970	0.6	0.6	-	1.7	21.6	0.9	25.4
	1976	0.7	0.4	-	1.5	18.3	1.3	22.2
	1982	0.3	0.3	-	1.0	25.7	3.0	30.3
	1987	0.5	0.8	-	1.8	18.0	2.8	23.9
Philippines	1970	0	0.2	0	-	0.7	0.3	1.2
	1976	0	0.5	0.2	-	2.2	0.3	3.2
	1982	0.1	1.1	3.6	-	2.2	0.3	7.3
	1987	0.8	1.1	2.0	-	3.4	21.7	29.2
Singapore	1970	1.6	-	21.9	0.3	-	3.3	27.1
	1976	1.5	-	15.2	0.8	-	3.0	20.8
	1982	1.7	-	17.7	1.6	-	3.8	24.8
	1987	1.2	-	14.2	1.5	-	4.2	21.1
Thailand	1970	0	2.3	5.6	0.1	7.0	-	15.0
	1976	0.1	5.2	4.2	1.0	6.8	-	17.2
	1982	0.1	2.0	5.4	0.5	6.8	-	14.7
	1987	0.1	3.3	3.1	0.6	8.7	-	15.8

Total value of intra-ASEAN exports as a percentage of the total value of members exports 1970 – 21.5%, 1976 – 14.8%, 1982 – 22.7%, 1987 – 17.1%.

Source : IMF *Directory of Trade Statistics Year Book*, Washington, various issues.

countries more aware of their economic vulnerabilities and contributed to moves towards regional cooperation. A second factor was the growing influence of business pressure groups in ASEAN member states with an interest in regional trade liberalisation. A third factor was political in nature. It stemmed from ASEAN's own desire to retain its relevance in the face of the proposals and formation of newer and wider regional institutions such as the Asia-Pacific Economic Cooperation.[55]

At the Singapore Summit in 1992, ASEAN decided to create an ASEAN Free Trade Area. Under AFTA, members were given until the year 2003 (although the new members were given an extension) to bring down their tariffs to between 0 to 5% (AFTA's original deadline for reducing tariffs to that level was a 15-year period beginning in January 1993, but it was brought forward for the original ASEAN-Six to 2003). AFTA's evolution, its scope and the extent of its institutionalisation conformed to the "ASEAN Way."[56] This meant a preference for informality, non-adversarial bargaining, consensus-building and non-legalistic procedures for decision-making rather than formal institutions and legal commitments.[57] ASEAN members agreed that AFTA be moved forward at a pace with which all governments felt comfortable.[58]

Apart from AFTA, ASEAN undertook a number of new initiatives to promote regional economic cooperation in the 1990s. These included cooperation in securing greater foreign investment through the creation of an ASEAN Investment Area, an ASEAN Investment Plan, and an ASEAN Investment Code. Another initiative, aimed at generating greater trade in services, would be achieved by liberalising market access and national treatment in key service sectors, such as tourism, maritime transport, air transport, telecommunications, construction, business, and financial services. Cooperation in intellectual property matters would be encouraged through the creation of an ASEAN Patent System and an ASEAN Trademark System.

Despite the AFTA and these other initiatives, state-centric trade liberalisation measures remained too modest to create a noticeably high degree of regional interdependence in Southeast Asia. The level of intra-ASEAN trade as proportion of total ASEAN trade remained around 16–17% in the 1980s.[59] From 1991 to 1995, trade among the ASEAN Six grew at an annual rate of 21.6%, totalling US $137 billion, or 23% of their total trade. This compared with the ASEAN Six's world trade which grew at a slower annual rate of 15% over the same period. (But if transhipment through Singapore is discounted, the level of intra-ASEAN trade falls to about 12%.)[60] Moreover, AFTA remained plagued by fears among ASEAN members concerning the unequal distribution of gains. This was aggravated by the differing levels of development between the ASEAN Six and the new ASEAN members, even though the latter were been allowed extensions beyond the 2003 deadline to bring down their tariffs to the required 0 to 5% level.

The low level of intra-regional trade was not the only challenge facing ASEAN in developing Southeast Asia as an economic region. A second challenge came from the global economic situation in the late 1980s and early 1990s. For the ASEAN states, one of the most troubling developments was the sign of rising protectionism in the West. This predated the crisis in the Uruguay Round of GATT talks in the late 1980s, but the latter contributed a sense of urgency. In March 1991, Singapore's Goh Chok Tong specifically argued that it was in ASEAN's interests to see free trade and GATT work but if this was not the case "and others [were] forming trading arrangements, then there would be no choice but for us to look after our own interests by following what others do".[61] A related development was the prospect of a declining flow of investment from Western countries to Southeast Asia as the East European market opened up. A former Finance Minister of Malaysia, Daim Zainuddin, warned that "... the expected diversion of private foreign capital to Eastern Europe would...necessitate that ASEAN lay greater stress on the intra-regional flow of capital, to lessen the dependence on external sources to maintain the momentum of growth."[62] Though overstated, the chances of a crunch in the availability of investment capital aggravated ASEAN's concerns regarding the competition it could face in attracting Western capital.

These perceived global economic trends shaped ASEAN's interest in, and attitude towards, the development of wider regional economic frameworks, especially the Asia-Pacific Economic Cooperation (APEC). APEC grew out of various academic and semi-official initiatives, especially the Pacific Economic Cooperation Conference set up in 1980 to explore and advance free trade and economic cooperation in the Asia Pacific region. APEC was conceived as a more formal inter-governmental vehicle for cooperation which could allow the region as a whole to co-ordinate an approach to GATT and increase the liberalization of trade in the area.[63] Growing support for Asia Pacific economic regionalism was partly a reaction to the anticipation of European integration and the Free Trade Agreement between Canada and the US. The first meeting of APEC, attended by ministers from 12 Pacific states (the US, Canada, Japan, Australia, New Zealand, South Korea and the six countries in ASEAN), met between 5–7 November 1989 in Canberra, Australia. ASEAN governments were initially lukewarm to APEC fearing that it would be dominated by non-Southeast Asian countries such as Japan, Australia and the United States. ASEAN wished to be the model for APEC and was keen to ensure that the new grouping should not on any account reduce the activities or status of ASEAN. ASEAN wished to remain as the core of multilateral processes in the region; other regional institutions should assess the ASEAN experience and proceed from there. Subsequently, ASEAN came to accept APEC, recognising ASEAN and APEC as "concentric circles."[64] But its endorsement of the wider regional economic body came with a number of conditions: (1) APEC should not deal with political and

152 THE QUEST FOR IDENTITY: INTERNATIONAL RELATIONS OF SOUTHEAST ASIA

security issues; (2) APEC should not lead to the formation of a trade bloc; (3) APEC's institutional arrangements should not reduce the importance and role of existing Asia Pacific institutions for cooperation; and (4) ASEAN's machinery should be the centre of the APEC process.[65]

ASEAN saw APEC as a useful forum for managing trade conflicts within the region, as well as a platform to advance ASEAN's interest in global multilateral trade negotiations.[66] Another contribution of APEC was seen to lie in countering some of the uncertainties in the regional investment climate caused by developments in Eastern Europe. At a time when Eastern Europe was attracting more attention from the Western countries, APEC would provide an extra incentive for Japan and other major regional economies to invest in Southeast Asia.[67]

Despite its acceptance of APEC, some ASEAN members felt that a regional economic group involving the developed and developing economies of the Asia Pacific was not the most desirable way to address the economic problems of the 1990s. Malaysia in particular resented the fact that APEC was an Australian initiative, that it was dominated by Western members at the expense of ASEAN, and that it did not reflect the level of de facto economic integration achieved within the East Asia region, which by some measures exceeded trans-Pacific integration. These factors led Malaysia's Prime Minister, Mahathir Mohamad, to call for the establishment of an exclusive East Asian Economic Grouping (EAEG) later changed to East Asian Economic Caucus or EAEC, in December 1990, soon after the collapse of the Uruguay Round talks over agriculture subsidies. Malaysia described the proposal as a move to "counter the threat of protectionism and regionalism in world trade".[68] The most striking aspect of the EAEC was the exclusion from its membership of the key members of APEC, including the US and Australia. The EAEC was to comprise the ASEAN countries, Taiwan, Hong Kong, and Japan, with the latter clearly being assigned the pivotal role.[69]

On the face of it, the EAEC concept was firmly rooted in the economic realities of the region.[70] Not only was trade among East Asian countries expected to exceed trans-Pacific trade in the 1990s in terms of invest-ment, the 1980s saw a massive increase in Japanese private investment in the region.[71] South Korean and Taiwanese investment in Southeast Asia had added to the massive influx of Japanese capital, creating a strong sense of East Asian economic interdependence.

However, if Malaysia's intention was to test the reaction of the ASEAN partners to the idea of a trade bloc that would "counter the emergence of protectionism and regionalism in world trade" through similar methods, then it clearly made little headway. Its ASEAN partners, not convinced that a genuine trade bloc would indeed be possible within the GATT framework and acceptable to the major trading partners of ASEAN, expressed reservation. Strong opposition from the US was clearly stated by Richard Solomon, Assistant Secretary of State for East Asia and Pacific, who argued that the EAEC would be a "very unwise direction to proceed".[72] In the face of US opposition and Japanese reluctance, the EAEC concept remained stagnant despite a compromise formula adopted by ASEAN which called for the EAEC to function as a caucus within APEC. But the subsequently convened summits under the Asia-Europe Meeting (ASEM) framework would see all the projected members of the EAEC participate with the members of the EU, prompting Malaysia to claim that the EAEC idea had in effect become a reality. Another significant development was the proposal for an East Asian Forum comprising ASEAN members and Japan, China and South Korea, which was given a strong push in November 1999. But the ASEAN countries continue to adhere to a conception of economic approach that rejects inward-looking trade structures and seeks the maintenance of an open and multilateral international trade regime.

Asia Pacific multilateral institutions like the APEC and EAEC were not the only entities raising questions about the concept of Southeast Asia as a distinctive economic region. Another challenge came from trends in transnational production, in the form of what has been known variously as "growth triangles", "natural economic territories" or "subregional economic zones" (here, the term "growth triangle" will be used as a generic concept). At least four such areas emerged in the first part of the 1990s: the Singapore-Johor-Riau (SIJORI) triangle; the Indonesia-Malaysia-Thailand Growth Triangle (IMT-GT); the East ASEAN Growth Area (EAGA) involving Sabah, Sarawak, and Labuan in Malaysia, North Sulawesi, East Kalimantan and West Kalimantan in Indonesia, the Mindanao region of the Philippines and Brunei; and finally, the Growth Quadrangle of Mainland Southeast Asia, consisting of China's Yunnan province, Laos, Thailand and Myanmar.

By their very nature, the growth triangles challenged the traditional state-centric regional concept of Southeast Asia consisting of officially defined state boundaries of the ten member countries of ASEAN. But they have contributed to enhanced intra-regional security accruing from greater economic integration and confidence-building.[73] They also re-established some of the intra-Southeast Asian economic linkages lost during the colonial period. Moreover, their emergence reflected a lessening of economic nationalism, which had in the past thwarted the development of a regional identity and regional cooperation. Many of the states involved in the growth triangles had been bitter enemies in the not-too-distant past. The emergence of a growth triangle linking Borneo and Mindanao, for example, was striking given the long-standing dispute between Malaysia and the Philippines over Sabah. The case of the Malaysia, Indonesia and Thailand (IMT-GT) triangle was also significant given the periodic strains in the Thai-Malaysian relationship over

Malaysian support for Thai Muslim separatists and the problems in Malaysia-Indonesia ties over the exodus of Acehenese refugees to Malaysia. Thus, the shared commitment of these states to a growth triangle suggested at the very least that the traditional element of the region's high politics was no longer a sufficient barrier to serious attempts at economic regionalism. On the other hand, these entities remained underdeveloped and their management was plagued by intra-mural differences. They could not overcome the political suspicions and differences in economic approach among Southeast Asian countries.

Globalisation and the Crisis of Regional Identity

The preceding sections have dealt with the challenges to Southeast Asia coming from the geographic "deepening" and "widening" of regional space managed by ASEAN. Another set of challenges which threatened regional identity swept through Southeast Asia during the last part of the decade, highlighting the impact of globalisation on regionalism. The Asian economic crisis which began in mid-1997 underscored the pitfalls of economic development strategies adopted by the Southeast Asian states based on an emphasis on foreign investment and export-oriented industralisation strategies without effective regulatory mechanisms.[74] While the crisis was not "Southeast Asian" in scope (apart from Korea, it acquired the attributes of a global crisis affecting countries as far apart as Russia and Brazil), the "contagion" effect of the crisis was most seriously felt in Southeast Asia. Moreover, the crisis was peculiarly Southeast Asian in the way it thretened to unravel and reshape intra-regional politics.

The crisis toppled the Suharto regime and generated intra-regional strains — especially evident in relations between Singapore, Indonesia and Malaysia. The rise of Islamic political forces in Indonesia following the downfall of Suharto rekindled anxieties in Singapore about being a "Chinese island in a sea of Malays". The forced repatriation of illegal workers, carried out by Malaysia and Thailand, challenged domestic stability (as evident in rioting by Indonesian workers) in Malaysia, fuelled interstate tension and regional insecurity. Singapore's leaders, for example, were apprehensive that instability in Indonesia would have spillover effects similar to the 1960s transition from Sukarno to Suharto. Moreover, in precipitating the downfall of Suharto, a founding father and key anchor of Southeast Asian regionalism, the crisis also cast a shadow over ASEAN's future.

The crisis undermined the "prosper-thy-neighbour" philosophy of ASEAN members. Singapore-Malaysia relations were poisoned by Malaysia's perception that Singapore was not interested in helping it out of the economic downturn by offering unconditional financial assistance that would have reduced its need for outside help with strings attached.

MANAGING "ONE SOUTHEAST ASIA" 155

Similar charges were levelled against Singapore by Suharto's immediate successor, President B.J. Habibie, who openly criticised Singapore as not being "a friend in need".[75] This was notwithstanding the US$5 billion in aid that Singapore had agreed to provide Indonesia in conjunction with the IMF rescue package. (The real reason for Habibie's anger was Lee Kuan Yew's earlier criticism of the choice of Habibie as Vice-President by Suharto, which Lee implied would be poorly received by the market and hinder Indonesia's recovery.)

The crisis exacerbated intra-Southeast Asian differences in national attitudes over human rights and democracy, with Thailand and the Philippines openly championing the virtues of democracy over authoritarianism in ensuring economic progress. The crisis also put the proponents of cultural relativism and "Asian values" on the defensive.[76] By showing the relative resilience and effectiveness of democratic political systems in Thailand and the Philippines in managing the dangers of globalisation, in contrast to the collapse of authoritarian Indonesia, the crisis provided a powerful argument to pro-democracy forces in the region.

A further challenge to regionalism was the perceived weakness of ASEAN in responding to the crisis. Despite initial hope that it might engender a greater sense of unity in ASEAN, the crisis diminished ASEAN's international standing. This was partly due to the limitations of the collective efforts by ASEAN to manage the crisis. An initial idea explored by ASEAN was to set up a "co-operative financing arrangement" or a "stand-by fund" which could be used to deal with future currency shocks and debt crises. The fund could be used only after an IMF-package had been put in place; in this sense it was not to be a substitute for global multilateral measures.[77] ASEAN economic ministers have since proposed a regional "framework" which will allow members to engage in "mutual surveillance" of each other's economic policies and provide "early-warning" on impending economic downturns.[78] But these measures hardly sufficed. Commenting on ASEAN's response to the crisis, Lee Kuan Yew likened it to the "solidarity of fellow chicken-flu suffers".[79] Apart from exposing the region's dependence on foreign capital and its vulnerability to global market and political forces, the crisis showed the limits of ASEAN's collective clout.[80]

Another challenge to ASEAN unity concerned its time-honoured principle of non-interference in the domestic affairs of states and the "ASEAN Way" of quiet and consensual diplomacy. The Economist argued that despite its achievements in settling old animosities in the early years of the organisation, "the 'ASEAN way' no longer works"[81]. Indeed, ASEAN's norm of non-interference was blamed as the reason why none of its ASEAN partners made any effort to warn Bangkok of its evident mismanagement of the national economy. Nor could anyone in ASEAN put a clamp on Malaysia's Mahathir despite the damage that his frequent outbursts against western capitalism and financial speculators did to the regional economy.[82] The new Thai Foreign Minister, Surin Pitsuwan, openly called for ASEAN to review its non-interference doctrine so that it could develop a capacity for "preventing or resolving domestic issues with regional implications." But Surin's initiative, dubbed "flexible engagement", received support from just one other ASEAN member, the Philippines. ASEAN foreign ministers, at their annual meeting in Manila in July 1998, decided to stick to the old principle of non-interference.[83] Subsequently, the sacking of Anwar Ibrahim, the proponent of the idea of "constructive intervention" as a framework for dealing with ASEAN's weaker and less stable members, further weakened the forces advocating more openness in ASEAN.[84]

Flexible engagement was not the only kind of reform that Southeast Asian regionalism confronted. The crisis generated demands for ASEAN to move away from the "ASEAN Way" and to be more receptive to formal and institutionalised mechanisms for cooperation. As Tommy Koh pointed out, East Asian leaders had pursued cooperation by "building trust, by a process of consultation, mutual accommodation and consensus" while displaying a "general reluctance to build institutions and to rely on laws and rules." But the economic crisis showed the need to supplement the "ASEAN Way" by institutions.[85] Similarly, the Foreign Secretary of the Philippines raised the possibility of an EU-style ASEAN. ASEAN's economic monitoring agreement, in his view, was already a step "towards institutionalising closer coordination of national economic policies and performance and fostering rule-based transparency in governance."[86]

The crisis not only highlighted the might of globalisation, but also the limits of national sovereignty and regional autonomy. It showed different conceptions of, and attitudes towards, globalisation within Southeast Asia. Malaysia's Mahathir became the most vocal critic of globalisation, pointing to its negative impact on sovereignty and security. In June 1998, Mahathir argued:

> We are moving inexorably towards globalisation ... globalisation, liberalisation and deregulation are ideas which originate in the rich countries ostensibly to enrich the world. But so far the advantages seem to accrue only to the rich.

Referring to the political and security turmoil in the region caused by the economic downturn, Mahathir asked:

> In a globalised world, should there be national governments? We have seen that market forces can change governments. What is the need for national elections if the results have to be approved by the market?[87]

Mahathir also warned that the Asian economic crisis, by forcing national economies to submit more closely to the forces of globalisation, would produce greater insecurity and violence. Warning of an impending "war" against globalisation in which Asians would fight foreign multinationals controlling their economic destiny, Mahathir noted:

> They [Asians] will regard this as a new war of liberation. Even if they want to avoid violence, violence must come as the new capitalists disregard the signs [of protest among the masses].[88]

In contrast, Singapore's leaders continued to affirm the positive impact of globalisation on economic well-being and security. Its Foreign Minister, S. Jayakumar, reminded that "it was the forces of globalisation that gave the developing countries in our region direct access to the financial resources, technology and markets of the developed world ... it was also globalization that allowed many developing countries, including those in East Asia, to enjoy decades of sustained economic growth, rapid industrialisation and massive improvement in their standards of living, health and education."[89] A retreat from globalisation, warned Deputy Prime Minister Lee Hsien Loong, would undermine not just the prospects for further development, but also security. "Globalization is an imperative ... for small countries .... The alternative is not just less competitive industries or lower standards of living, but a world in which countries will be *less secure, and more prone to conflicts* (emphasis added)."[90]

Conclusion

Challenges to the regional concept of Southeast Asia in the post-Cold War era fall into three categories. The first stemmed from intra-regional problems, both old and new, which affected political unity among the ASEAN countries and exacerbated existing differentiation among them in terms of domestic politics and foreign policy. Some of these problems threatened to undermine the sense of regional identity that had been painstakingly constructed by ASEAN over the past three decades. The second set of challenges came from Southeast Asia's closer interdependence and integration with the wider Asia Pacific region. Of particular significance here was ASEAN's involvement in Asia Pacific multilateral institutions. The third challenge arose from the impact of economic globalisation. Globalisation not only affected the "regionness" of Southeast Asia, but differing responses to globalisation became a source of discord among the states of the region. The negative impact of globalisation, as manifested through the economic crisis plaguing the region since mid-1997, also exposed the precarious dependence of Southeast Asian countries on external forces and called into question their professed aspirations for regional autonomy. Together, these developments created pressures on Southeast Asia's regional unity and identity.

Notes

1. Thai Prime Minister Anand Panyarachun, cited in the *The Straits Times*, 25 June 1991.

2. Statement by H.E. Ali Alatas, Minister for Foreign Affairs and Co-Chair of the Paris Peace Conference on Cambodia, 23 October 1991, p.4.

3. *The Straits Times*, 17 February 1992, p.11.

4. S. Paribatra, "ASEAN Ten and Its Role in the Asia Pacific", Paper Prepared for the Conference "Asia in the XXI Century", Organized by the Institute for International Relations, Hanoi, on 28–29 April 1997, p.5.

5. C. Hernandez (1995) "One Southeast Asia in the 21st Century: Opportunities and Challenges", Paper Presented to the 1995 Convention of the Canadian Council for Southeast Asian Studies on *The Dynamism of Southeast Asia*, University of Laval, Quebec City, 27–29 October 1995, p.4.

6. "Vietnam Joins ASEAN", *Strategic Comments*, no. 5, 8 June 1995, p.2.

7. M. Gainsborough (1992) "Vietnam II: A Turbulent Normalisation with China", *The World Today*, vol. 48, no. 11, November 1992, p.207.

8. K. Chaipipat (1997) "ASEAN Agrees to Burma's Entry", *The Nation*, 1 June 1997.

9. "Coping with a Larger Family", *Bangkok Post* (editorial), 13 June 1997 (internet).

10. Commodore A. Ramli Nor (1989) "ASEAN Maritime Cooperation", paper presented to the Defence Asia '89 Conference on "Towards Greater ASEAN Military and Security Cooperation: Issues and Prospects", Singapore, 22–25 March 1989, pp.2–6.

11. M. Milivojevic, "The Spratly and Paracel Islands Conflict: *Survival*, vol.31, no.1 (January/February 1989), pp.

12. "Spratly Islands: Jakarta's next target for peace", *The Sunday Times* , 6 January 1991, p.10.

13. *The Straits Times*, 24 August 1992, p.12.

14. See T. Huxley (1990) "South-East Asia's Arms Race: Some Notes on Recent Developments", *Arms Control*, vol.11, no.1, May 1990, pp.69–76; M. Vatikiotis (1992) "Measure for Measure: Malaysia, Singapore, Poised to Acquire New Arms", *Far Eastern Economic Review*, 30 April 1992, p.18.

15. See S. Kondo (1992) "The Evolving Security Environment: Political", paper presented to the Workshop on "Arms Control and Confidence-Building in the Asia-Pacific Region", Organised by the Canadian Institute for International Peace and Security, Ottawa, 22–23 May 1992, pp.4–5; A. Mack (1991) "Asia's New Military Build-up", *Pacific Research*, February 1991, p.12.

16. The procurement of fighter aircraft became a key region-wide trend in the mid and late 1980s, when three countries, Indonesia, Thailand and Singapore acquired the F-16 from the U.S., as well as advanced airborne early warning capabilities. Other states entered the fray since with Indonesia, Malaysia and Brunei acquiring *Hawk* advanced jet trainer/strike aircraft from Britain, Russian-built MiG-29 *Fulcrum* fighters and US built FA-18 fighters. Singapore's Air Force, already the region's most advanced, further increased its combat aircraft strength by acquiring additional F-16s fighter aircraft from the US. Thailand also purchased additional F-16A/B fighters as well as E-2C *Hawkeye* Airborne Early Warning and Control aircraft from the US. See A. Acharya (1995) *An Arms Race in Post Cold War Southeast Asia: Propects for Control*, Pacific Strategic Paper No.7, Singapore: Institute of Southeast Asian Studies.

MANAGING "ONE SOUTHEAST ASIA" 159

[17] M. Richardson (1993) "For the Planners, a Time to Decide", *International Herald Tribune*, 18 November 1993, p.5.

[18] G. Fairclough (1993) "Standing Firm", *Far Eastern Economic Review*, 15 April 1993, p.22.

[19] "Vienna Showdown", *Far Eastern Economic Review*, 17 June 1993, p.17.

[20] K. Mahbubani, (1992)" News Areas of Asean Reaction: Environment, Human Rights and Democracy", *Asean-ISIS Monitor*, Issue no.5, October-December 1992, p.15 and at www.aseansec.org.

[21] Joint Communique of the Twenty-Sixth ASEAN Ministerial Meeting, Singapore, 23–24 July 1993, p.7.

[22] Y. Ghai (1994) *Human Rights and Governance: The Asia Debate*, San Franscisco: The Asia Foundation, Center for Asian Pacific Affairs, p.10.

[23] C. Hernandez (1995) "ASEAN Perspectives on Human Rights and Democracy in International Relations: Problems and Prospects", Working Paper 1995-1, Centre for International Studies, University of Toronto, p.13.

[24] See A. Acharya (1995) "Human Rights and Regional Order: ASEAN and Human Rights Management in post-Cold War Southeast Asia", in James T.H. Tang, ed. *(1995) Human Rights and International Relations in the Asia-Pacific*, London: Pinter, pp.167–182; Amitav Acharya (1995) *Human Rights in Southeast Asia: Dilemmas of Foreign Policy*, Toronto: JCAPS.

[25] On the role of human rights NGOs in Asia, see: S. Jones (1993) "The Organic Growth", *Far Eastern Economic Review*, 17 June, p.23.

[26] S. Jones (1995) "The Impact of Asian Economic Growth on Human Rights", Asia Project Working Paper, New York: Council on Foreign Relations.

[27] "Thailand: Rights Activists Get Cold Reception", *Bangkok Post*, 26 July 1994, p.10.

[28] M. Vatikiotis (1994) "Going Regional" *Far Eastern Economic Review*, 20 Oct, p.16.

[29] T.R. Leinbach and R. Ulak (2000) *Southeast Asia's Diversity and Development*, Upper Saddle River, New Jersey: Prentice-Hall, p.136.

[30] M. Seda, 'Global environmental concerns and priorities: implications for ASEAN', chpt. 1 in M. Seda, ed. (1993) Environmental Management in ASEAN: Perspectives on Critical Regional Issues, Singapore: Institute of Southeast Asian Studies, p.24.

[31] "Fires Again Ravage Indonesia's Forests", *The Los Angeles Times*, 23/3/1998, http://forests.org/

[32] M. Hiebert & J. McBeth (1997) 'Trial by fire: smog tests Asean's vaunted cooperation', *Far Eastern Economic Review*, October 16, http://www.singapore-window.org/1016feer.htm

[33] Ibid.

[34] "Suharto says Indonesia doing its best to combat fires", Agence France-Presse, 10/4/97, Worldwide Forest/Biodiversity Campaign News, http://forests.org/gohper/indonesia/allcando.tx. Officials in Indonesia said that 6 people in total have died from respiratory diseases. In March of 1998, the Suara Pembaruan newspaper in the capital, Jakarta, reported that smoke from the fires had caused 297 cases of pneumonia and that two people had died.

[35] "Envrionment Minister to make fighting fires a priority", *The Straits Times Interactive*, 18 March, 1998, http://web3.asia1.com.sg/archive/st/5/pages/p031803.htm

[36] H. Singh (1993) "Prospects for Regional Stability in Southeast Asia in the Post-Cold War Era", *Millennium*, vol.22, no.2, pp.279–300.

160 THE QUEST FOR IDENTITY: INTERNATIONAL RELATIONS OF SOUTHEAST ASIA

[37] L. Buszynski (1990) "Declining Superpowers: The Impact on ASEAN", *The Pacific Review*, vol.3, no.3, 1990, p.258.

[38] M. Richardson, "Soviets cutting Vietnam force", *International Herald Tribune*, 16 January 1990, p.1.

[39] "Asia shudders in the Grip of new fears after the Cold War", *The Straits Times*, 29 December 1990, p.23.

[40] "Asean talks about security at last, but how far will it go", *The Straits Times* (Singapore), 1 February 1992, p.24.

[41] M.C. Tai (1991) "China's Regional Military Posture", *International Defense Review*, June 1991, pp.618–622.

[42] K.Y. Lee (1992) "Japan's Key Role in the Industrialisation of East Asia", *The Straits Times*, 14 February 1992, p.22.

[43] M. Richardson (1991) "Asians urge Japan to be peacekeeper", *International Herald tribune*, 8 March 1991, p.1.

[44] S.W. Simon (1990) "United States Security Policy and ASEAN", *Current History*, vol.89, no.545 (March 1990), p.98.

[45] K.Y. Lee (1992), *The Straits Times Weekly Overseas Edition*, 14 November 1992, p.24.

[46] M. Alagappa (1991) "Regional Arrangements and International Security in Southeast Asia", *Contemporary Southeast Asia*, vol.12, no. 4, March 1991, pp.269–305

[47] "Asean must stick to Zopfan plan, says Alatas", *The Straits Times*, 31 December 1990, p.11.

[48] For a discussion of the evolution of ideas and initiatives concerning a multilateral security system in the Asia-Pacific region, see: Amitav Acharya (1993) *A New Regional Order in Southeast Asia: ASEAN in the Post-Cold War Era*, Adelphi Paper no. 279, London: International Institute for Strategic Studies.

[49] *Singapore Declaration of 1992*, ASEAN Heads of Government Meeting, Singapore, 27–28 January 1992, p.2.

[50] "The ASEAN Regional Forum: A Concept Paper", Document Circulated at the Second Annual Meeting of the ASEAN Regional Forum, Brunei, 1 August 1995.

[51] *The Straits Times*, August 4, 1994, p.2.

[52] *The ASEAN Regional Forum: A Concept Paper*, op. cit., Annex A and B, pp.8–11.

[53] "New Framework for Security", *The Straits Times*, July 26, 1994, p.15.

[54] R. Stubbs (1999) "Signing on to Liberalization: AFTA and the Politics of Regional Economic Cooperation", Manuscript, pp.6–8.

[55] P. Bowles (1997) "ASEAN, AFTA and the New Regionalism", *Pacific Affairs*, vol.70, no.2, Summer 1997, p.221.

[56] R. Stubbs (1999), "Signing on to Liberalization: AFTA and the Politics of Regional Economic Cooperation", op.cit., p.27.

[57] Ibid., p.27.

[58] Ibid., pp.28–29.

[59] M. Hadi Soesastro (1990) "Prospects for Pacific-Asian Regional Trade Structures", in R. Scalapino et. al., eds. (1990) *Regional Dynamics: Security, Political and Economic Issues in the Asia-Pacific Region*, Jakarta: Centre for Strategic and International Studies, p.391.

[60] For an excellent study of the economic implications of an expanded ASEAN, which is the main source for the discussion in this paragraph, see *The New ASEANs: Vietnam, Burma, Cambodia and Laos*, Canberra: Department of Foreign Affairs and Trade, 1997.

[61] He was of course referring to worries about the apparent formation of trade blocs in Europe and North America and making the point that ASEAN might be forced to consider similar measures in response. See *The Straits Times*, 5 March 1991.

[62] *The Straits Times* (Weekly Overseas Edition), 31 March 1990.

[63] For instance see J. Cotton (1990) "APEC: Australia hosts another Pacific acronym" in *The Pacific Review* vol.3, no.2, 1990, pp.171–173.

[64] *Far Eastern Economic Review*, 16 November 1989.

[65] N. Sopiee (1989) "Pan-Pacific Talks: ASEAN is the Key", *International Herald Tribune*, 4–5 November 1989, p.4.

[66] Text of speech by Lee Hsien Loong, Minister for Trade and Industries, Singapore, before the Indonesia Forum, Jakarta, 11 July 1990, p.9.

[67] Ibid.

[68] *Far Eastern Economic Review*, 31 January 1991, p.32.

[69] Later, in the wake of concerns regarding the exclusion of important regional actors, such as Australia, Malaysia was to insist that there was no "exclusion list" for EAEG and that Australia's participation would be possible at a subsequent stage.

[70] See P. Evans (1990) "The Changing Context of Security Relations in Eastern Asia", Paper prepared for the workshop on "Korea and the Changing Asia-Pacific Region", 8–9 February 1990.

[71] *International Herald Tribune*, 8–9 December 1990.

[72] *The Straits Times*, 22 December 1990.

[73] A. Acharya (1995) "Transnational Production and Security: Southeast Asia's Growth Triangles", *Contemporary Southeast Asia*, vol.17, no.2 , September 1995, pp.173–185.

[74] For general discussions of development strategies in Southeast Asia, see: R.F. Doner (1991) "Approaches to the Politics of Economic Growth in Southeast Asia" in *Journal of Asian Studies*, no.50, Nov. 1991, pp.818–849. K. Hay (1989) "ASEAN and the Shifting Tides of Economic Power at the End of the 1980s." *International Journal*, no.44, Summer, pp.640–59. J. Clad (1990) *Behind the Myth: Business, Power and Money in Southeast Asia*. London; Hyman Press. W. Bello and S. Rosenfeld (1990) *Dragons in Distress: Asia's Miracle Economies in Crisis*, San Francisco: Institute for Food and Development Policy. K. Yoshihara (1985) *Philippine Industrialization: Foreign and Domestic Capital*, New York: Oxford University Press. A. Suehiro (1985) *Capital accumulation and Industrial Development in Thailand*. Bangkok. Social Research Institute.

[75] *The Straits Times*, 5 August 1998, p.16

[76] *The Straits Times*, March 1, 1998 SECTION: Sunday Review; Viewpoints; Global Village; Pg. "Only clear laws can stem the tide".

[77] "Beggars and Choosers", *The Economist*, 6 December 1997, p.43.

[78] Ibid.

[79] "The Limits of Politeness", *The Economist*, 28 February 1998, p.43.

[80] "Out of Depth", *Far Eastern Economic Review*, 19 February 1998, p.25.

[81] "The limits of politeness", *The Economist*, February 28, 1998, p.43.

[82] Ibid.

[83] "Thais Retract Call for Asean Intervention", *The Straits Times (Interactive)*, 27 June 1998, web3.asia1.com.sg.

[84] "ASEAN Loses Critic Anwar", *Asiaweek*, 18 September 1998, p.54.

[85] T. Koh, "What E. Asia Can Learn from the EU", *The Straits Times*, 10 July 1998, p.48.

[86] "EU-Style Asean Possible", *The Straits Times*, 19 August 1998, p.21.

[87] Text of Speech at the Fifth Symposium of the Institute for International Monetary Affairs, Tokyo Japan, reproduced in the *New Straits Times*, 4 June 1998, p.12.

[88] "Perhaps Mahathir Will Have the Last Laugh", *The Sunday Nation*, editorial, 14 June 1998, p.A5.

[89] "Singapore Urges No retreat From Globalization", Xinhua News Agency Dispatch, 3 September 1998 (From Lexis-Nexis).

[90] H.L. Lee (1998) "Whither Globalism — A World In Crisis", Speech at the Economic Strategy Conference, Washington, D.C., 6 May 1998, cited in C.K. Wah (1998)"Globalization and Its Challenges to ASEAN Political Participation", Paper presented to the ISEAS 30th Anniversary Conference, "Southeast Asia in the 21st Century; Challenges of Globalization", 30 July – 1 August 1998, Singapore, Institute of Southeast Asian Studies, p.3.

CONCLUSION

The Making and Possible Unmaking
of Southeast Asia

"Nations come and go — why shouldn't regions?" (Don Emmerson[1])

*"'Southeast Asia' was once a term used by outsiders far more than
by those living in the region; but now it is becoming something of
an economic and political reality, and its leaders themselves are
moving to make ASEAN an organisation of and for the region,
instead of an organisation designed to add to the security of some
of its states vis-à-vis others." (Nicholas Tarling[2])*

The aim of this book, as stated in the Introduction, is to study Southeast
Asia's international relations by using region and regionalism as the
central analytical concepts. The two are closely linked and mutually
reinforcing. The notion of Southeast Asia as a region, based on such
traditional attributes of "regionness" as proximity, shared history, similarities in culture and heritage, as well as more dynamic variables such
as commercial, strategic and political interactions before and after the
colonial period, has been a central basis of regionalism in Southeast Asia.
At the same time regional cooperation, including the development of
norms and institutions, has been crucial to the development of Southeast
Asia's regional identity.

In a previous paper, I had argued:

> Southeast Asia is a region built on shared human and physical characteristics
> and endeavours, external geopolitical and economic currents, and collective
> social imagination. But its claim to be a region should be seen as being based
> as much on the construction of a regional identity as on the sum total of
> shared physical attributes and functional interactions among its units. The
> development of a regional identity may not necessarily conform to the "facts"
> of geography, history, culture, or politics. The notion of Southeast Asia as a
> homogenous cultural or geographic entity can indeed be overstated. But its
> social and political identity, derived from the conscious promotion of the
> regional concept by its states, societies, and peoples, is what makes it a
> distinct idea in the latter part of the 20th century.[3]

A key argument of this book has been that as with nationalism and
nation-states, regions may be "imagined", designed, constructed and even
defended.[4] But just as the nation-state cannot be viable without a sense
of nationalism, regions cannot be regions without a sense of regionalism.
This explains the heavy emphasis on regionalism in the book. Moreover,
there are many parallels between "imagining the nation" and "imagining
the region".

164 THE QUEST FOR IDENTITY: INTERNATIONAL RELATIONS OF SOUTHEAST ASIA

Of course, region and regionalism are both relatively new ideas, much more recent than the concept of nationalism and the nation-state. But as historians of Southeast Asia tell us, before regionalism in its modern, institutional sense made its mark on the area east of India and south of China, "region-wide" patterns of inter-state relations and a degree of interaction and interdependence did exist among the political units inhabiting that area. Any serious study of Southeast Asia's international relations and its claim to be a region must therefore begin with a historical framework that includes the inter-state system during the pre-colonial period. Drawing upon the work of a variety of scholars, the first chapter of this book looked at the role of traditional political-cultural frameworks and commercial interactions in creating the basis of the idea of Southeast Asia. It must not be forgotten that the *mandala* system, or the "galactic polity" is a historical reconstruction; there is no way of saying whether Southeast Asians themselves saw it in this way, or considered themselves to be part of a region. Even then, the study of the pre-colonial state-system should occupy an important place in Southeast Asia's claim to be a region, because its constituent units shared important characteristics, as well as a degree of interaction and interdependence which served to reduce, if not eliminate, the diversity of Southeast Asia.

Moreover, the pre-colonial regional pattern did provide a framework to study the political impact of colonialism in fragmenting the region. It also reinforced the claim of latter-day nationalists and regionalists that Southeast Asia's claim to be a region was not simply a figment of Western imagination or an accidental by-product of Western geopolitics, such as the Southeast Asia Command (SEAC). But the relationship between nationalism and regionalism, one of the key determinants of the modern Southeast Asian identity, was not always easy or complementary. Initially, nationalism undermined the prospects for regionalism. This was certainly the case with Indonesia's Sukarno, whose belligerent nationalism threatened his Southeast Asian neighbours and left little scope for the idea of Southeast Asian (as opposed to Afro-Asian) regionalism to flourish. Nationalism and nation-building also undercut regionalism in another way. Preoccupied with domestic nation-building issues, and facing historical, political and economic conditions which varied widely from country to country (as discussed in Chapter 2), Southeast Asia's early post-colonial leaders were not only prevented from paying sufficient attention to regionalism, but they also produced conflicting responses. While some nationalists saw regionalism as helpful for their cause, this was not necessarily framed within a Southeast Asian context. In fact, in some cases, wider regionalist concepts conflicted with incipient ideas about Southeast Asian regionalism. And both were overwhelmed by the great power geopolitics of the early Cold War period.

Indeed, during the first two decades of the post-Second World War peiod, Southeast Asia's international relations were determined by a struggle between continued Western dominance (including competitive great power interactions) on the one hand and nationalism on the other. Regionalism played a marginal role in this contestation. Southeast Asia as a region was defined not just by geopolitical currents in which external powers were the central actors, but also by academic writings and policy debates in which Westerners played a dominant role. The situation during the next twenty years was dramatically different, however. During this period, Southeast Asian regionalism came into its own. After a shaky start, Southeast Asian regionalists, who espoused the cause of "moderate nationalism" (to borrow Wang Gungwu's useful term) succeeded in creating and sustaining a regionalist framework which proved effective in containing intra-regional conflicts and projecting a collective regional identity. These leaders recognised a sufficient congruence between the nationalist and regionalist project, despite significant cultural, linguistic, political and economic differences among the regionalist-minded nations themselves.

It was during the 1960s that the moderate nationalist leaders of Southeast Asia saw regionalism as a way of preserving their state security and regime survival not from neo-colonial pressures, but from the twin dangers of Cold War superpower rivalry and domestic communist insurgencies. Thus, the Cold War, while helping to polarise Southeast Asia into two ideologically hostile segments, might have inadvertently contributed to the regionalist cause, by promoting a solidarity among like-minded regimes despite their recognition that such a regionalism would be less than Southeast Asian in scope and would be greeted by the excluded actors (the Indochinese countries) with open hostility.

At its origin, regionalism in Southeast Asia was limited in scope and objective. It comprised the anti-communist states of the region and was ostensibly geared to the fulfilment of vague economic and political objectives. It was geared as much to maintainance of peaceful relations among the participants themselves as to creating a common front against potential adversaries within and outside the region. But even this limited framework of regionalism did make an important contribution to the idea of the region.

Southeast Asian regionalists contributed to the idea of region in two distinct ways. The first was by maintaining regional unity and preventing any serious escalation of intra-mural conflicts. This was done, among other things, through an effort to adhere to certain norms of inter-state behaviour as well as through development of bilateral and multilateral mechanisms for consultations and consensus-building. Moreover, even in conflicts which involved non-regionalists, such as the Indochinese states led by Vietnam, they pursued a moderate path and left the door open to negotia-

166 THE QUEST FOR IDENTITY: INTERNATIONAL RELATIONS OF SOUTHEAST ASIA

tions and the eventual incorporation of the latter into their regionalist vision and framework.

A second way in which regionalism might have contributed to the regional idea of Southeast Asia was the pursuit of what could be called regional autonomy and self-reliance. The regionalists developed a *modus vivendi* with larger, more powerful external players through collective bargaining without seeking their complete exclusion from regional affairs. Through proposals for regional self-reliance and autonomy, as manifested in the idea of neutralisation and the Zone of Peace, Freedom and Neutrality, Southeast Asian regionalists articulated a common stance vis-à-vis the outside world which reinforced Southeast Asia's claim to be a region. What is striking is that during these years, Southeast Asia's regional identity was indigenously constructed, rather than exogenously determined.

ASEAN's region-building project should not, however, simply be seen as an example of newly-liberated Third World states attempting to exert control over affairs within their region by means of a communal organisation. It served a purpose that independent nationalisms were not able to, that is, the reclamation of a regional identity whose historical foundations had been severely disrupted by colonialism.

To be sure, regionalism has had a mixed impact on the regional identity of Southeast Asia. On the one hand, ASEAN reflected the polarisation of Southeast Asia. Discourses on regionalism and competing visions of regionalism before and after the formation of ASEAN highlighted the problematic nature of Southeast Asia as a region. But despite its mixed impact, regionalism played a central role in making Southeast Asia an even more distinct region in external perceptions. In 1966, a year before ASEAN's birth, Kenneth T. Young, a former US ambassador to Thailand, observed about Southeast Asia: "This is a so-called region without any feeling for community, without much sense of shared values and with few common institutions."[5] Less than twenty years later, Russell Fifield would reach the conclusion that "the regional concept of Southeast Asia, as perceived by decision makers in and outside the area, is a living reality."[6] Leonard Andaya would even be more forceful; relating the rediscovery of a regional identity specifically to the major project of regionalism in Southeast Asia:

> In participating in ASEAN activities and using the term "Asean", these nation-states are reaffirming the existence of Southeast Asia. Southeast Asia is being reborn by means of a solid core consisting of the ASEAN nations. Through participation in ASEAN, the ASEAN Business Forum, cooperative academic ventures among ASEAN universities...the peoples of Southeast Asia have come to accept as a matter of course their identification as "Southeast Asians".[7]

This amounts to a powerful endorsement of the role of ASEAN and the impact of regionalism in the making of Southeast Asia as a region. It also suggests that the development of the regional concept should be seen as a process of *identity-building*. While the pre-colonial inter-state system had a regional scope, albeit weak and impermanent, it was the regionalism of the 1970s and 80s which gave Southeast Asia a regional identity. Similarly, while the recognition of Southeast Asia as a political region during the Cold War was the result of global geopolitical currents and outside perceptions and influences, genuine and lasting recognition came only in the course of the efforts by Southeast Asian regionalists to manage regional conflicts (such as the Cambodia conflict) and seek out collective positions vis-à-vis outside powers. While the very idea of the nation-state as an "imagined community" came into prominence in Southeast Asia (as in other areas under colonial rule) through the adaptation of a somewhat alien concept by the local elite, region-building in Southeast Asia was based primarily, but not exclusively, on indigenous frameworks of socialisation. While the main forces shaping recognition of Southeast Asia during the early post-World War II period were the "orientalist" scholarship on the region and great power geopolitics, in the 1970s and 80s, an inward-looking and exclusionary concept of regionalism developed by ASEAN proved crucial to developing a sense of regional destiny and identity.

Will this unravel? The international relations of Southeast Asia in the 1990s have been transformed as the result of developments in the global arena. While several of these changes have been positive, new sources of conflict and tension have emerged. Unless carefully managed, these could seriously undermine prospects for regional unity and the very idea of Southeast Asia as a region. In the post-Cold War era, the international relations of Southeast Asia have been increasingly linked to developments in the wider Asia Pacific region, especially relations among the major powers, such as the US, China, Japan and India. While a new regional order might emerge based on the foundations laid by ASEAN, this has clear limitations in ensuring a balance of power that would preserve stability. Issues related to the role of the major powers, such as the US military presence in the region, the power projection potential of China and Japan, will have a major bearing on the security milieu of Southeast Asian states in the 21st century. This could challenge the concept of Southeast Asia as a distinctive security region.

On the economic front, the regional concept of Southeast Asia is being challenged by the forces of globalisation. For some, Southeast Asia has always been too closely integrated into Northeast Asia and the Western countries to be considered a distinctive economic region. Efforts to develop a pan-Asia Pacific economic institution, now joined by efforts to develop an East Asian grouping (ASEAN plus China, Japan and South Korea), recognised this reality. But the contagion effect of the Asian economic crisis during the 1997–99 period, encompassing South Korea, Russia, Thailand, Brazil and Indonesia, underscored this point in a much more powerful way.

Moreover, the view of ASEAN as an organisation "of and for the region" must be seen against the backdrop of lingering tensions and animosities which have surfaced with alarming regularity among its original core members, Indonesia, Malaysia, Singapore, Thailand, and the Philippines. The Asian economic crisis provided the latest and some of the most dramatic illustrations of this. The fact that some of these quarrels are about questions of ethnicity (as between Singapore and Malaysia), while others question colonial territorial allocations is particularly troubling to those who have come to expect a nascent regional identity replacing particular national ones. While regionalism has given an additional measure of clout to Southeast Asian countries in dealing with the outside world, the limits of such clout must not be overlooked. In dealing with the larger powers in security, economic or political matters (such as human rights), Southeast Asian countries have found themselves suffering as much from a lack of resources as of resolve. The poor record of ASEAN in dealing with the economic crisis or the rise of Chinese power attests to this.

The confidence which marked the entry of Southeast Asian regionalists into the post-Cold War period led them not only to embark on a project of regionalist expansion ("One Southeast Asia"), but also to aspire to a "leadership" role in wider Asia Pacific regional institutions. This is a striking feature of modern Southeast Asian history. Not long ago, these states were considered "objects" rather than leaders of international relations in Asia Pacific, not to mention the larger international system. But the euphoria of the early 1990s appeared to have been unwarranted. By the late 1990s, there was a more realistic assessment of the limits and possibilities of collective Southeast Asian regional clout. The "One Southeast Asia" project had run into considerable trouble, especially with the issue of accession by Myanmar and Cambodia into ASEAN. Expansion, while diluting the decision-making homogeneity of regionalism, also presented the regionalist project with new economic and security burdens which had not been fully anticipated.

Against this backdrop, it may be too optimistic to argue that the regional concept of Southeast Asia will become a permanent reality or endure indefinitely into the future. A lot will depend on external economic (globalisation) and strategic (great power relations) events which are beyond the control of Southeast Asian countries. These forces could unravel the regional unity and identity of Southeast Asia. Yet this would not be an entirely new challenge since, as this book has argued, for much of the post-Second World War period, the idea of one Southeast Asia has been consciously nurtured by regional elites. It has been altered, re-invented and managed to suit the exigencies of shifting external political, economic and strategic currents. Southeast Asia has been an imagined community during much of its recent past. It may well continue to do so in the future, provided there continues to exist a strong measure of collective political will on the part of Southeast Asian states and societies to adapt the regional concept to changing external and domestic circumstances, including the forces of globalisation.

Notes

[1] D.K. Emmerson (1984) "Southeast Asia: What's in a Name?", *Journal of Southeast Asian Studies*, XV, No.1 , March 1984, p.20.

[2] N. Tarling (1998) *Nations and States in Southeast Asia*, Cambridge: Cambridge University Press, p.viii.

[3] A. Acharya, (1999) "Imagined Proximities: The Making and Remaking of Southeast Asia as a Region", *Southeast Asian Journal of Social Science*, vol.27, no.1, p.73.

[4] B. Anderson (1991) *Imagined Communities*, London: Verso.

[5] K.T. Young (1966) *The Southeast Asia Crisis*, p.5.

[6] R. Fifield "'Southeast Asia' and 'ASEAN' as Regional Concepts", in R.A. Morse, ed. (1984) *Southeast Asian Studies: Options for the Future*, Lanham: University Press of America, p.128.

[7] L.Y. Andaya, "Ethnonation, Nation-State and Regionalism in Southeast Asia", in Proceedings of the International Symposium, "Southeast Asia: Global Area Studies for the 21st Century", organized by Project Team: An Integrated Approach to Global Area Studies (funded by Monbusho Grant-in-Aid for Scientific Research on Priority Areas), and Center for Southeast Asian Studies, Kyoto University, Kyoto International Community House, October 18–22, 1996, p.135.

Bibliography

Books and Monographs

Acharya, A. (1990) *A New Regional Order in Southeast Asia: ASEAN in the Post Cold War Era*, Adelphi Paper no.279. London: International Institute of Strategic Studies, 1983.

Acharya, A. (1995) *Human Rights in Southeast Asia: Dilemmas of Foreign Policy*, Eastern Asia Policy Papers No.11. Toronto: University of Toronto-York University Joint Centre for Asia Pacific Studies.

Acharya, A. (1995) "An Arms Race in Post-Cold War Southeast Asia: Prospects for Control", Pacific Strategic Paper No.7. Singapore: Institute of Southeast Asian Studies.

Andaya, B.W. & Andaya, L.Y. (1982) *A History of Malaysia*. Macmillian, London.

Anderson, B. (1991) *Imagined Communities*. (Revised and Expanded Edition). London: Verso.

Bello, W. and Rosenfeld, S. (1990) *Dragons in Distress: Asia's Miracle Economies in Crisis*. San Fransisco: Institute for Food and Development Policy.

Bello, W. & Yoshihara, K. (1985) *Philippine Industrialization: Foreign and Domestic Capital*. New York: Oxford University Press.

Boeke, J.H. (1953) *Economics and Economic Policy of Dual Societies as Exemplified by Indonesia*. New York, Institute of Pacific Relations.

Bresnan, J. (1994) *From Dominoes to Dynamos: The Transformation of Southeast Asia*. New York: Council on Foreign Press.

Buzan B. (1990) *People, States, and Fear: An Agenda for International Security Studies in the Post-Cold War Era*. Boulder: Lynne Rienner;

Caldwell, J.A.(1974) *American Economic Aid to Thailand*. Lexington, Mass.: D.C. Heath.

Cameron, A.W. (1976) *Indochina: Prosepects After 'the End'*. Washington, D.C.: American Enterprise Institute for Public Policy Research.

Cantori, L.J. and Spiegel, S.L. (Eds.) (1970) *The International Politics of Regions: A Comparative Approach*. Englewood Cliffs, N.J.: Prentice Hall.

Chin, K.W. (1974) *The Five Power Defence Arrangement and AMDA: Some Observations on the Nature of an Evolving Partnership*, Occasional Paper No. 23. Singapore: Institute of Southeast Asian Studies.

Clad, J. (1990) *Behind the Myth: Business, Power and Money in Southeast Asia*. London: Hyman Press.

Coedes, G. (1968) *The Indianized States of States of Southeast Asia*. Kuala Lumpur: University of Malaya Press (edited by Walter F. Vella, translated by Susan Brown Cowing).

Daw, T.H. (1988) *Common Vision: Burma's Regional Outlook*, Occasional Paper. Washington, D.C.: Institute for the Study of Diplomacy.

Dixon, C. (1991) *South East Asia in the World-Economy: A Regional Geography*. London: Cambridge University Press.

Economist Intelligence Unit (1968) *The Economic Effects of the Vietnam War in East and Southeast Asia*, QER Special no.3. London: Economist Intelligence Unit.

Federspiel, H.M., & Rafferty, K.E. (1969) *Prospects for Regional Military Cooperation in Southeast Asia*. McLean, Virginia: Research Analysis Corporation.

Fisher, C.A (1964) *South-East Asia: A Social, Economic and Political Geography*. London: Methuen and Co.

Furnivall, J.S. (1956) *Colonial Policy and Practice : A Comparative Study of Burma and Netherlands India*. New York: New York University Press.

Geertz, C. (1980) *Negara: The Theatre State in Nineteenth-Century Bali*. Princeton, NJ: Princeton University Press.

Ghai, Y. (1994) *Human Rights and Governance: The Asia Debate*. San Franscisco: The Asia Foundation, Center for Asian Pacific Affairs.

Gill, Ranjit. (1987) *ASEAN: Coming of Age*. Singapore: Sterling Corporate Services.

Girling, J.L.S. (1981)*Thailand: Society and Politics*. Ithaca: Cornell University Press.

Golay, F.H., Anspach, R., Pfanner, M.R. and Eliezer B.A. (1969) *Underdevelopment and Economic Nationalism in Southeast Asia*. Ithaca: Cornell University Press.

Gordon, B.K. (1966) *The Dimensions of Conflict in Southeast Asia*. New Jersey: Prentice Hall.

Goscha, C.E. (1999) *Thailand and the Southeast Asian Networks of the Vietnamese Revolution, 1885–1954*. Surrey: Curzon Press.

Haas, E.B. (1986) *Why We Still Need the United Nations: The Collective Management of International Conflict*. Berkeley: University of California, Institute of International Relations.

Hall, D.G. E. (1968) *A History of South East Asia*. London: Macmillan.

Hall, K.R. (1985) *Maritime Trade and State Development in Early Southeast Asia*. Honolulu: University of Hawaii Press.

Hanggi, H. (1991) *ASEAN and the ZOPFAN Concept*. Singapore: Institute of Southeast Asian Studies.

Hatch, W. and Yamamura, K. (1996) *Asia in Japan's Embrace: Building a Regional Production Alliance*. New York: Cambridge University Press.

172 THE QUEST FOR IDENTITY: INTERNATIONAL RELATIONS OF SOUTHEAST ASIA

Hernandez, C. (1995) *ASEAN Perspectives on Human Rights and Democracy in International Relations: Problems and Prospects*, Working Paper 1995–1. Centre for International Studies, University of Toronto, 1995.

Hervouet, G. (1988) *The Return of Vietnam to the International System*, Occasional Paper no.6. Ottawa: Canadian Institute for International Peace and Security.

Higham, C. (1989) *The Archeology of Mainland Southeast Asia from 10,000 B.C. to the Fall of Angkor*. Cambridge: Cambridge University Press.

Huxley, T. (1986) *The ASEAN States' Defence Policies, 1975-81: Military Response to Indochina?*, Working Paper No.88. Canberra: Australian National University, Strategic and Defence Studies Centre.

Institute of Southeast Asian Studies (1991) *Regional Outlook 1991*. Singapore: Institute of Southeast Asian Studies.

Institute of Strategic and International Studies (1987) *Proceedings of the Second ASEAN Roundtable, Kuala Lumpur, 20–21 July 1987*. Kuala Lumpur: Institute of Strategic and International Studies.

International Institute for Strategic Studies (1983) *Strategic Survey 1982–1983*. London: International Institute for Strategic Studies.

Japan Economic Institute (various dates) *JEI Reports*. Washington: Japan Economic Institute.

Jones, Sidney (1995) *The Impact of Asian Economic Growth on Human Rights*, Asia Project Working Paper. New York: Council on Foreign Relations.

Jorgensen-Dahl, A. (1982) *Regional Organisation and Order in Southeast Asia*. London: Macmillan.

Kahin, G.M. (1964), *Governments and Politics of Southeast Asia*. Ithaca: Cornell University Press.

Lake D. and Morgan P. (1997) (Eds.) *Regional Orders: Building Security in a Modern World*. University Park: The Pennsylvania State University Press.

Leifer, M. (1980) *Conflict and Regional Order in Southeast Asia*. London: International Institute for Strategic Studies.

Leifer, M. (1983) *Indonesia's Foreign Policy*. London: George Allen and Unwin.

Leinbach, T.R. and R. Ulak (2000) *Southeast Asia: Diversity and Development*. Upper Saddle River, New Jersey.

Leur, J.C. van (1955) *Indonesian Trade and Society*, van Hoeve, The Hague.

Lim, J. and Vani, S. (1984) (Eds.) *Armed Communist Movements in Southeast Asia*. Aldershot: Gower.

Luhulima, C.P. (1995) *ASEAN's Security Gamework*, CAPA Reports No.22. San Francisco: Center for Asia Pacific Affairs, The Asia Foundation.

Mahapatra, C. (1990) *American Role in the Origin and Growth of ASEAN*. New Delhi: ABC Publishing House.

Mason, M. (1994) *Foreign Direct Investment in East Asia: Trends and Critical Issues*. CFR Asia Project Working Paper. New York: Council on Foreign Relations.

McCloud, D.G. (1986) *System and Process in Southeast Asia: The Evolution of a Region*. Boulder, CO: Westview Press.

Mason, M. (1994) *Foreign Direct Investment in East Asia: Trends and Critical Issues*, CFR Asia Project Working Paper, 1994.

Morgan, T. and Spoelstra, N. (1969) *Economic Interdependence in Southeast Asia*. Madison: University of Wisconsin Press.

Murray, M.J. (1980) *The Development of Capitalism in Colonial Indochina, 1870–1940*. Los Angeles: University of California Press.

Muscat, R.J. (1990) *Thailand and the United States: Development, Security and Foreign Aid*. New York: Columbia University Press.

Myint, H. (1972) *Southeast Asia's Economy: Development Policies in the 1970s*. NY: Praeger Publishers.

Nair, K.K. (1984) *ASEAN-Indochina Relations Since 1975: The Politics of Accommodation*. Canberra Papers on Stategy and Defence No.30. Canberra: Australian National University, Strategic and Defence Studies Centre.

Nguen Duy Quy (Ed.) (1992) *Unity in Diversity: Cooperation Between Vietnam and Other Southeast Asian Countries*. Hanoi: Social Science Publishing House.

Osborne, M. (1970) *Region of Revolt: Focus on Southeast Asia*. New South Wales, Pergamon Australia.

Osborne, M. (1990) *Southeast Asia: An Illustrated Introductory History*, 5th Edition. St. Leonards, NSW: Allen and Unwin.

Pace, B. et al. (1970) *Regional Cooperation in Southeast Asia: The First Two Years of ASEAN — 1967–1969*. McLean, Va.: Research Analysis Corporation.

Palmer, R.D. (1987) *Building ASEAN: 20 Years of Southeast Asian Cooperation*, The Washington Papers, No.127. New York: Praeger for the Centre for Strategic and International Studies.

Paribatra, S. (1997) *ASEAN Ten and Its Role in the Asia Pacific*, Paper Prepared for the Conference on Asia in the XXI Century, Organized by the Institute for International Relations, Hanoi, on 28–29 April 1997.

Peterson, E. (1988) *The Gulf Cooperation Council Search for Unity in a Dynamic Region*. Boulder, CO: Westview Press.

Pye, L.W. (1967) *Southeast Asia's Political Systems*, 2d ed. Englewood Cliffs, New Jersey: Prentice-Hall Inc.

Pye, L.W. (1998) *International Relations in Asia: Culture, Nation and State*, Sigur Center Asia Papers, no.1. Washington, D.C.: The Sigur Center for Asian Studies, The George Washington University.

Reid, A.(1988) *Southeast Asia in the Age of Commerce 1450–1680, Volume One: The Lands Below the Winds*. New Haven: Yale University Press.

174　THE QUEST FOR IDENTITY: INTERNATIONAL RELATIONS OF SOUTHEAST ASIA

Reid, A. (1993) *Southeast Asia in the Age of Commerce 1450–1680, Volume Two: Expansion and Crisis.* New Haven: Yale University Press.

Ricklefs, M.C. (1993) *A History of Modern Indonesia Since c.1300,* 2nd edition. Stanford: Stanford University Press.

Robison, R., Hewison, K., and Higgott, R.A. (1987) (Eds.) *South East Asia in the 1980s: The Politics of Economic Crisis.* Allen and Unwin, Sydney.

Russett, B.M. (1967) *International Regions and the International System: A Study in Political Ecology.* Chicago: Rand McNally.

Seah, C.M. (1979) *Singapore's Position in ASEAN Cooperation,* Occasional Paper No.38, Department of Political Science, National University of Singapore.

Simon, S.W. (1982) *ASEAN States and Regional Security.* Stanford, California: Hoover Institution Press.

Solidum, E.D. (1974) *Towards a Southeast Asian Community.* Quezon City: University of the Philippines Press.

Spencer, J.E. (1964) *Oriental Asia: Themes Towards A Geography.* Prentice-Hall, Englewood Cliffs, New Jersey.

Steinberg, D.J. (1987) *In Search of Southeast Asia: A Modern History.* Honolulu: University of Hawaii Press.

Stubbs R., and G.R.D. Underhill (1999) (Eds.) *Political Economy and the Changing Global Order.* Second Edition, London: Macmillan.

Suehiro, A. (1985) *Capital Accumulation and Industrial Development in Thailand.* Bangkok: Social Research Institute.

Suriyamongkol, M.L. (1988) *Politics of ASEAN Economic Co-operation.* Singapore. Oxford University Press.

Tambiah, S.J. (1985) *Culture, Thought, and Social Action: An Anthropological Perspective.* Cambridge: Harvard University Press.

Tarling, N. ed. (1992) *The Cambridge History of Southeast Asia, Volume 2, "The Nineteenth and Twentieth Centuries".* Cambridge: Cambridge University Press.

Tarling N. (1998) *Nations and States in Southeast Asia.* Cambridge: Cambridge University Press.

Tillman, R.O. (1987) *Southeast Asia and the Enemy Beyond: ASEAN Perceptions of External Threats.* Boulder, CO: Westview Press.

Vanderbosch, A. & Butwell, R. (1966.) *The Changing Face of Southeast Asia.* Lexington: University of Kentucky Press.

Weinstein, F. (1969) *Indonesia Abandons Confrontation.* Interim Report Series, Ithaca: Modern Indonesia Project, Southeast Asia Program, Department of Asian Studies, Cornell University.

Wolters, O.W. (1982) *History, Culture, and Region in Southeast Asian Perspectives*. Singapore: Institute of Southeast Asian Studies.

Wolters, O.W. (1999) *History, Culture, and Region in Southeast Asian Perspectives*, Revised Edition. Ithaca: Cornell University Southeast Asia Program Publications.

Yoshihara, K. (1985) *Philippine Industrialization: Foreign and Domestic Capital*. New York: Oxford University Press.

Young, K.T. et al. (1965) *The Southeast Asia Crisis*. New York: The Association of the Bar of the City of New York.

Zacher, M.W. (1977) *International Conflicts and Collective Security, 1946–1977*. New York: Praeger.

Articles and Book Chapters

Acharya, A. (1987) "The Asia-Pacific region: Cockpit for superpower rivalry", *The World Today*, vol.43, nos.8-9, August–September 1987, pp.155–58.

Acharya, A. (1988) "The US Versus the USSR in the Pacific: Trends in the Military Balance", *Contemporary Southeast Asia*, vol.9, no.4, March 1988, pp.282–99.

Acharya, A. (1995) Transnational Production and Security: Southeast Asia's Growth Triangles, *Contemporary Southeast Asia*, vol.17, no.2, September 1995, pp.173–85.

Acharya, A. (1995) "Human Rights and Regional Order: ASEAN and Human Rights Management in post-Cold War Southeast Asia", in James T.H. Tang, ed. (1995) *Human Rights and International Relations in the Asia-Pacific* , London: Pinter, pp.167–182.

Acharya, A. (1997) "Ideas, Identity, and Institution-Building: From the 'ASEAN Way' to the 'Asia-Pacific Way'?", *The Pacific Review*, vol.10, no.3, 1997, pp.319–46.

Acharya, A. (1999) "Imagined Proximities: The Making and Unmaking of Southeast Asia as a Region", *Southeast Asian Journal of Social Science*, vol.27, no.1, 1999, pp.55–76.

Acharya, A. and Rajah, A. (1999) Introduction: Reconceptualising Southeast Asia, Special issue, *Southeast Asian Journal of Social Science*, vol.27, no.1, pp.1–6.

Acharya, A., and Stubbs, R. (1995) "The Perils of Prosperity? Security and Economic Growth in the ASEAN Region", in Jane Davis, ed., *Security Issues in the Post-Cold War World*. London: Edward Elgar, pp.99–112.

Alagappa, M. (1989) "Bringing Indochina into Asean", *Far Eastern Economic Review*, 29 June 1989, pp.21–22.

Alagappa, M. (1991) "Regional Arrangements and International Security in Southeast Asia", *Contemporary Southeast Asia*, vol.12, no.4 , March 1991, pp.269–305.

Andaya, L.Y. (1996) "Ethnonation, Nation-State and Regionalism in Southeast Asia", in Proceedings of the International Symposium, "Southeast Asia: Global Area Studies for the 21st Century", Organized by Project Team: An Integrated Approach to Global Area Studies (funded by Monbusho Grant-in-Aid for Scientific Research on Priority Areas), and Center for Southeast Asian Studies, Kyoto University, Kyoto International Community House, October 18–22, 1996, pp.131–49.

Anderson, B. (1972) "The Idea of Power in Javanese Culture", in C. Holt, ed., *Culture and Politics in Indonesia*, Ithaca: Cornell University Press, pp.1–69.

Awanohara, S. (1987) 'Look East' — The Japan Model, *Asian-Pacific Economic Literature*, vol.1, no.1, May 1987, pp.75–89.

Becker, E. (1987) "Stalemate in Cambodia", *Current History*, vol. 86, no. 519, April 1987, pp.156–59.

Benda, H.J. (1969) "The Structure of Southeast Asian History: Some Preliminary Observations", in Robert O. Tilman, ed., *Man, State, and Society in Contemporary Southeast Asia*, London: Pall Mall Press, pp.23–44.

Bentley, G.C. (1985) "Indigenous States of Southeast Asia", *Annual Review of Anthropology* 76, pp.275–305.

Bernard, M. (1996) "Regions in the Global Political Economy: Beyond the Local-Global Divide in the Formation of the Eastern Asian Region", *New Political Economy*, vol.1, no.3, pp.335–53.

Bernard, M. and Ravenhill J. (1995) "Beyond Product Cycles and Flying Geese: Regionalisation, Hierarchy and Industrialisation in East Asia", *World Politics*, vol.47, no.2, pp.171–209.

Bowles, P (1997) "ASEAN, AFTA and the New Regionalism", *Pacific Affairs*, 1997, vol.70, no.2, pp.219–33.

Buszynski, L. (1990) "Declining Superpowers: The Impact on ASEAN", *The Pacific Review*, vol.3, no.3, 1990, pp.257–61.

Chan, H.C. (1980) "The Interests and Role of ASEAN in the Indochina Conflict", paper presented to the International Conference on Indochina and Problems of Security and Stability in Southeast Asia" held at Chulalongkron University, Bangkok, 19–21 June 1980.

Chan, H.C. (1982) "Political Stability in Southeast Asia" paper presented to the Seminar on "Trends and Perspectives in ASEAN", Singapore, Institute of Southeast Asian Studies, 1–3 February 1982.

Cheung, T.M. (1991) "China's Regional Military Posture", *International Defense Review*, June 1991, vol.24, no.6, pp.618–622.

Chn'g, M.K. (1985) "ASEAN Economic Cooperation: The Current Status", *Southeast Asian Affairs 1985*, Singapore: Institute of Southeast Asian Studies, pp.31–53.

Christie, J.W. (1986) "Negara, Mandala, and Despotic State: Images of Early Java", in D.G. Marr and A.C. Milner, *Southeast Asia in the 9th to 14th Centuries*, Singapore: Institute of Southeast Asian Studies and Canberra: Australian National University, Research School of Pacific Studies, pp.65–93.

Cotton, J. (1990) "APEC: Australia hosts another Pacific acronym", *The Pacific Review*, vol.3, no.2, 1990, pp.171–73.

Devan, J. (1987) " The Economic Development of the ASEAN Countries", in P. West and F.A. Alting von Geusau, eds., *The Pacific Rim and the Western World*, Westview, London, pp.159–78.

Dirlik, A. (1992) "The Asia-Pacific Region: Reality and Representation in the Invention of the Regional Structure", *Journal of World History*, vol.3, no.1, 1992, pp.55–79.

Djiwandono, J.S. (1983) "The Political and Security Aspects of ASEAN: Its Principal Achievements", *Indonesian Quarterly*, vol.11, July 1983, pp.19–26.

Doner, R.F. (1991) "Approaches to the Politics of Economic Growth in Southeast Asia", *Journal of Asian Studies*, vol.50, no.4, Nov. 1991; pp.818–49.

Emmerson, D.K. (1984) "Southeast Asia: What's in a Name?", *Journal of Southeast Asian Studies*, vol. XV, No.1, March 1984, pp.1–21.

Evans, P. (1990) "The Changing Context of Security Relations in Eastern Asia", Paper prepared for the workshop on *Korea and the Changing Asia-Pacific Region*, 8–9 February 1990.

Evers, Hans-Dieter (1980) "The Challenge of Diversity: Basic Concepts and Theories in the Study of South-East Asian Societies", in Evers, ed., *Sociology of South-East Asia*, Kuala Lumpur: Oxford University Press, pp.2–7.

Fairclough, G. (1993) "Standing Firm", *Far Eastern Economic Review*, 15 April 1993, p.22.

Fifield, R. (1984) "'Southeast Asia' and 'ASEAN' as Regional Concepts", in R.A. Morse, ed., *Southeast Asian Studies: Options for the Future*, Lanham: University Press of America, pp.125–28.

Fifield, R. (1992) "The Southeast Asia Command", in K.S. Sandhu et al., *The ASEAN Reader*, Singapore: Institute of Southeast Asian Studies, pp.20–24.

Fisher, C.A. (1962) "Southeast Asia: The Balkans of the Orient? A Study in Continuity and Change", *Geography 47*, pp.347–67.

Frost, F. (1980) "The Origins and Evolution of ASEAN", *World Review*, vol.19, no.3, August 1980, pp.5–16.

Frost, F. (1991) "Vietnam and Asean: From Enmity to Cooperation", *Trends*, Singapore: Institute of Southeast Asian Studies, 29 December 1991, p.29.

Gainsborough, M. (1992) "Vietnam II: A Turbulent Normalisation with China", *The World Today*, vol.48, no.11 (November 1992), pp.205–07.

Haas, E.B. (1983) "Regime Decay: Conflict Management and International Organizations", *International Organization*, vol.37, no.2, Spring 1983, pp.189–256.

Hay, K. (1989) "ASEAN and the Shifting Tides of Economic Power at the End of the 1980s", *International Journal*, no.44, Summer 1989, pp.640–59.

Hernandez, C. (1995) *One Southeast Asia in the 21st Century: Opportunities and Challenges,* Paper Presented to the 1995 Convention of the Canadian Council for Southeast Asian Studies on The Dynamism of Southeast Asia, University of Laval, Quebec City, 27–29 October 1995.

Henderson, W. (1955) "The Development of Regionalism in Southeast Asia", *International Organization*, vol.9, no.4, pp.463–76.

Hirono, R. (1988) "Japan: Model for East Asia Industrialization?", in H. Hughes, ed., *Achieving Industrialization in East Asia*, Cambridge: Cambridge University Press, pp.241–59.

Huxley, T. (1990) "South-East Asia's Arms Race: Some Notes on Recent Developments", *Arms Control*, vol.11, no.1 (May 1990), pp.69–76.

Irvine, D. (1982) "Making Haste Slowly: ASEAN from 1975", in Alison Broinowski, *Understanding ASEAN*, London: Macmillan, pp.37–69.

Ispahani, M.Z. (1984) "Alone Together: Regional Security Arrangements in Southern Africa and the Arabian Gulf", *International Security*, vol.8, no.4 , Spring 1984, pp.152–75.

Johnson, C. (1987) "Political Institutions and Economic Performance: The Government-Business Relationship in Japan, South Korea and Taiwan", in F.C. Deyo, ed., *The Political Economy of the New Asian Industrialism*. Ithaca: Cornell University Press, pp.136–64.

Jones, S. (1993) "The Organic Growth", *Far Eastern Economic Review*, 17 June, 1993, p.23.

Kahn, G.M. (1973) "The Role of the United States in Southeast Asia", in Lau, T.S., ed., *New Directions in the International Relations of Southeast Asia*, Singapore: Singapore University Press.

Kitamura, H. and Bhagat, A.N. (1969) "Aspects of Regional Harmonization of National Development Plans", in T. Morgan and N. Spoelstra, eds., *Economic Interdependence in Southeast Asia*. Madison: University of Wisconsin Press, pp.39-56.

Kondo, Shigekatsu (1992) *The Evolving Security Environment: Political,* paper presented to the Workshop on "Arms Control and Confidence-Building in the Asia-Pacific Region", Organised by the Canadian Institute for International Peace and Security, Ottawa, 22-23 May 1992.

Kulke, H. (1986) "The Early and Imperial Kingdom in Southeast Asian History", in David G. Marr and A.C. Milner, *Southeast Asia in the 9th to 14th Centuries,* Singapore: Institute of Southeast Asian Studies and Canberra: Australian National University, Research School of Pacific Studies, pp.1–22.

Lau, T.S. (1980) "The Role of Singapore in Southeast Asia",*World Review*, vol.19, no.3, August 1980, pp.36–44.

Legge, J.D. (1992) "The Writing of Southeast Asian History", in *The Cambridge History of Southeast Asia vol.1*, Cambridge: Cambridge University Press, pp.1–50.

Leifer, M. (1978) "The Paradox of ASEAN: A Security Organization Without the Structure of an Alliance", *The Round Table*, vol.68, no.271, July 1978, pp.261–68.

Leifer, M. (1992) "Power-sharing and Peacemaking in Cambodia", *SAIS Review*, vol.12, no.1, Winter-Spring 1992, pp.139–53.

Leifer, M. (1992) "Debating Asian Security: Michael Leifer Responds to Geoffrey Wiseman", *The Pacific Review*, vol.5, no.2, 1992, pp.167–69.

Lieberman, V. (1995) "An Age of Commerce in Southeast Asia? Problems of Regional Coherence", *The Journal of Asian Studies*, vol.54, no.3, August 1995, pp.796–807.

Mack, A. (1991) "Asia's New Military Build-up", *Pacific Research*, February 1991, pp.12–13.

Mahbubani, K. (1992) "News Areas of Asean Reaction: Environment, Human Rights and Democracy", *Asean-ISIS Monitor*, Issue no.5, October–December 1992, pp.13–17.

Mak, J.N. (1995) *The ASEAN Process ("Way") of Multilateral Cooperation and Cooperative Security: The Road to a Regional Arms Register?*, Paper Presented to the "MIMA-SIPRI Workshop on An ASEAN Arms Register: Developing Transparency", Kuala Lumpur, 2–3 October 1995.

Malik, A. (1970) "Djakarta's Conference and Asia's Political Future", *Pacific Community*, vol.2, no. 1, October 1970, pp.66–76.

Malik, A. (1975) "Regional Cooperation in International Politics", *Regionalism in Southeast Asia*, Jakarta: Yayasan Proklamasi, Centre for Strategic and International Studies, pp.157–69.

Melchor, A. Jr. (1975) "Security Issues in Southeast Asia", *Regionalism in Southeast Asia*, Jakarta: Centre for Strategic and International Studies, pp.39–53.

Milivojevic, M. (1989) "The Spratly and Paracel Islands Conflict", *Survival*, vol.31, no.1, January/February 1989, pp.70–78.

Miller, L.B. (1967) "Regional Organization and the Regulation of Internal Conflict", *World Politics*, vol.19, no.4, July 1967, pp.582–600.

Nair, K.K. (1975) "Defence and Security in Southeast Asia: The Urgency of Self-Reliance", *Asian Defence Journal*, no.1, 1975, pp.9–17.

Neher, C.D (1984) "The Social Sciences", in Ronald A. Morse, ed., *Southeast Asian Studies: Options for the Future*, Lanham: University Press of America, pp.129–36.

Nor, Commodore A. Ramli (1989) "ASEAN Maritime Cooperation", paper presented to the Defence Asia '89 Conference, "Towards Greater ASEAN Military and Security Cooperation: Issues and Prospects", Singapore, 22–25 March 1989.

Nuechterlein, D.E. (1967) "Thailand: Another Vietnam?" *Asian Survey*, vol.7 no.2, February 1967, pp.126–30.

Owen, N. (1992) "Economic and Social Change" in Nicholas Tarling, ed., *The Cambridge History of Southeast Asia*, Volume 2, "The Nineteenth and Twentieth Centuries", Cambridge: Cambridge University Press, pp.467–527.

Paribatra, S. and Samudavanija, C-A. (1986) "Internal Dimensions of Regional Security in Southeast Asia", in Mohammed Ayoob, ed., *Regional Security in the Third World*, London: Croom Helm, pp.57–94.

Rajaratnam, S. (1989) "Riding the Vietnamese Tiger", *Contemporary Southeast Asia*, vol.10, no.4 , March 1989, pp.343–61.

Ravenholt, A. (1964) *Maphilindo: Dream or Achievable Reality*, New York: American University Field Staff Reports, Southeast Asia Series, vol. xii, no.1, 1964, pp.1–14.

Reid, A. (1999) "A Saucer Model of Southeast Asian Identity", Special issue of *Southeast Asian Journal of Social Science*, vol.27, no.1, pp.7–23.

Reynolds, C. (1995) "A New Look at Old Southeast Asia", *Journal of Asian Studies*, vol.54, no.2 pp.419–46.

Rieger, H.C. (1989) "Regional Economic Cooperation in the Asia-Pacific Region", *Asia-Pacific Economic Literature*, vol.3, no.2, September 1989, pp.5–33.

Robison, R., Higgott, R. and Hewison, K. (1987) "Crisis in Economic Strategy in the 1980s: The Factors at Work", in R. Robison, R. Higgott and K. Hewison, eds., *South East Asia in the 1980s: The Politics of Economic Crisis*. Sydney: Allen and Unwin, pp.1–15.

Russett, B.M. (1968) "Delineating International Regions", in Singer, J.D., ed., *Quantitative International Politics: Insights and Evidence*, New York: Free Press, pp.317–52.

Seda, M. (1993) "Global Environmental Concerns and Priorities: Implications for ASEAN", in M. Seda, ed., *Environmental Management in ASEAN: Perspectives on Critical Regional Issues*. Singapore: Institute of Southeast Asian Studies, pp.1–54.

Shafie, M.G. bin (1971) "The Neutralisation of Southeast Asia", *Pacific Community*, vol.3, no.1, October 1971, pp.110–17.

Shafie, M.G. bin (1975) "ASEAN's Response to Security Issues in Southeast Asia", in Centre for Strategic and International Studies (1975) *Regionalism in Southeast Asia*. Jakarta: Centre for Strategic and International Studies, pp.17–37.

Shafie, M.G. bin (1982) "Confrontation Leads to ASEAN", *Asian Defence Journal*, February 1982, pp.30–35.

Simon, S.W. (1978) "The ASEAN States: Obstacles to Security Cooperation", *Orbis*, vol.22, no.2, Summer 1978, pp.415–34.

Simon, S.W. (1990) "United States Security Policy and ASEAN", *Current History*, vol.89, no.545, March 1990, pp.97–100, 130–32.

Singh, H. (1993) "Prospects for Regional Stability in Southeast Asia in the Post-Cold War Era", *Millennium*, vol.22, no.2, pp.279–300.

Singh, H. (1997) "Vietnam and ASEAN: "The Politics of Accommodation", *Australian Journal of International Affairs*, vol.51, no.2, pp.215–29.

Singh, H. (1999) "Understanding Conflict Resolution in Cambodia: A Neorealist Perspective", *Asian Journal of Political Science*, vol.7, no.1, pp.41–59.

Singh, H. (1999), "Hegemonic Construction of Regions: Southeast Asia as a Case Study", in Sarah Owen, ed., *The State and Identity Construction in International Relations*. London: Macmillan, forthcoming.

Soesastro, M.H. (1987) "ASEAN's Participation in GATT", *Indonesian Quarterly*, vol.15, no.1, January 1987, pp.107–27.

Soesastro, M.H. (1990) "Prospects for Pacific-Asian Regional Trade Structures", in Robert Scalapino et. al., eds., *Regional Dynamics: Security, Political and Economic Issues in the Asia-Pacific Region*, Jakarta: Centre for Strategic and International Studies, pp.374–94.

Sopiee, N. (1986) "ASEAN and Regional Security", in Mohammed Ayoob, ed., *Regional Security in the Third World*. London: Croom Helm, 1986, pp.221–234.

Sopiee, N. (1995) "The Neutralization of Southeast Asia" in Hedley Bull, ed., *Asia and the Western Pacific: Towards A New International Order*, Melbourne & Sydney: Thomas Nelson, pp.132–58.

Srichratchanya, P. (1989) "Wait and See", *Far Eastern Economic Review*, 11 May 1989, pp.21–24.

Stockwell, A.J. (1992) "Southeast Asia in War and Peace: The End of European Colonial Empires, in N. Tarling, ed., *The Cambridge History of Southeast Asia*, vol.2, Cambridge: Cambridge University Press, pp.329–85.

Stubbs, R. (1989) "Geopolitics and the Political Economy of Southeast Asia", *International Journal*, vol.44, Summer 1989, pp.517–40.

Stubbs, R. (1999) "Signing on to Liberalization: AFTA and the Politics of Regional Economic Cooperation", *The Pacific Review* vol.13, no.2 (2000), forthcoming.

Stubbs, R. (1999) "Regionalization and Globalization", in Richard Stubbs and Geoffrey Underhill, eds., *Political Economy and Global Order*, 2nd edition, Toronto: Oxford University Press, pp.231–34.

Taylor, K. (1986) "Authority and Legitimacy in 11th Century Vietnam", in David G. Marr and A.C. Milner, *Southeast Asia in the 9th to 14th Centuries* (Singapore: Institute of Southeast Asian Studies and Canberra: Australian National University, Research School of Pacific Studies, pp.139–76.

Thayer, C.A. (1992) "The Challenges Facing Vietnamese Communism", *South-east Asian Affairs 1992*, Singapore: Institute of Southeast Asian Studies, pp.349–64.

Than, M. (1991) "ASEAN, Indochina and Myanmar: Towards Economic Coopera-tion", *ASEAN Economic Bulletin*, vol.8, no.2, November 1991, pp.173–93.

Thomson, W.R. (1973) "The Regional Subsystem: A Conceptual Explication and a Propositional Inventory", *International Studies Quarterly*, vol.17, no.1, March 1973, pp.89–117.

Trocki, C.A. (1992) "Political Structures in the Nineteenth and Early Twentieth Century", in Nicholas Tarling, ed., *The Cambridge History of Southeast Asia*, Volume 2, Cambridge: Cambridge University Press, pp.79–130.

Turnbull, C.M. (1992) "Regionalism and Nationalism", in Nicholas Tarling, ed., *The Cambridge History of Southeast Asia*, Volume 2, Cambridge: Cambridge University Press, pp.585–645.

Van der Kroef, J.M. (1981) "ASEAN, Hanoi, and the Kampuchean Conflict: Between Kuantan and a Third Alternative", *Asian Survey*, vol.21, no.5, May 1981, pp.515–35.

Vatikiotis, M. (1992) "Measure for Measure: Malaysia, Singapore, Poised to Acquire New Arms", *Far Eastern Economic Review*, 30 April 1992, p.18.

Vatikiotis, M. (1994) "Going Regional", *Far Eastern Economic Review*, 20 October 1994, p.16.

Wah, C.K. (1998) "Globalization and Its Challenges to ASEAN Political Participation", paper presented to the ISEAS 30th Anniversary Conference, "Southeast Asia in the 21st Century: Challenges of Globalization", Singapore, 30 July – 1 August 1998.

Walton, J. (1996) " Economics" in Mohammed Halib & Tim Huxley, eds., *An Introduction to Southeast Asian Studies*, London: I.B., Tauris, pp.189–208.

Wanandi, J. (1984) "Security Issues in the ASEAN Region", in Karl D. Jackson and M. Hadi Soesastro, eds. (1984) *ASEAN Security and Economic Development*, Research Papers and Policy Studies No. 11, Berkeley: Institute of East Asian Studies, University of California, Berkeley, pp.297–308.

Wang Gungwu (1986) "Nation Formation and Regionalism in Southeast Asia", in Margaret Grant, ed., (1964) *South Asia Pacific Crisis: National Development and World Community*, New York: Dodd, Mead and Company, pp.125–35.

Wang Gungwu (1986) "Introduction", in David Marr and A.C. Milner, eds. *Southeast Asia in the 9th to 14th Centuries*, Singapore: Institute of Southeast Asian Studies, pp. xi–xviii.

Weaver, O. (1993) "Culture and Identity in the Baltic Sea Region", in P. Joenniemi, ed., *Cooperation in the Baltic Sea Region*, London: Taylor and Francis, pp.23–48.

Wolters, O.W. (1981) "Culture, History and Region in Southeast Asian Perspective", in R.P. Anand and P.V. Quisumbing, eds., *ASEAN: Identity, Development and Culture*, Quezon City: University of the Philippines Law Center and Honolulu: East-West Center Culture Learning Institute, pp.1–40.

Zarkovic, M. (1977) "The Revival of ASEAN", *Review of International Affairs*, 5 October 1977, pp.29–31.

BIBLIOGRAPHY **183**

Official Documents

Association of Southeast Asia (April 1962) *Report of the Special Session of Foreign Ministers of ASA*, Kuala Lumpur/Cameron Highlands: Federation of Malaya.

Association of South-East Asian Nations (1995) *The ASEAN Regional Forum: A Concept Paper.* Jakarta: ASEAN Secretariat.

Association of South-East Asian Nations (1993) "Joint Communique of the Twenty-Sixth ASEAN Ministerial Meeting, Singapore, 23–24 July 1993." Jakarta: ASEAN Secretariat.

Association of South-East Asian Nations (1992) *Singapore Declaration of 1992.* Singapore: ASEAN Heads of Government Meeting, 27–28 January 1992.

Association of South-East Asian Nations (1967) *The ASEAN Declaration.* Bangkok: Association of South-East Asian Nations, 8 August 1967.

Australia, Department of Foreign Affairs and Trade (1997) *The New ASEANs: Vietnam, Burma, Cambodia and Laos.* Canberra: Department of Foreign Affairs and Trade.

The Parliament of the Commonwealth of Australia, Joint Committee on Foreign Affairs and Defence (1981) *Power in IndoChina Since 1975*, Canberra: Australian Government Publishing Service.

Indonesia, H.E. Ali Alatas, Minister for Foreign Affairs (1991) Text of statement as Co-Chair of the Paris Peace Conference on Cambodia, 23 October 1991.

Singapore, Ministry of Information and the Arts (1991) *Speeches*, Singapore: Ministry of Information and the Arts.

Singapore, Lee Hsien Loong, Minister for Trade and Industries (1990) Text of speech to Indonesia Forum, Jakarta, 11 July 1990.

South-East Asia Treaty Organization (n.d.) *History of SEATO.* Bangkok: Public Information Office, SEATO Headquarters.

Internet Sources

ASEAN Secretariat (www.aseansec.org)

The Burmanet News (burmanet-1@igc.apc.org)

Singapore Window (www.singapore-window.org)

The Straits Times Interactive (web3.asia1.com.sg)

Worldwide Forest/Biodiversity Campaign News (forests.org/gopher/indonesia/allcando.tx)

Others

Agence France Presse (AFP)

Xinhua News Agency Dispatch

Syriyamongkol, M.L. (1982) *The Politics of Economic Cooperation in the Association of Southeast Asian Nations*, Ph.D. Dissertation, University of Illinois at Urbana-Champaign.

Asian Defence Journal

Asiaweek

Bangkok Post

The Economist

Far Eastern Economic Review

International Herald Tribune

The Los Angeles Times

Manila Journal

The Nation

The New Straits Times

The Straits Times (Singapore)

The Straits Times (Weekly Overseas Edition)

Strategic Comments (International Institute for Strategic Studies)

The Sunday Nation

The Sunday Times (Singapore)

Huxley, T. (1986) *Indochina as a Security Concern of the ASEAN States 1975–81*, Ph.D. Dissertation, Australian National University.

Phanit, T. (1980) *Regional Integration Attempts in Southeast Asia: A Study of ASEAN's Problems and Progress*, Ph.D. Dissertation, Pennsylvania State University.

Thongswasdi, T. (1979) *ASEAN after the Vietnam War: Stability and Development Through Regional Cooperation*, Ph.D. thesis, Claremont Graduate School.

Young, E. (1981) *Development Cooperation in ASEAN: Balancing Free Trade and Regional Planning*, Ph.D. Dissertation, The University of Michigan, Ann Arbor.

Index

A

Abdul Rahman, Tunku 61, 79–80, 82
Acheson, Dean 65
Afro-Asian 43–44, 51, 164
    Conference in Bandung (1955) 50, 66
Alatas, Ali 134, 136, 139
Anand Panyarachun 123, 134
Andaya, Leonard 9, 24, 166
Anderson, Benedict 2, 98
Angkor 19–21, 23, 24, 26
Anglo-Malaysian Defence Agreement
    (AMDA) (1957) 61, 70
Asia-Europe Meeting (ASEM) 153
Asia Pacific Economic Cooperation
    (APEC) 148, 151, 153
Asia Pacific multilateral institutions
    143, 157
Asian Collective Security Arrangement
    86
Asian Commonwealth 47
Asian Development Bank (ADB) 53
Asian economic crisis 13, 133, 154–157,
    168
Asian Potsdam Conference 47
Asian Relations Conference (1947) 46,
    66, 81
Asian values 140
Association of Southeast Asia (ASA) 13,
    78–82, 91
Association of Southeast Asian Nations
    (ASEAN) 3, 12, 59, 62, 69, 74, 78,
    83–87, 89–93, 95–98, 105–108,
    110–116, 118, 120, 145–146, 151,
    163, 166, 168
    ASEAN-10 83, 135–136
    and APEC 151–152
    ASEAN Free Trade Area (AFTA)
        136, 150
    ASEAN Post-Ministerial
        Conferences 146

ASEAN Regional Forum (ARF)
    146–148
ASEAN Way 12, 29, 127–128, 133,
    135, 140, 150, 155–156
Bali summit (1976) 94–95
and Cambodia conflict 111–116
and China 119, 144
Declaration of ASEAN Concord
    (1976) 94
defence cooperation 94–95
economic cooperation 96–98
and environmental issues 142–143
High Council 128
and human rights 138–142
intra-ASEAN relations 137
intra-ASEAN trade 125, 148
and Japan 144
political cooperation 117
and Sabah dispute 91–93
Secretariat 143
security cooperation 117
and Soviet Union 113
Vietnam relations 117–123
Aung San 43–44, 47, 49–50
Ayutthya 19, 21–24, 26, 30

B

Ba Maw 34
Bangkok Declaration 85
Boeke, J.H. 7
Britain
    East of Suez policy 69
Burma 12

C

Cambodia 12, 105, 111–117, 118
    Paris Peace Agreement (1991) 12,
        120
    Paris Peace Conference 120
    Vietnamese invasion of 3

Champa 19, 30
Chan, Heng Chee 59
Chatichai Choonhavan 121
Chiang, Kai-Shek 65
Churchill,Winston 44
Cold War 11–13, 43, 69, 72–73, 116,
    164–165
Colombo Plan 50, 64, 76 (n.34)
Colombo Powers 50
Colonialism, European 33
Commerce 29
    age of commerce 32
Communist insurgency 55, 136
Communist Party of Malaya (CPM)
    55–56
Constructive engagement 140, 142
Constructive intervention 156

D
Daim Zainuddin 151
Domino theory 10, 64, 65, 110

E
East Asia
    regionalisation 123–127
East Asian Economic Caucus (EAEC)
    152–153
Economic and Social Commission for
    Asia and the Pacific (ESCAP) 96
Emmerson, Don 163
Erlangga, King 26
Ethnic separatism 55, 137
Evers, Hans-Dieter 4
Export-oriented industrialisation (EOI)
    52, 88–89

F
Federation of Free Peoples of Southern
    Asia 45
Fifield, Russell 10, 98, 166
Fisher, C.A. 7–9, 36–37
Five Power Defence Arrangements
    (FPDA) 70
Flexible engagement 156
Flying geese 126

Funan 5, 19
Furnivall, J.S. 7, 33

G
Galactic polity 20, 22, 24, 27, 164
Garcia, President 79
Geertz, Clifford 11, 20, 22–23, 27–29
Geneva Accords on Indochina (1954)
    66–67, 76 (n.37)
Ghazali Shafie, Mohammed 68, 90
Giang, Vo Dong 109
Giap, Vo Nguyen, General 48, 66
Goh, Chok Tong 151
Gorbachev, Mikhail 119
Gordon, Bernard 72, 82
Greater East Asian Co-Prosperity
    Sphere 34
Growth triangles 153–154
Guided Democracy 53, 60–61

H
Habibie, B.J. 155
Hall, D.G.E. 6–7
Heng Samarin 111, 114, 115
Hernandez, Carolina 140
Hirono, R. 127
Hla Myint 53
Ho Chi Minh 45, 106
Hun Sen 111, 121, 135
Hussein Onn 86, 94

I
Imagined communities 9
Import-substituting industrialisation
    (ISI) 52, 89
Indochina 12
International Conference on
    Kampuchea (ICK) (1981) 114

J
Jakarta Informal Meetings (JIM I
    and II) 120
Jayakumar, S. 157
Johnson, Chalmers 125

K

Khmer Rouge 55–56
Kiet, Vo Van 123
Koh, Tommy 156
Konfrontasi 58, 60, 73, 84–85
Kukrit, Promoj 62
Kulke, Kulke H. 23

L

Lee, Hsien Loong 157
Lee, Kuan Yew 85–86, 91, 138, 145, 155
Legge, John 2
Leifer, Michael 59
Lon Nol 52

M

Macapagal, Diasdado, President 82
Mahathir Mohamad 123, 156–157
   "Look East" policy 126
Majapahit 19, 21, 24, 30
Malik, Adam 68, 84, 86, 99
Mandala 11, 20–28, 31–32, 37, 164
Manila Pact (1954) 67
Maphilindo 13, 78, 82–83, 91
Marcos, Ferdinand 61, 91, 110
Mataram 20
McCloud, Donald 5
Melchor, Alejandro 98
Mindoro 25
musyawarah 83, 128

N

Nai Pridi Phanomyong 53
Nanhai 2
Nanyang 2
National resilience 110
Nationalism 2, 11, 13, 37, 43–51, 78, 164
Ne Win 58, 60
Neher, Clark 3, 33
Nehru, Jawaharlal 46–47, 50
New Delhi Conference (1949) 66
Nixon Doctrine 70–72
Non-interference 58, 91, 135, 156
Noordin Sopiee 128

O

Osborne, Milton 5, 20, 72
Owen, Norman 52, 88–89

P

Pagan 19, 26, 30
Pan-Asianism 34, 43–47, 51, 66, 78
Paracels 112
Paris Peace Conference 120
Pathet Lao 55–56
Pelaez, Emmanuel 80
Phibun Songkram 34, 62
Pol Pot 111
Prapat Charusathien 62
Pridi Banomyong 48
Promoj, Seni 62
Pye, Lucian 18, 20

Q

Quirino, Elpidio 43, 65

R

Rajaratnam, S. 70, 74, 99
Ravenholt, Albert 78
Reagan Doctrine 117
Reagan, Ronald 119
Regional identity 1, 3, 11–12, 24, 29, 80,
   133, 143, 157, 163
Regional resilience 110
Regionalism 10–11, 13, 37, 43–51, 54, 62,
   78, 86, 98–99, 164
Reid, Anthony 1, 6, 9, 30–31
Reynolds, C. 21, 28–29
Romulo, Carlos P. 46, 94

S

Sabah 82, 91
   dispute 81, 91–93
Sarit Thanarat 62
Second World War 2, 11
Seni, Promoj 62
Sihanouk, Norodom 53, 83, 108
Sino-Soviet rivalry 112
Souphanouvong, Prince 48
Southeast Asia 1, 7, 17, 31, 37, 43, 54,
   112, 116

and China 113, 135
diversity 5–6
economic development 53
international relations 3
Japanese investment in 124
Official Development Assistance,
    Japanese 125
languages 6
neutralisation 93
One Southeast Asia 12–13, 129,
    134, 143, 145
Orientalist construction 29
political economy 89
pre-colonial inter-state system 17,
    28, 32
regional cooperation 73
regionalism 2, 13, 51, 63, 86, 165
regionness 4, 11, 29
Soviet policy toward 116, 143
unity 8
Southeast Asia Collective Defence
    Treaty (1954) 67
Southeast Asia Command (SEAC) 10,
    17, 20, 34–35, 37, 64, 164
Southeast Asia Nuclear Weapon Free
    Zone Treaty (1995) 128
Southeast Asia Treaty Organization
    (SEATO) 66–69, 79, 96
Soviet Union 112, 116
Spratly Islands 112
Srivijaya 5, 19–21, 24, 26
Stockwell, A.J. 66
Suharto 49, 52, 61, 63, 84, 123
Sukarno 50, 51, 58, 61, 63, 65, 72, 81–82
Sukhothai 19, 26, 30
Sutan Sjahrir, 45
Suvarnabbhumi 2

T
Tambiah, Stanley 11, 20, 22, 27
Tarling, Nicholas 1, 163

Thai-US security alliance 113
Thamrong Nawasawat 48
Thanat Khoman 79, 81–82, 84
Thanom Kittikachorn 62
Theatre state 20, 25, 28
Treaty of Amity and Cooperation (1976)
    95, 128
Trickle down effect 90
Trinh, Nguyen Duy 108
Turnbull, C.M. 43

U
U Nu 53
United States-Philippines Mutual
    Defence Treaty (1951) 63, 69
United States 65–66
    policy toward Southeast Asia 63–64,
        88
    military presence in Pacific 144
Unity in diversity 3, 5, 6
Upadit Pachariyangkun 109

V
Viet Cong 55
Vietnam 106–107
    invasion of Cambodia 3

W
Wan Waithayakon, Prince 34
Wang, Gungwu 3, 49, 165
Wolters, O.W. 9–11, 17, 20, 22, 24–25,
    27–28, 31

Y
Young, Kenneth T. 73, 166

Z
Zone of Peace, Freedom and Neutrality
    (ZOPFAN) 93–95, 99, 109, 117, 127,
    145, 166